John Mackay, Adam Gunn

Sutherland and the Reay Country

History, antiquities, folklore, topography, regiments, ecclesiastical records, poetry and music, etc.

John Mackay, Adam Gunn

Sutherland and the Reay Country
History, antiquities, folklore, topography, regiments, ecclesiastical records, poetry and music, etc.

ISBN/EAN: 9783337428471

Printed in Europe, USA, Canada, Australia, Japan

Cover: Foto ©ninafisch / pixelio.de

More available books at **www.hansebooks.com**

Sutherland and the Reay Country.

DUKE OF SUTHERLAND.

DUCHESS OF SUTHERLAND.

SUTHERLAND
AND THE
REAY COUNTRY:

HISTORY, ANTIQUITIES, FOLKLORE, TOPOGRAPHY,
REGIMENTS, ECCLESIASTICAL RECORDS,
POETRY AND MUSIC, ETC.

WITH NUMEROUS PORTRAITS AND ILLUSTRATIONS.

EDITED BY
REV. ADAM GUNN, M.A.,
AND
JOHN MACKAY.

GLASGOW:
JOHN MACKAY, "CELTIC MONTHLY" OFFICE,
9 BLYTHSWOOD DRIVE.
1897.

"I will venture to say that in the whole of this island there exists not a more intelligent population connected with the labouring and industrial interests, than the population of the County of Sutherland." —*Speech in Parliament*, by the RIGHT HON. W. E. GLADSTONE.

DEDICATED

TO

THE DUKE AND DUCHESS OF SUTHERLAND,

AND

LORD AND LADY REAY,

THE PRESENT REPRESENTATIVES OF THE ANCIENT AND

NOBLE FAMILIES OF

"SUTHERLAND AND REAY,"

BY

THE EDITORS.

PREFACE.

WHILE a great many works have already appeared bearing more or less remotely on the County of Sutherland, only two of these can be said to possess much historical value, viz. Sir Robert Gordon's "Earldom of Sutherland" and Robert Mackay's "House and Clan of Mackay." Copies of these are somewhat scarce, and their price puts them beyond the reach of many. The want of such a work as the present has been long felt, and the Editors considered it would greatly enhance its value if each subject were treated separately by the best authority procurable. It will be readily understood that a considerable time was necessary in bringing together contributions from a variety of authors, and this accounts for the delay in the publication of the book. Subscribers, however, have lost nothing by the delay, as the volume has greatly exceeded the dimensions indicated in the prospectus, and contains 100 pages more than anticipated.

It was intended at first to include chapters on the Natural History and Geology of Sutherland; but the exigencies of space, combined with the recent appearance of exhaustive works on these subjects by Mr. Harvie-Brown, of Larbert, and Mr. Cadell, of Grange, induced the Editors to depart from their original intention.

The Editors record, with thanks, their indebtedness for valuable assistance in the preparation of the work to Mr.

John Mackay of Hereford, whom all Highlanders recognise as one of the best representatives of their race ; to Colonel Duncan Menzies of Blairich, the popular Commanding Officer of the Sutherland Volunteers ; to the Rev. James Aberigh-Mackay, D.D., the present representative of the famous Clan Abrach of Strathnaver ; to Mr. John Munro, Hanley; to the late Mr. Thomas Bantock, of Wolverhampton ; to Mr. Henry Whyte (Fionn), the distinguished Celtic scholar ; to Dr. Anderson of the Society of Antiquaries (Scotland), for the use of a number of engravings which illustrate the Rev. Robert Munro's paper on the "Antiquities"; and to Mr. Fred Box, House of Tongue, through whose kind assistance several interesting views of the Reay country have been secured ; and, above all, to the various authors of the valuable papers relating to the County which appear in this volume.

In preparing a list of notable men, the Editors found that the number of names deserving of notice was so large as to preclude adequate treatment of each. They therefore resolved to include only those who have kept in close touch with the affairs of their native county, a goodly number of whom are contributors to this work.

The Editors, having now completed their labours, feel satisfied that Sutherland men at home and abroad will find in these papers something to interest them, and possibly to add to their knowledge of the past history of their native county ; while they also hope that the volume will not be without interest to other workers in the Celtic field.

ADAM GUNN,
JOHN MACKAY, } Joint-Editors.

CONTENTS.

	PAGE
History, to 1560,	1
History, 1560-1800,	43
A Short Treatise on Homespun,	78
Antiquities,	87
Folklore,	116
Topography,	141
Language,	172
Regiments,	183
Volunteers,	260
Poetry and Music,	283
Rob Donn,	285
Religious History before the Reformation,	321
Religious History of the Reay Country after the Reformation,	333
Distinguished Men,	367

LIST OF ILLUSTRATIONS.

A Glimpse of Strathnaver at Loch Naver,	5
Loch Hope, looking towards Strathmore,	9
The Field of Bannockburn, from Gillies Hill,	12
Dunrobin Castle, Seat of the Duke of Sutherland,	15
Kyle of Tongue,	17

CONTENTS.

The Watch Hill, Tongue,	24
Castle Varrich, Kyle of Tongue,	27
Strathnaver at Syre, near Rossal,	29
Mackay (from M'Ian's " Clans of the Scottish Highlands "),	35
Site of Borve Castle, Farr,	41
Tombstone on grave of Murchadh Macleod,	43
Ruins of Helmsdale Castle,	45
The White Banner of the Clan Mackay,	49
Coat of Arms of the Sutherland family,	54
Tongue House, the ancient seat of the Mackay Chiefs,	59
Coat of Arms of Donald, first Lord Reay, in Tongue House,	61
Corner in Tongue House gardens,	65
Kirkiboll Churchyard, Tongue,	68
Clans Sutherland and Mackay (from "The Queen's Book"),	74
Dunrobin Castle,	76
View and Plan of Rhinavie Cairns,	91
Doorway from first to second chamber of long Cairn,	92
North end of Cairn No. 3,	93
Balblair Blade,	98
Bronze Anvil,	99
Bronze Vessels found near Helmsdale,	100, 101
Torish Necklace,	102
Eirde House, Erribol (cross section),	109
Ancient Gravestone in Farr Churchyard,	111
Colours of Mackay's Regiment in the service of Holland,	188
Colours of the Reay Fencibles,	233
Place at Syre, where the Strathnaver men enlisted in 93rd,	236
The "Thin Red Line" at Balaclava,	243
Officer, Sergeant, Piper, and Privates of Sutherland Co.'s,	261
,, Caithness Companies,	263
Sergeant and Privates of the Caithness Companies,	265

Group of Officers of Battalion, - - - - 267
Group of Pipers ,, ,, - - - - - 269
Battalion at Invergordon Camp, - - - - 271
  ,, marching past, Jubilee Review, Inverness, - 273
Colour-Sergeant Robert Mackay, Queen's Prizeman,- 278

PLATE PORTRAITS.

The Duke and Duchess of Sutherland,	Frontispiece.
Lord and Lady Reay, - - - - -	To face page 1
Rev. Robert Munro, M.A., B.D., F.S.A. Scot.,	,, 87
The late John Mackay (Ben Reay), - -	,, 183
General Sir John A. Ewart, K.C.B., 93rd S. H.,	,, 235
Lieut.-Col. Duncan Menzies, 1st S. H. R. Vol.,	,, 260
John Mackay, C,E., J.P., Hereford, - -	,, 285
Rev. John S. Mackay, Fort-Augustus, - -	,, 333
George J. Campbell, Sheriff of the Lews, -	,, 371
James Macdonald, W.S., Edinburgh, - -	,, 372
Rev. Adam Gunn, M.A., Durness, - - -	373
Donald Matheson, of Achany, - - -	374
William Mackay, Provost of Thurso - -	,, 375
Rev. John Murray, Convener of the County, -	,, 378
Donald Munro, M.E., Manchester, - - -	,, 379
John Mackay, Editor *Celtic Monthly*, Glasgow,	,, 380
George Murray Campbell, C.E., Siam, - -	,, 381
Rev. James Aberigh-Mackay, D.D., - -	,, 382

List of Subscribers.

Adam, Frank, Esq., F.S.A., Scot., Sourabaya, Java.
Anderson, J. L., Esq., Northumberland Street, Edinburgh.
Ansell, W. J., Esq., Larnacia, Cyprus.
Bannerman, Hugh, Esq., Southport.
Bantock, George Granville, Esq., M.D., London.
Bantock, Thomas, Esq., Wolverhampton.
Bickley, Thomas, Esq., J.P., Hanley.
Bignold, Arthur, Esq., of Lochrosque, Ross-shire.
Black, Robert, Esq., Bangkok, Siam.
Bolton, Mrs., Moor Court, N. Staffordshire.
Bolton, Miss Beatrice, Moor Court, N. Staffordshire.
Box, John, Esq , House of Tongue, Sutherland.
Box, Fred., Esq., Johannesburg, South African Republic.
Bruce, Alexander, Esq., Clyne House, Pollokshields, Glasgow.
Burgess, Captain A., Gairloch, Ross-shire.
Cameron, A. F. H., Esq., M.D., Camden, Glos.
Cameron, John, Esq., J.P., Ex-Provost of Kirkintilloch.
Campbell, A. D., Esq., Komgha, Cape Colony, South Africa.
Campbell, George J., Esq., Sheriff of the Lews.
Campbell, John, Esq., Tongue, Sutherland.
Carmichael, Dr., Tarbert.
Chaplin's Library, Keswick.
Chisholm, Kenneth Mackenzie, Esq., M.D., Radcliffe.
Clarke, G. G., Esq., Eriboll, Sutherland.
Colquhoun, Sir James, of Colquhoun and Luss, Bart.
Colquhoun, Lady, Rossdhu, Loch Lomond.
Cowan, George, Esq., Edinburgh.
Crerar, Rev. A., Kinlochbervie.
Cumming, Miss, Secretary, Sutherland Home Industries, Golspie.
Cunyngham, Miss Ethel A., London.

LIST OF SUBSCRIBERS. xiii.

Dennis, Mrs. Matilda Mackay, Conneaut Lake, Penn., U.S.A
Ewart, General Sir John Alex., K.C.B., of Craigcleuch.
Fraser, Alex., Esq., Solicitor, Inverness.
Finlayson, Rev. D., Kinlochbervie, Sutherland.
Gilmour, James, Esq., Mansion House Road, Paisley.
Gilmour, William Ewing, Esq., Alexandria.
Graham, William, Esq., J.P., of North Erines.
Gray-Buchanan, A. W., Esq., Polmont.
Gray, George, Esq., J.P., Rutherglen.
Gunn, A. M., Esq., M.A., Brora, Sutherland.
Gunn, Alexander, Esq., Parkhead, Glasgow.
Gunn, Lieut. Gilbert, The Royal Scots, Bangalore, India.
Gunn, Hugh, Esq., Strathy, Sutherland.
Gunn, John, Esq., Golspie.
Gunn, William, Esq., Strathpeffer.
Harradence, R. W., Esq., Ware, Herts.
Harvie-Brown, John A., Esq., Larbert.
Hedderwick, J. C. H., Esq., M.P., Biggar.
Hay, Colin, Esq., Ardbeg, Islay.
Holmes, W. & R., Booksellers, Glasgow.
Hopkinson, J. Garland, Esq., Monaughty, Forres.
Houston, Major William, Kintradwell, Sutherland.
Hunter, John England, Esq., Douglas, Gairloch.
Hunter, W. Sutherland, Esq., Kildonan, Pollokshields, Glasgow.
Joass, Rev. Dr., Golspie.
Kemp, Daniel William, Esq., J.P., Trinity, Edinburgh.
Kerr, Rev. Cathel, Melness, Tongue, Sutherland.
Leason, George, Esq., J.P., Stoke-on-Trent.
Lightbody, W., Esq., Nairn.
Lindsay, Councillor Andrew, Merchant, Golspie.
Littlejohn, Alex., Esq., J.P., D.L., of Invercharron.
Macandrew, Sir Henry C., Aisthorpe, Inverness.
Macaulay, A. N., Esq., Solicitor, Golspie.
Macbean, William M., Esq., New York, U.S.A.

Macbeth, John, Esq., Kinbrace, Sutherland.
MacCoy, Daniel, Esq., Grand Rapids, Michigan, U.S.A.
Macdonald, Rev. A. J., Killearnan.
Macdonald, D. S., Esq., M.B., C.M., Armadale, Isle of Skye.
Macdonald, D. T., Esq., J.P., Calumet, Michigan, U.S.A.
Macdonald, H. L., Esq., of Dunach.
Macdonald, Allan, Esq., LL.D., Glenarm, Co. Antrim.
Macdonald, Alexander, Esq., of Balranald and Edenwood.
Macdonald, Alexander, Esq., Doncaster Street, Glasgow.
Macdonald, Charles Donald, Esq., Rosario, Argentine Republic.
Macdonald, George, Esq., Merchant, Lairg.
Macdonald, Hugh, Esq., Balcharn, Lairg.
Macdonald, Hugh, Esq., Solicitor, Aberdeen.
Macdonald, James, Esq., W.S., Edinburgh.
Macdonald, Keith Norman, Esq., M.D., Edinburgh.
Macdonald, Lachlan, Esq., of Skeabost, Isle of Skye.
Macdonald, Ranald, Esq., Carloway, Lewis.
Macfarlane, Malcolm, Esq., Elderslie.
Macgregor, George, Esq., Cannon Street, London.
MacIvor, Evander, Factor, Scourie.
Mackay, Captain A. Leith-Hay, Inverness.
Mackay, Major A. Y., Grangemouth.
Mackay, Sheriff Æneas J. G., M.A., LL.D., Edinburgh.
Mackay, Alexander, Esq., J.P., Holt Manor, Wilts.
Mackay, Alexander, Esq., St. Andrew Square, Edinburgh.
Mackay, Alexander, Esq., Bank of Scotland, Thurso.
Mackay, Alexander, Esq., Hutchison Square, Glasgow.
Mackay, Alexander, Esq., Bath Street, Glasgow.
Mackay, Alexander H., Esq., B.A., LL.D., B.Sc., Minister for Education, Nova Scotia.
Mackay, Andrew, Esq., The Mound, Sutherland.
Mackay, Colin J., Esq., of Bighouse, Kurnoul, India.
Mackay, D. J., Esq., Greencroft Gardens, London.
Mackay, David, Esq., Tain, Ross-shire.

LIST OF SUBSCRIBERS.

Mackay, Donald, Esq., J.P., Braemore, Caithness.
Mackay, Donald, Esq. (of Ceylon), Hereford.
Mackay, Donald, Esq., "Strathnaver," Edinburgh.
Mackay, Donald, Esq., Bromley, Kent.
Mackay, Donald, Esq., Helmsdale.
Mackay, Donald Hugh Petrus, Esq., Amsterdam, Holland.
Mackay, Duncan, Esq., Struan, Perthshire.
Mackay, His Excellency Baron Eneas, late Prime Minister of the Netherlands, The Hague, Holland.
Mackay, Eneas, Esq., Bookseller, Stirling.
Mackay, Eppe Roelof, Esq., Amsterdam, Holland.
Mackay, Eric, Esq., Royal Exchange, London.
Mackay, Mrs. Eric, Cheltenham.
Mackay, Surgeon-General George, M.D., J.P., of Bighouse.
Mackay, George, Esq., M.D., Drumsheugh Gardens, Edinburgh.
Mackay, George, Esq., Seedhill Road, Paisley.
Mackay, George J., Esq., J.P., Ex-Mayor of Kendal.
Mackay, Hector M., Esq., Town Clerk, Dornoch.
Mackay, Hugh, Esq., Spens Crescent, Perth.
Mackay, Hugh, Esq., Coleraine, Ireland.
Mackay, Ian Donald, Esq., B.A., C.M., M.B., Knaresborough.
Mackay, Captain James, Trowbridge, Wilts.
Mackay, Rev. James, Shrewsbury.
Mackay, James, Esq., Swansea.
Mackay, James, Esq., Roxburgh, Otago, New Zealand.
Mackay, James, Esq., Aberdeen.
Mackay, James, Esq., George IV. Bridge, Edinburgh.
Mackay, Rev. James Aberigh, D.D., Chieftain of Clan Abrach.
Mackay, James Hayward, Esq., Primrose Hill, London.
Mackay, James R., Esq., British Linen Bank House, Edinburgh.
Mackay, Miss Joan, "Mackay Institute," Paris, France.
Mackay, John, Esq., C.E., J.P., Hereford.
Mackay, John, Esq., M.I.M.E., Bangkok, Siam.
Mackay, John, Esq., Bristol.

LIST OF SUBSCRIBERS.

Mackay, John C., Esq., Battlefield Gardens, Langside, Glasgow.
Mackay, Councillor John, Peterborough.
Mackay, John, Esq., Gosforth, Newcastle-on-Tyne.
Mackay, John, Esq., Laidmore, New Zealand.
Mackay, John, Esq., Baffin Street, Dundee.
Mackay, John G., Esq., C.C., Portree, Isle of Skye.
Mackay, John S., Esq., LL.D., Edinburgh Academy.
Mackay, Joseph, Esq., High Street, Belfast.
Mackay, Mrs. C. (of Kinlochbervie House), Edinburgh.
Mackay, Miss, St. Giles, Lincoln.
Mackay, Mrs. Neil, Rosemarkie, Ross-shire.
Mackay, Neil, Esq., West 24th Street, New York, U.S.A.
Mackay, R. A., Esq., Durban, South Africa.
Mackay, R. Gunn, Esq., Stamford Hill, London.
Mackay, R. J., Esq., Darlington.
Mackay, R. Whyte, Esq., Union Street, Aberdeen.
Mackay, Richard, Esq., Merchant, Durness, Sutherland.
Mackay, Richard, Esq., M'Aslan Street, Glasgow.
Mackay, Stewart J., Esq., Conneaut Lake, Penn., U.S.A.
Mackay, Thomas, Esq., Largs.
Mackay, Thomas A., Esq., British Linen Bank House, Inverness.
Mackay, W. W., Esq., Ex-Provost, Dunoon.
Mackay, Councillor William, Solicitor, Inverness.
Mackay, William, Esq., Provost of Thurso.
Mackay, William, Esq., Dungannon, Co. Tyrone.
Mackay, William, Esq., Garriochmill Road, Glasgow.
Mackenzie, Alexander, Esq., Bath.
Mackenzie, Rev. D., Farr, Sutherland.
Mackenzie, Rev. Duncan S., Gairloch, Ross-shire.
Mackenzie, Rev. John, Golspie.
Mackenzie, John, Esq., Kirn.
Mackenzie, John, Esq., Town Clerk, Tain.
Mackenzie, Roderick Fraser, Esq., Fortrose.
Mackenzie, Sheriff, Dornoch.

Mackenzie, Miss, Durness.
Mackenzie, Wm., Esq., Secy., Crofters' Commission, Edinburgh.
Mackey, Edward, Esq., M.D., Brighton.
Mackey, Robert, Esq., Coleraine, Ireland.
Mackey, Thomas, Esq., Coleraine, Ireland.
Mackey, William J., Esq., Londonderry.
Mackillop, James, Jun., Esq., Polmont.
Mackinnon, Alexander K., Esq., South Kensington, London.
Mackintosh, Alexander, Esq., Forfar.
Mackintosh, Charles Fraser, Esq., of Drummond.
Mackintosh, D. A. S., Esq., Shettleston.
Mackintosh, Duncan, Bank of Scotland, Inverness.
Maclauchlan, J. D., Esq., M.E., Edinburgh.
Maclean, Alexander Scott, Esq., Bank Street, Greenock.
Maclean, Charles, Esq., Merchant, Golspie.
Maclean, Daniel, Jun., Esq., Roxburgh Street, Greenock.
Maclean, Lieut. Hector F., Younger of Duart, Scots Guards.
Macleod, John, Esq., Ardgay, Ross-shire.
Macleod, Norman, Esq., Bookseller, Edinburgh.
Macleod, Peter B. H., Esq., M.D., New Deer.
Macpherson, Alexander, Esq., Provost of Kingussie.
Macpherson, Donald, Esq., Postmaster, Falkirk.
Maitland, Bailie Andrew, Tain.
Matheson, Donald, Esq., J.P., of Achany and the Lews.
Matheson, Hugh Mackay, Esq., J,P., Hampstead, London.
Maybrick Library, Oxford.
Melville, Mullen and Slade, Booksellers, London.
Menzies, Colonel Duncan, 1st Sutherland Rifle Volunteers.
Menzies & Co., Messrs. John, Booksellers, Glasgow.
Morrison, Captain John, Dunrobin, Golspie.
Morrison, James, Esq., British Linen Coy.'s Bank, Golspie.
Morrison, Mrs. M. S., Partick, Glasgow.
Morrison, Captain William, Edinburgh.
Munro, Alexander, Esq., Breadalbane Street, Glasgow.

LIST OF SUBSCRIBERS.

Munro, Bailey, Esq., Hope Street, Glasgow.
Munro, Donald, Esq., M.I.C.E., Manchester.
Munro, Donald, Esq., Armadale, Melbourne, Victoria.
Munro, Rev. Donald, Ferintosh.
Munro, George M., Esq., C.-on-M., Manchester.
Munro, The Hon. James, late Premier of Victoria, Melbourne.
Munro, John, Esq., Hanley, Staffordshire.
Munro, Rev. Robert, M.A., B.D., F.S.A., Scot., Old Kilpatrick.
Murray, Bailie Alexander, J.P., Glasgow.
Murray, Alexander, Esq., Merchant, Strath Halladale.
Murray, Rev. John, Convener of the County of Sutherland, Brora.
Napier, Theodore, Esq., " Magdala," Essenden, Victoria.
Nicol, John, Esq., Golspie.
Noble, Kenneth D., Esq., Helensburgh.
Patience, James, Esq., Clutha Street, Glasgow.
Polson, Dr. J. Ronald, Worcester.
Pratt, Miss Maud, Secy. to the Duchess of Sutherland, Trentham.
Reay, The Right Hon. Lord, D.C.L., G.C.I.E., G.C.S.I.
Reay, Lady, Carolside, Berwickshire.
Reid, Donald, Esq., Struy, Beauly.
Robson, A. Mackay, Esq., Edinburgh.
Ross, A., Esq., Leicester.
Ross, Rev. Henry, LL.D., Lancaster.
Ross, John M., Esq., Devonshire Gardens, Glasgow.
Ross, William George, Esq., Forres.
Salmond, Rev. Dr., Aberdeen.
Sandison, A. K., Esq., Southampton.
Scobie, Miss, Keoldale, Durness.
Scott, Rev. A. B., Helmsdale.
Scott, Miss Jean Macfarlane, Sunderland.
Simpson, Dr. J. B., Golspie.
Sinclair, Archibald, Publisher, 10 Bothwell Street, Glasgow.
Sinclair, Rev. Colin, Kirkhill, Inverness-shire.
Sinclair, Donald, Esq., Stempster, Caithness.

LIST OF SUBSCRIBERS.

Sinclair, James, Esq., Fresno City, Cal., U.S.A.
Sinclair, Rev. A. Maclean, Belfast, Prince Edward Island.
Smith, Rev. Hunter, Edinburgh.
Smith, Captain J., Rhiconich Hotel, Sutherland.
Stewart, Hugh, Esq., Maxwell Street, Partick, Glasgow.
Steven, Frank, Esq., Station Hotel, Inverness.
Sutherland, His Grace the Duke of, Dunrobin Castle.
Sutherland, Dr. D. G., Brora.
Sutherland, Dr. L. R., Kersland Terrace, Glasgow.
Sutherland, Alexander, Esq., Prestonkirk.
Sutherland, A. Munro, Esq., Newcastle-on-Tyne.
Sutherland, Benjamin John, Esq., Newcastle-on-Tyne.
Sutherland, Charles H., Esq., Montreal, Canada.
Sutherland, Charles J., Esq., M.D., South Shields.
Sutherland, George, Esq., Hatfield, Herts.
Sutherland, George Miller, Esq., Wick.
Sutherland, James, Esq., Berriedale, Clapham Common, London.
Sutherland, John, Esq., Stoke-on-Trent.
Sutherland, John, Esq., Cefu Coed, South Wales.
Sutherland, John A., Esq., M.D., Cleckheaton, Yorks.
Sutherland, George, Esq., Portskerra, Sutherland.
Symon, A., Esq., The Mound, Golspie.
Thompson, Frederick, Esq., South Street, London.
Thomson, J. J. P., Esq., C.C., London.
Tongue Reading Room, Sutherland.
Tunnicliff, Major, J.P., Hanley.
Turnbull, Mrs., Durness Hotel, Sutherland.
Urquhart, R., Esq., Commercial Bank, Douglas, Lanark.
Waddell, James, Esq., Gallowgate, Glasgow.
Warrand, Colonel A. J. C., Ryefield, Conon-Bridge.
Westminster, His Grace the Duke of, Benmore Lodge.
White, Hon. Montague, Antigua, West Indies.
Whyte, Henry, Esq., 4 Bridge Street, Glasgow.
Wilson, J. Mackay, Esq., Currygrane, Co. Longford, Ireland.
Yule, Miss Amy Frances, Tarradale, Ross-shire.

LADY REAY.

SUTHERLAND AND THE REAY COUNTRY.

HISTORY, PART I.

BY JOHN MACKAY, C.E., J.P., HEREFORD.

OUR earliest knowledge of this district is obtained from the Greek geographers of Alexandria, Strabo and Ptolemy, of the first and second century of our era. They compiled maps and charts of the world so far as it was then explored, and in their works it is interesting to meet with such names as Nabarus, (Naver), Ila, (Illigh), Logi, (Loth), and Abona, (Bonar). The tribal names of the period are not so easily identified now, but it is clear they were a Celtic race, and closely allied with the British or Brythonic family.

From the Roman era to the seventh century, the story of these Northern Caledonian Picts is shrouded in obscurity. A feeble light begins to glint upon its horizon by the advent of the Columban Missionaries, in the end of the sixth century. It is a matter of regret that neither the Scottish, nor Irish annalists of this period, record anything of the Northern Picts. There is abundant evidence, however, in the pages of Adamnan, Columba's biographer, and of Dicuil, an Irish Monk, that the Orkneys were converted to the Christian faith before the 7th century, and the same may be fairly inferred about Caithness and Sutherland. Shortly after this the inhabitants were destined to a rude awakening, from the Norse pirates on the one hand, and the Dalriadic Scots on the other.

It is indeed impossible to say how early the North Coast received occasional visits from the Vikings. They did not, however, come to stay, until Orkney was first colonized by them, and made the base of operations. The earliest Norse settlers there were refugees from Norway, and they did not hesitate to make raids upon the mother country as well as upon the mainland, and the Western Isles of Scotland. To put an end to these plundering expeditions Harold Fairhair, King of Norway, in 872, fitted out a large fleet, subdued the Orkney Islands and continued his course to the Hebrides, which he also subjugated. Orkney was then given to Rognwald, Earl of Moeri, who was thus the first Earl, and he, in less than a year, presented the Earldom to his brother Sigurd, uncle of Rolf, the conqueror of Normandy.

In 875, Sigurd, along with Thorstein the Red, leader of the Norse settlers in Ireland, subdued the Northern Counties as far south as Moray. The Sagas relate with much detail his encounter with Maolbragd, the Celtic mor-mhaor of Ross, surnamed Buck-tooth. The Celtic chief challenged him to fight with forty men a side on horseback, but the Norse Jarl, suspecting treachery, put two men on each horse, and so won the victory. It was, however, dearly bought, for as Sigurd rode off, with the chieftain's head fastened to his saddle-straps, the protruding tooth grazed his foot, and inflicted a wound of which he died. He was buried in "Sigurd's Hoch," now Siderha (Cyderhall). From this date, until the final expulsion of the Norsemen in 1196, the county of Sutherland had little peace. Its position exposed it to perpetual inroads from the Norsemen of Caithness on the one hand, and the Celts of Moray on the other. The Mor-mhaor of ancient Moravia vied with the Scottish Kings in power and influence. Again and again this district was overrun by the victorious Norse, but native chiefs soon arose after each invasion, and kept the foreigners well within the bounds of Caithness. The Reay country did not fare so badly in this perpetual strife, although the native population was more or less dominated by the Norse colonies at Durness, Tongue, Farr, and Halladale. That sanguinary conflicts took place in this remote district is clear alike from the pages of Torfæus, and the Sagas, and the battle-fields along the banks of the Naver, and the North Coast, which bear Norse names. But the South East part of the County suffered most, as it lay in the way of the opposing armies, and to this period must be ascribed the construction of such fortifications as remain at Loch Brora, and the many walled caves along the coast, such as those of Kintradwell, and in the hill face above Dunrobin, visited by Pococke and Pennant.

It was during the fierce and sanguinary warfare carried on for centuries between the Norse and the descendants of the Northern Picts, that the Scottish kingdom of the Dalriads extended its borders, and ultimately obtained complete control over all Scotland. As early as the tenth century the Scottish

Kings claim the right to interfere in matters of this Northern Earldom. In 1008, King Malcolm confirms the Earldom of Sutherland and Caithness to Sigurd, the Stout, and gives him his daughter in marriage. Their son Thorfinn, was created Earl at the early age of five, by his grandfather, and deputies were appointed to govern his possessions during his minority. He became one of the most influential of the Norse Earls, and disputed the right of his cousin, King Duncan, to the tribute usually paid to the Scottish Kings. This brought about war, and Moddan, the King's nephew, was created Earl of Caithness, and furnished with an army to dispossess his rival. Moddan's army was defeated, and King Duncan now resolved to attack Thorfinn by land and sea. He himself went with the fleet, and Moddan was sent by land with a large army. Thorfinn was again victorious. King Duncan made a third attempt to crush this formidable vassal. This time the scene of operations was in the district of Moray. A great battle was fought, and victory for a time was doubtful, but the Norse Earl again prevailed, and the country was overrun as far south as Fife. Torfæus says "his vengeance was terrific, destroying whole countries with fire and sword." King Duncan was slain either in the battle, or by his General, Macbeth, who succeeded him on the throne. The Kingdom was divided between himself and Thorfinn, the latter receiving the North and Eastern provinces to the Tay. He died in 1064, leaving a widow Ingibiorg, who became the first wife of Malcolm Ceannmor.

Thorfinn's successors, however, were not able long to keep possession of the Southern districts. On the accession of Malcolm Ceannmor to the Scottish throne, one after another fell away from their Norse allegiance. His sons

A GLIMPSE OF STRATHNAVER AT LOCH NAVER.

quarrelled among themselves, and in 1139 Rognald, the son of Kol, and Harold, the son of Maddad, Earl of Athol, by Margaret, daughter of a Sutherland Norse magnate, obtained forcible possession of the Northern Earldom. About 1187, a rival to Harald Maddadson appeared in the person of Harald, the younger, grandson of Earl Rognwald. Hostilities began afresh, and Harald, the younger, was slain. King William the Lion commissioned Reginald of the Isles to levy troops, and proceed to the scene of disturbance. A battle was fought at Dalharold, Strathnaver, which ended in the defeat of Harald Maddadson; and three deputies were appointed to rule in the name of the King of Scots, at Tongue, Thurso, and Dunrobin respectively. Shortly afterwards, Harald returned from Orkney, whither he had fled, and mutilated the Bishop at Scrabster, (who intervened on behalf of his countrymen), and ravaged the county with fire and sword. This outburst of Norse savagery moved King William to come in person to the North, with a large army. He had with him a contingent from Galloway, and another from Moray, under command of Hugh Freskyn. After fining the Earl in 2000 pounds of silver, and separating Reay and Sutherland from his jurisdiction, and taking hostages, he returned, leaving Hugh Freskyn commander in Sutherland, and the chief of the Galloway contingent, Alex. (Mackay) in the Reay Country. These respective chiefs were the progenitors of the Houses of Sutherland and Mackay. They soon expelled the Norsemen, applied themselves to restore and maintain order, pacify the country, and consolidate the power and influence vested in them by the King of Scotland, whose authority was now firmly established in the North. In 1222 they rendered material assistance to Alexander II., in his expedition into Caithness, to punish those implicated in the barbarous and tragical burning of Bishop Adam, at Brawl. The Mackay chief met the King at Halkirk, and the Sutherland contingent led by William De Moravia, Hugh Freskyn's son, joined him as he passed through by the coast. This gallant young warrior was a constant attendant upon William the Lion in his expeditions to quell mutinies in Moray and Ross, fomented by the Celtic population in these provinces, against the feudal rule of the Norman lords, introduced by King David and William the Lion himself. He also assisted Alexander II., in quelling a Celtic rebellion in Ross, for which he was ennobled and styled, "Dominus Sutherlandiae," and in 1228 Alexander created him Earl of Sutherland, the first Earl of his race. He died about 1248, and his son William succeeded him as 2nd Earl. It was during the 1st Earl's rule in Sutherland that Bishop Gilbert of Moravia, a cousin, reorganised the bishopric of Caithness and Sutherland, built the cathedral of Dornoch, divided the counties into parishes, provided ministers to officiate in them, and made provision for their support, and the maintenance of conventual worship in the cathedral. It is said that he translated the Psalms of David and the Gospels into Gaelic for the benefit of all within his diocese. This eminent ecclesiastic was held in the highest esteem by Alexander II. He died in 1245, and was afterwards canonized.

In 1259, the date given by Sir Robert Gordon, was fought the battle of Dornoch. Tradition has it that Bishop Gilbert, like other ecclesiastics of his time, with his younger brother Richard, baron of Skelbo, were first in the fray. The Bishop's shield-bearer, as soon as he saw the Norsemen, ran away, so that the Bishop had to fight without his shield.

The incident became a common proverb ever after—"He was like the Bishop's lad; when wanted he was not to be found." Earl William soon appeared on the scene, and the Norsemen were defeated and chased to their ships at the Little Ferry. The fight was severe, and among the killed was Sir Richard De Moravia of Skelbo. The Earl of Sutherland was disarmed by the Norse commander, but finding the leg of a horse near him, hurled it at his antagonist and killed him. A stone on the battlefield marks the place of his fall and interment; another named the Earl's Cross, was reared to commemorate the victory. This was the last raid of the Norsemen into Sutherland. If the Bishop took part in this battle, its date would probably be 1239, not 1259.

In 1263, the whole county was thrown into a state of great consternation by rumours of a Norwegian invasion. Norwegian troops had landed in Caithness, and were levying contributions far and near. Watch fires were alight everywhere, but Haco passed on to Durness, brought his fleet to anchor, and sent some men on shore to plunder. The people being forewarned, retired into the interior with their goods and chattels. Foiled in their expectation of plunder, the remorseless invaders destroyed twenty hamlets, and demolished a fort on the shore, the ruins of which still remain, now called "Sean chaisteal," (old castle).

On the return of Haco, after the disaster of Largs, he put into Loch Erribol for provisions and fresh water. A strong party was sent out to forage. The natives were on the alert, and drove their cattle and flocks into the inland valleys. Some were discovered in Glengollie, which were being driven away when the natives intercepted the Norsemen, and after some fighting the plunderers retreated into the adjacent valley of Strathmore. Here they were again intercepted, and all slain except one, who by fleetness of foot, escaped to carry his tale of woe to Haco. In memory of this event the valley became known as "Urra-Dal," or the Dale upon which the Norse leader fell, and in which he was interred. Haco immediately set sail for Orkney.

LOCH HOPE, LOOKING TOWARDS STRATHMORE.

The spirited rule of the successors of William the Lion, the two Alexanders, caused law and order to prevail in the North and the South. The prosperous reign of the last Alexander, for thirty-seven years, became the theme of poets. Wars, internal and external, had ceased in the land. Everyone enjoyed security. It was the "golden age" in Scotland, when every yeoman and every peasant cultivated his fields, and tended his flocks in peace and tranquility. The merchant plied his trade on land and sea without dread or apprehension, commerce at home and with foreign countries prospered to an extent hitherto unknown or unheard of, Scottish ships and merchantmen were known in almost every seaport in Europe.

Sutherland, north and south, shared in this general prosperity. The two chiefs of Sutherland succeeded in moulding their heterogeneous followers to their will, and uniting them into a compact body of clansmen devoted to their service. This wise and conciliating policy had its due reward. The chiefs became respected and revered, the clansmen felt proud of their chiefs, and acknowledged the kindness shown them by complete devotion to their interests in peace or war, and the spirit of clanship was in consequence fostered to an extent previously unknown.

Evil days were impending; the disastrous and tragic death of Alexander III., in 1286, threw the country into the hands of the designing and warlike Edward I. of England. The selfish and craven hearted Scots nobility bowed their necks to the yoke, and swore fealty to Edward in 1296, William, the 2nd Earl of Sutherland, being of the number. The Scottish yeomen and peasantry gloomily stood aloof anticipating a leader; the rapacity of the English soldiery aroused the greatest indignation amongst all classes. The leader arose in the person of Wallace, who like another Samson, went forth almost singly and slew the "Philistines," in almost every encounter. He became a real hero, the magic of his name and fame encouraged the middle and lower classes of his countrymen, while it terrified the enemy far and wide. Emboldened by such rapid successes, the bravest of his countrymen soon rallied round the standard of freedom and justice, determined, like their leader, to free their country from the arrogant oppressions of Edward's soldiery One stronghold after another was captured from the invaders, till Scotland, north of the Tay, was set free. Then an opportunity presented itself, which was to set free the whole south of Scotland by one fell stroke. Edward, furious at the rapid progress made by Wallace in capturing and expelling his garrisons from so many strongholds throughout the country, ordered his Lord Deputy, Warrender, to collect all the soldiery of the North of England and South of Scotland, and crush the "robber and rebel," Wallace, who was at the time besieging Dundee. Wallace immediately sent the fiery-cross into the North Lowlands and Highlands, for every chief to come to his aid, with his contingent of men. He raised the siege of Dundee, and with the forces he had in hand took post on the Ochill hills, behind Dunblane, to watch the movements of the invading army. Here came to his aid the Menzies, Murray, and other clans of Perthshire and Moray, the yeomen of Fife, Angus, and the Mearns, a goodly array; indeed, the Scottish army was mostly composed of Highlanders. By dint of strategy and generalship, a glorious victory at Stirling Bridge was achieved by Wallace, and Scotland set free.

The calamitous effects of the envy and jealousy of the craven hearted Scottish nobility, at these astounding successes being achieved without their aid or countenance, became manifest next year at Falkirk, when all of them again bowed the knee to Edward, and the independence of Scotland was once again lost for a time. Nevertheless, Wallace showed the way to attain it; his mantle fell upon Robert Bruce, who,

THE FIELD OF BANNOCKBURN, FROM THE GILLIES' HILL.

following the tactics of Wallace, eventually succeeded in giving the "coup de grace" to English arrogance and claim of supremacy, on the field of Bannockburn, by the united military forces of the Kingdom, amongst whom were the chiefs and retainers of Sutherland and Mackay.

A deep and general panic seized the English after Bannockburn. Their wonted energy forsook them. Robert Bruce, taking advantage of this dejection, very soon after the battle, invaded England three times in 1314, enriched his army, and sent every member of it home laden with spoil. These expeditions were continued almost every year, with little opposition. In 1323, Bruce personally conducted a large army into England, comprising the whole military strength of Scotland, from North to South, and meeting the King of England, with all the array of his kingdom, at Biland Abbey, inflicted upon him a crushing defeat, pursuing him to the gates of York. The chiefs of Sutherland distinguished themselves at this battle; the "Redshanks," as the English called the kilted men of the North, proved themselves brave warriors. Earl William of Sutherland died two years after this great victory.

In 1333, his son and successor Kenneth, was slain at the battle of Halidon Hill, leading the van; many of his men fell with him. In 1349, Earl William, son of Kenneth, led an expedition into England, and on returning captured Roxburgh Castle. This Earl became a great favourite with King David, after returning to Scotland from his nine years' exile in France, in 1341.

In 1341-3, this Earl with his men accompanied David in his expeditions and invasions into England. David rewarded him for his services by giving him his sister,

Margaret Bruce, in marriage, by whom he had two sons, Alexander and John.

In 1346, David, at the instigation of the King of France, who was then hard pressed by Edward III., mustered the whole military forces of Scotland, and burst into England, ravaging the country as he advanced, right up to Durham. The Earl of Sutherland, with the barons and men of the North, were in this army. David, although no general, was as brave and daring as his uncle, Edward Bruce, but he wholly lacked the admirable judgment, prudence, and military skill of his great father. After very severe fighting at Neville's Cross, he was defeated and taken prisoner, with his brother-in-law, the Earl of Sutherland, and several of his nobility. He attributed his defeat and capture to the Steward of Scotland and the Earl of March, commanding the third division, retiring from the field without making an effort to come to his aid while hard pressed in the centre. This was the supposed cause of the bitter enmity he afterwards manifested towards the Steward, who was his presumptive heir. After eleven years' captivity in England he was ransomed, his nephew, the young master of Sutherland, being one of the hostages for the payment. David, after his return, obtained the consent of parliament to disinherit the Steward, and elect the young master of Sutherland his heir presumptive. He then largely endowed the Earl of Sutherland with baronies in various counties, which the Earl afterwards reconveyed to noblemen in those districts on promise to support the rights granted to his son, against any claims the Steward might make upon the demise of the King. The young master of Sutherland died in England before the King's ransom was paid, and the whole scheme became void

DUNROBIN CASTLE—SEAT OF THE DUKE OF SUTHERLAND.

and of no effect. The Steward succeeded to the throne as Robert II.

During the time of William, fifth Earl of Sutherland, who was much in the south engaged in the continual warfare on the borders, frequent aggressions were made by Sutherland men upon the Mackays, who as frequently retaliated. Upon the return of the Sutherland chief, Mackay demanded reparation, the Sutherlands being the aggressors. The Earl offered to submit their differences to the Lord of the Isles, and other noblemen of Ross; Mackay assented. The parties met at Dingwall, and submitted their relative cases to arbitration. It would appear that the Mackay chief seemed likely to get the best of it. The Earl sought an interview with Mackay and his son Donald. In the heat of the discussion high words ensued, and the Earl getting very angry drew his dagger and mortally stabbed both father and son. Hastily making his escape out of the castle, he rode off to Dunrobin, pursued by the Mackay retainers so closely that it was with some difficulty he succeeded in effecting his escape. This was the commencement of the feuds and conflicts which lasted for two centuries, between the Sutherlands and Mackays. The successor of this Earl arranged the whole dispute afterwards with the successor of the chiefs assassinated at Dingwall, and amity was re-established for a time.

The Mackay chief, Angus, who succeeded his father Donald, killed at Dingwall in 1370, married a daughter of MacLeod of Lewis, by whom he had two sons, Angus Du, and Rorie Gallda, (Roderick the foreigner), so called from his being by custom reared in Lewis amongst his mother's relatives. Their father, having died at an early age, left

KYLE OF TONGUE.

his family and estates in the guardianship of his brother Hugh, till his son Angus Du came of age. Hugh was a stern man of business, and proved himself worthy of the trust reposed in him by his brother. During his guardianship the mother of the young chief was desirous of having some share in the management of affairs, and probably a larger allowance than had been allotted to her. Hugh declined to accede to her demands. She then complained to her brother, MacLeod of Lewis, who came to Tongue with a large and select company of his men, with the determination of compelling Hugh by entreaty or force, to comply with his sister's demands. Finding the guardian inflexible, and not a man to be cajoled by fair words, or overawed by force, he departed in high dudgeon, and on his way homewards drove off a large number of cattle from Mackay's lands. No sooner was this reported than Hugh and his brother Neil, getting as many men together as they could, went in pursuit of the men of Lewis, whom they overtook in Strathoykell. The Mackays immediately attacked the Lewis men, and as Sir R. Gordon says, "a terrible battle was fought," in which the islanders were annihilated, one only escaping to tell the woful tale. Hugh, the guardian, died two years after this event, and Neil did not long survive, leaving three sons, Thomas, Morgan, and Neil, who played an important part in the story of the life of Angus Du.

Upon the death of his uncle Hugh, the young chief assumed the reins of government, well prepared by his guardian in all the accomplishments of the period to govern and lead men in peace and war. He soon proved himself to be no ordinary leader of men. From the associations he had formed, and the influence he had acquired in the earlier years of his rule, we find him to have been a young man of great capacity, attaining within the three northern counties an ascendancy second only to the Lord of the Isles, when that potentate rebelled against the Regent of Scotland, to assert his pretended right to the Earldom of Ross, during the long imprisonment of James I. in England.

The Munro, Ross, and other clans in that Earldom were on the side of the Regent, and were not well inclined to the Lord of the Isles. Instigated probably by the Regent, these clans formed a confederacy to resist the pretensions of the turbulent Lord of the Isles, who had been plotting with the King of England to divide Scotland between them. Angus Du was appealed to for assistance. Being the most powerful of the confederates, he was elected to command in chief, and thus became "leader of 4000 men." The Lord of the Isles, informed of this confederacy, resolved at once to force these refractory clans into submission. Collecting an army in the Isles, he invaded Ross, and came up to his opponents at Dingwall, where after a stubborn conflict he defeated them, and took Angus Du prisoner. The defeated Ross-shire clans were obliged to submit, and Angus Du was confined in Caisteal Tirrim. Situated as he then was, the Lord of the Isles was politic enough to perceive that the friendship of so influential a chief would be a great accession of strength to himself, in keeping possession of Ross against the wiles of the Regent; he therefore proposed to set him at liberty, give him his sister Elizabeth in marriage, and endow them with large grants of land, the superiority of which he possessed in right of his wife, the Countess of Ross.

An agreement upon these terms was effected. Angus Du was liberated, and married the sister of Donald of the

Isles and the famous Alistair "Carrach," at Caisteal Tirrim, and returned with his wife to Tongue. A charter (1414-15) confirmed to them those lands, on the south west of Sutherland, extending from the church lands of Skibo to the confines of Assynt, and thence to Lochbroom, and on the north coast, the whole of Strath Halladale.

Angus Du life-rented these lands to his cousins Thomas, Morgan, and Neil, the sons of his uncle Neil. To Thomas he assigned Strath Halladale, Pulrossie, and Criech to the river Shin; to Morgan, the whole of Strathoykell; and to Neil all the Ross-shire lands.

Such an extensive acquisition of territory adjoining his own patrimonial estates gave the Mackay chief a preponderance of power and influence much superior to the Earl of Sutherland,—anything but agreeable to him—and moreover a source of great disquietude, as his own territory was now surrounded on three sides by those of the Mackay chief, who in reality became "Angus the absolute" in the county, in point of territory and command of men. Thus, Robert Earl of Sutherland, became extremely jealous of the martial Mackay chief. He was aware he could not openly counteract his influence, but what could not be done by force might be accomplished by underhand policy, in fomenting quarrels and disturbances in that lawless age. The Earl had willing allies in the Murrays in Sutherland, and his own relatives, and the Mowatts in Caithness, who began to make incursions into Strath Halladade. Thomas Mackay accused Mowatt of fostering or permitting such raids, and demanded redress. Mowatt haughtily refused. Thomas, being some time afterward in Criech, where he generally resided, heard of Mowatt having passed southward with a retinue of men; he pursued him, and overtook him near Tain. Redress of the injuries complained of was again demanded and refused, swords were drawn, Mowatt was slain, and his followers took refuge in St. Duffus' chapel. The infuriated Mackays pursued them and set fire to the chapel. This atrocity was reported to the Regent, who declared Thomas Mackay an outlaw, his possessions, goods, and chattels forfeited, and offered as a reward for his apprehension. The difficulty was, who would dare do it. Angus Du would not apprehend his own near relative. The Earl of Sutherland was not anxious to embroil himself with the Mackays, but a fitting instrument was found in Angus Murray of Pulrossie, who had two daughters of whom Thomas Mackay's brothers, Morgan and Neil were enamoured. Angus Murray consulted the Earl, who promised him his protection; he then cajoled the two brothers to assist him, promising them his two daughters in marriage, and sharing with them their brother's forfeited property. The unnatural miscreants assented. Their brother was inveigled into Angus Murray's power, taken to Inverness and there executed. Murray and they had their reward, but neither of them long enjoyed the fruits of their perfidy.

Meanwhile, the Caithness folk and friends of Mowatt, indignant at one of their lairds being slain by Thomas Mackay, made several raids into Strath Halladale, considering his forfeited property fair plunder, but continuing them too far into Angus Du's own territory in Farr, the redoubtable old chief was provoked to make reprisals. Gathering together his men and taking his young son Neil with him, he marched into Caithness, and at Harpsdale, a few miles from Thurso, met the whole forces of Caithness. A furious battle soon began, fought out with equal valour, and in the end the Caithness men were overthrown with great slaughter; many members of the best families in the county fell in this engagement. Loud complaints from Caithness reached King James I., who a few years previously had returned from his captivity in England, and having many more similar complaints from various quarters of the Highlands, he determined to summon all the Highland chiefs to meet him at Inverness, (1427). Some of these he ordered to be executed forthwith, others he imprisoned, and a few men, amongst whom was the Mackay chief, upon their justifying their acts, he forgave and released, upon giving their eldest sons as hostages. This was a device of James to get the heirs of the Highland chiefs into his possession, and near his court to be educated and "civilized" as he himself had been at the English court, and so make them better subjects, and more amenable to law and order when permitted to return home. The Mackay chief gave the King his eldest son and heir, Neil, who for a time was imprisoned in the Bass, under the care and tutelage of Sir Robert Lauder, a relative. Ever after this young chief was nicknamed Neil Wass (Neil of the Bass).

Angus Murray, now in possession of Strath Halladale and Criech, still plotted against Angus Du, whose brother-in-law, Donald Lord of the Isles, was now dead, and Alexander his successor, and cousin of Angus, under the ban of the crown, and his own son and heir prisoner in the Bass, whose return was uncertain. He thought it a fitting opportunity to carry out his scheme of getting entire possession of the Reay country, in which he was encouraged by Robert, Earl of Sutherland. He was well aware that his sons-in-law, Morgan and Neil Mackay, had incurred the hatred of their near relative and chief Angus Du, for the base and unnatural part they acted in the apprehension of their brother Thomas, and representing to them the old age of their father's nephew, the uncertainty of his son's ever returning from the Bass, he prevailed upon them to lay claim to the succession, and immediate surrender to them of the inheritance which was now their right, as nearest heirs. This illegal demand Angus Du well knew to be supported by influences of a dangerous nature He was now from his years less able to lead his men in battle, he also considered that his son and heir was a hostage, and that it was imperative upon him to keep the King's peace, he therefore offered to surrender to his ungrateful cousins some of his territory, reserving to himself the district of Kintail, the original patrimony. This great concession was declined.

Angus Murray now persuaded them to enforce their demands by the sword. He consulted the Earl of Sutherland, who promised him his assistance, or as Sir R. Gordon puts it, "they had Earl Robert his attollerance."

Intelligence reached Angus Du that an invasion of his country was in preparation. The aged hero was astonished: he consulted his head men, and his young son Ian Abrach, as his clansmen then named him from having been reared by his mother's relatives in Lochaber, and still delight to keep his name in remembrance as the hero of the clan. The resolution come to was, to defend the territory and the honour of their chief and clan to the last extremity, or die in their defence.

The fiery cross was sent through every hamlet, clansmen were aroused and prepared to resist the threatened invasion to the uttermost. This stern determination of his men

THE "WATCH HILL," TONGUE—(CNOC-AN-FHREACADAIN).

roused in the old warrior chief much of the animation of his younger days. Scouts and spies were sent into Sutherland to observe and report upon the movements going on. It was soon ascertained that Angus Murray and his coadjutors were gathering men from all quarters, and a day had been appointed to march into the Reay country to take possession. The veteran old chief, like Bruce before his day, now looked out for an advantageous position near Tongue, upon which his comparatively few men could oppose the superior numbers of the invaders in a defensive battle. His practised eye soon marked out Druim-na-cupa, two miles south of Tongue, on the shortest track to it from the south. There were no roads in those days. There was, however, a doubt as to the actual route the invaders might choose, and a party was posted on the south face of Ben Loyal to watch. From this point a view of the whole country round was obtained for miles in front and flanks. The approach of the invaders was reported inclining to the direct route to Tongue. There was no longer any doubt. The Mackay commanders marshalled their men in compact order on the upper slopes of Druim-na-cupa, sending forward a detachment to the gorge of a pass in front, to conceal themselves in a copse on the side of the pass and attack the rear of the enemy in coming through it. These arrangements made, Ian Abrach and the other commanders entreated the aged chief to retire to the top of the ridge, where he could survey the impending conflict and be out of harm's way. He consented, and relinquished the command to his gallant young son.

The invaders were seen advancing through the pass, in a disorderly manner, leaders in front, as if there was no danger of opposition. Emerging from the pass, and seeing only a small compact body of Mackays right in front, they thought they were marching to an easy victory. One of the leaders shouted, "come on, we shall soon shackle those calves," to which another replied, "look out for yourself, the calves may jump too high for you to shackle them."

The van of the invaders rushed across the intervening hollow and advanced up the slope to the onset in desultory order. They were firmly and fiercely met by Ian Abrach and his men. Their front ranks, out of breath, soon bit the dust, the next met with no better fate, but still the fight was continued, the Sutherland men fighting resolutely as they came up Meanwhile the party in ambush attacked the rear going through the pass. So sudden and unexpected was this attack that the disorderly resistance made was unavailing, and the party of scouts coming up from the rear at nearly the same time and falling in on the flanks, this portion of the invaders was nearly, if not wholly annihilated. The victors in the pass now pushed on to the aid of their countrymen fighting the main battle. They fell upon the left rear and flank of the enemy, but the Sutherland men still fought on with their accustomed bravery. They were, however, outgeneraled, their leaders slain, numbers were of no avail, and taken now in front, flank, and left rear, the survivors fled away to their right up the slopes of the northern end of Ben Loyal, pursued by the Mackays for some miles, till, it is said, the last man of them was slain at Ath-charrie.

Such was the battle of Druim-na-cupa, the "Bannockburn" of the Reay country, and as momentous to it in its results. Sir R. Gordon is obliged to admit in his "Earldom of Sutherland," "the memory of this 'skirmish' remaineth in that country (Reay country) with the posterity to this day,' and "Morgan and Neil with their father-in-law Angus Murray were slain, and as they had undertaken this enterpryse upon ane evill ground, they perished therin accordinglie," but Sir Robert does not say that Earl Robert was cognisant of it and aided the actors, and further he says, that on being informed of the fall of Angus Murray "he pursued John

CASTLE VARRICH, KYLE OF TONGUE.

Abrach so hotely, that he constrained him, for saiftie of his lyff to fly into the Isles." There is no foundation in fact or tradition for this assertion, but there is a traditionary foundation for asserting that the Earl had several times sent assassins to the Reay country to kill him, and a cave in the face of the rock beneath Castle Varrich is named in the vernacular, "the hidden bed of John Abrach." Sutherland had received such a blow by the issue of the battle of Druim-na-cupa, that peace was preserved between the two clans for a century, till the advent of the Gordons into Sutherland. The differences of the Mackays in the meantime were with the people of Caithness, in which as we shall see they still proved their prowess and superiority in fighting.

After the fighting on the slopes of Druim-na-cupa was over, and the whole survivors of the Mackays were in pursuit of the flying Sutherland men, as already noted, Angus Du came upon the field to view the slain, wounded, and dying. He soon recognised Angus Murray and his own two ungrateful and unnatural cousins among the slain. While standing contemplating the unhappy, though deserved fate that so swiftly overtook their vile ingratitude, he was killed by an arrow shot by a cowardly Sutherland man lurking in a bush near the battlefield. Years after, this assassin was slain by William Du, son of John Abrach and grandson of Angus Du. This important engagement took place about 1431.

In consequence of its decisive and signal result John Abrach was greatly distinguished in the north. Young as he was he governed his clan with a firm and judicious hand, and preserved the peace during the absence of his elder brother in the Bass. He made himself so much beloved by the people that they solicited him to assume the chiefship, as it was uncertain whether or not his brother would ever return, but the loyal and gallant young man declined all such solicitations as derogatory to himself, and to his heroic father, and exiled brother kept in durance by the will of the King, as a hostage for the maintenance of peace. John Abrach, the hero of the Mackay clan, possessed great bodily strength, fortitude, and courage; reared amongst the Lochaber warriors, he excelled in swordsmanship and athletic exercises. His clansmen and neighbours respected him for his prowess and conciliatory conduct. He was no less respected for his social virtues. He married a daughter of the Mackintosh chief, with whom he became acquainted in his youth in Lochaber. On his brother's return after the assassination

STRATHNAVER AT SYRE, NEAR ROSSAL.

of James I., he resigned all authority to him. So pleased was his brother with his excellent administration of his clan affairs that he resigned to him in perpetuity a large portion of the estate, extending from Mudale to Rossal in Strathnaver. Taking up his seat in Achness, he became the progenitor of the sept of his clan styled the Abrach Mackays.

Shortly after Neil of the Bass' return, upon some provo

cation given by the people of Caithness, he and his brother John Abrach collected their forces and marched into Caithness to punish them. They left a reserve force at Sandside, and went further into the country, gathering a great spoil, with which they returned. The Caithness men overtook them at Downreay, when a fierce conflict took place. The Caithness men had the worst of it and fled, pursued by the Mackays to the river Forse, when a large number of Caithness men were seen speedily marching to the aid of their countrymen. The Mackays retired upon their reserve; coming up to them, they again faced their foes and a most desperate engagement was began, which ended in the complete rout of the men of Caithness, who were pursued, with great slaughter, for three miles. This event is locally known as "The Sandside chase."

Neil of the Bass died about 1450, and by his wife, a lady of the Munro clan, left two sons, Angus and John Roy. Angus succeeded his father and lived in peace till about 1464, when broils broke out in Caithness between the Keiths of Ackergill and the clan Gunn. The Gunns prepared for war, and many other districts of Caithness espoused their cause. The Keith, mistrustful of his own ability to cope with the Gunns and their allies, applied to his friend Mackay for aid, which was readily granted. Collecting all the men he could, he made a forced march of thirty miles through Caithness and joined the Keiths. The hostile forces met on the moor of Tannach, three miles from Wick, where a most desperate engagement ensued, attended with great slaughter on each side. At length victory declared itself for the Keiths and Mackays, chiefly through the extraordinary prowess of a herculean Mackay delighting in the euphonious appellation of John Mor-Mac-Ian Riabhaich Mackay, who with a battle-axe proportionate to his strength, cut down every opponent who came within its reach ; but this decisive battle did not terminate the differences between the Keiths and the Gunns.

Meanwhile peace was maintained between the Sutherlands and Mackays, but during the rule of Earl John in Sutherland, 1455, the MacDonalds of Glengarry to the number of some hundreds made an irruption into Sutherland and encamped at Skibo. They began to maraud and gather spoil. Before they did much harm the Sutherlands and Murrays were upon them and defeated them. A year or two afterwards a larger party of them penetrated into Sutherland as far as Strathfleet; but the gallant Murrays were not far off. They quickly and quietly gathered men enough to give them battle, in which the MacDonald marauders were again defeated and chased away as far as Bonar. This was the last raid made by the MacDonalds into Sutherland in any numbers, but from tradition and songs sung by the old inhabitants commemorating smaller marauding incidents in after years, it is evident they had been continued.

About 1475, Angus, the Mackay chief, it is recorded, was burnt by the Rosses of Balnagown in the church of Tarbet, probably on account of some raids he had made into Eastern Ross in conjunction with the MacKenzies, when letters of fire and sword enjoined them to proceed against the Earl of Ross, Lord of the Isles, who was at the time under the ban of the Crown. This murder was avenged a few years after by John, the son and successor of Angus, who invaded Strathoykell and at Allta-charrish defeated the Rosses of Balnagown with great loss, no less than seventeen landed proprietors of Ross were killed, and as usual a great booty carried away. The Mackays in this battle were led, under the command of the chief, by William Du, son of the renowned John Abrach. After the battle, an incident occurred as to the division of the spoil, which evinced the noble spirit and character of the gallant son of a gallant father. There was a contingent of Assynt men and another of Sutherland men, assisting the Mackays. The Assynt men proposed to the Mackay chief to slay the Sutherland men that they might not participate in the booty. When William Du heard of the infernal proposal he immediately went to the Sutherland commander, advised him of it, and asked him to stand to his arms and wait for him while he got his own contingent ready to come to his protection. This was done forthwith. The plot was foiled and the spoil was fairly divided. The Assynt men got their share and marched away. William Du and the Sutherland men left together for their homes to the great satisfaction of both. From this incident arose the saying, "Ceartas nan Abrich" (the justice of the Abrachs; fair play to all). The date given of this event is 1478.

John Riabhach Mackay died about 1495, and was succeeded by his brother Iye, or Hugh 2nd. He was held in great esteem by James 4th, who in 1499 commissioned him to apprehend Sutherland of Dilred, for the murder of Sir James Dunbar. This commission the Mackay chief performed to the satisfaction of the King, who by charter, dated 4th November, 1499, granted him all Sutherland's lands in Caithness and Sutherland, Armadile, Strathy, Rynevie, Kenauld, Gollespy, Kilcalmkill, Dilred, &c. The prompt execution of this commission recommended him to the spirited King for a more difficult one in 1506, to apprehend MacLeod of Lewis. This was effected with equal expedition and success, and a charter was granted him by the King, of lands in Assynt and Ross.

From 1431, (date of the battle of Druim-na-cupa) to a few years after the battle of Flodden, 1513, when the death of James IV. threw the whole of Scotland into disorder and anarchy, there was internal tranquillity and peace in Sutherland, with the exception of the MacDonald irruptions. During this period the chiefs of Sutherland took little or no part in war or politics. They were content to stay at home controlling their private affairs, keeping their men in order, and leaving the southern nobles to foment and compose their own quarrels, and make their periodical raids over the borders with little credit to themselves, and less credit to their prowess or generalship.

The advent of the Gordons into Sutherland by the marriage of Elizabeth, eldest daughter of John Earl of Sutherland, in 1500, with Adam Gordon, second son of the Earl of Huntly, had a dire effect on the whole of Sutherland, the Reay Country, and Caithness, for more than a century after the battle of Flodden. Earl John died in 1508, and was succeeded by his son John, the last of the Freskyn race, in the male line, a young man of easy disposition, caring little for business and leaving all his affairs to the control of others, chiefly to Adam Gordon, his brother-in-law, which was very galling to the native gentlemen of the county, always jealous of the interference of strangers. This young Earl had two half-brothers, Alexander and George, whose mother was a daughter of Ross of Balnagown, his own mother being a daughter of the Lord of the Isles. It was pretended that these two brothers were bastards, their father being only handfasted to the Balnagown lady. Adam Gordon soon aspired to the Earldom, seeing that the young Earl, as he thought, was unfit to govern, and unlikely to marry. Sir Robert Gordon says "he begines to lay a foundation to settle that estate upon himself and to his successors by the lawes of the Kingdome, for besyds himself there was Alexander Sutherland, the 'bastard' brother of this Erle John, that pretended some right to the Erledome." Alexander was a young man, a minor. Adam Gordon took him to Aboyne, induced him to renounce all rights to the Earldom, and took legal proceedings to procure the succession to his wife.

Meanwhile the disastrous Battle of Flodden took place, so fatal to the King, nobility and Kingdom of Scotland. It threw the government of the country into the hands of a weak Regency, and the control of a turbulent and unscrupulous oligarchy. This was advantageous to the designs and ambitious aspirations of Adam Gordon. Next year, 1514, he procured the Earl, his brother-in-law, to be decerned an idiot unfit to rule, and his own wife to be declared his heir and successor. Earl John died soon after, and in 1515 Adam Gordon became Earl of Sutherland, in right of his wife.

Now began a century of turmoil, disorder and violence, plots, counter-plots and intrigues, feuds, raids, battles, spoliations, ravages, mutual hatred and animosity, triangular fighting between the three principal races in the two counties, Sutherlands, Murrays, and Gordons in the south, Mackays in the north, and Sinclairs in the east. Well might Sir Robert Gordon say "In 1516 Adam, Earl of Southerland, forseing great trubles liklie to fall furth in his countrey, he entered in familiaritie and friendship with John Sinckler,

MACKAY.

"The figure wears a flat bonnet, on which the clan badge is displayed, and an eagle's feather. The doublet, or jacket, is of strong cloth formerly much worn, to which a dull red colour was imparted by a native dye. The tartan is that recognised as peculiar to the Clan Aodh, the brogs are molach or of hide, from which the hair is not removed; the sword and targe are of the forms in common use among the Highlanders."—James Logan, in R. R. M'Ian's "Clans of the Scottish Highlands."

Earl of Catteynes for assisting him against his enemies." To cement this familiarity and friendship he gave Caithness a charter for "ten davachs" of land east side of Helmsdale river, but says Sir Robert, "he keipt the lands bot joyned afterwards Earle Adam his foes." These two Earles then set to work to create dissensions amongst the Mackays as to the succession on the death of Iye, the Mackay chief, in 1516. They succeeded for some time in their machinations, but the Mackays perceiving that their ruin was intended, composed the succession differences, entered into an alliance with Caithness, and in revenge for Earl Adam's treachery, were soon on the "war-path," invading Sutherland with varying success till 1529, when Donald Mackay, the second son of Iye and brother of John, succeeded.

Meanwhile, in 1518, Alexander Sutherland, the rightful heir who had been supplanted by Earl Adam, raised a revolt against him. "The clans and trybes of the countrie were hierupon broken into factions. Alexander had gained a great favour among them, he was followed by manie, and manteyned by the Earl of Catteynes and Macky." Alexander so far succeeded as to cause the Gordons to fly to Strathbogie, took the castle of Dunrobin, and for a short time kept possession of it. He now married the sister of the Mackay chief, and during his absence in Strathnaver a party of Gordons sent from Aboyne, assisted by the Murrays, retook Dunrobin. Thereupon Alexander invaded Sutherland. The Gordons surprised him on the links of Brora, defeated his small force, and being taken prisoner, he was immediately killed, his head cut off and placed in triumph on the highest pinnacle of Dunrobin Castle. The descendants of this Alexander Sutherland resided afterwards at

Kilpheder, above Helmsdale, and were noted for generations for their great size and strength. The last of them lived in Edinburgh during the great law-suit for the Earldom in 1782. It has been said that the guardians of the young Countess, in the event of Sutherland of Forse, one of the claimants, succeeding in establishing his claim, intended to bring him forward as the true heir in the male line. The House of Lords having decided in favour of the Countess, no more was heard of him, except that the Countess allowed him a pension for the rest of his life.

In 1529 Donald Mackay succeeded his brother John. Peace was maintained by him while Earl Adam lived. Sir Robert, contrary to his usual estimate of Mackay chiefs, states that he "was a politic and wise gentleman, a good soldier and a valiant captain." This is great praise from Sir Robert Gordon. This Mackay chief was in high favour with James V. When Henry VIII. threatened invasion James called out his feudal army. Amongst others Mackay came with his contingent, and when at Falamuir, noble Earls and Lords refused to invade England, Lord Maxwell, Mackay, and a few more stood by the King. He was indignant, he remonstrated, he implored. All in vain; the King, overwhelmed with disappointment and chagrin, disbanded the army. Maxwell, Mackay, and others escorted the King to Edinburgh. Some peers and barons, ashamed of what had happened, proposed to collect the loyal part of the army and invade England by the west coast. This was agreed to, the army now consisting of only 10,000 men was speedily and secretly on the march, accompanied by the King as far as Caerlaverock. The army went on and encamped on English ground, when the nobles refused to proceed any further under the command of Oliver Sinclair. While thus discussing and disputing, three hundred English horsemen were amongst them full tilt with levelled lances. A panic ensued, a rout followed, few were killed, but upwards of 1000 men, and some peers and barons, were made prisoners.

Mackay and others on their return from this disgraceful affair picked up the King at Caerlaverock, and accompanied him to Edinburgh. James, grateful to Mackay for his courage and steadfast loyalty, conferred upon him several estates, and within a month died of a broken heart.

The untimely death of the young King again threw Scotland into a regency and disorder. The nobles ran riot, and the whole country was convulsed by aristocratic factions, each one of them for himself or party, none for the State.

The Mackay chief on his return, finding that the Sutherlands had committed several depredations upon his people in his absence, was again on the "war-path," invaded Sutherland several times, and though repelled appeared again fresh and willing to fight and retaliate.

The bishop of the diocese, brother of Lennox, was called to the south; before leaving he gave the charge of his lands in Caithness to the Earl of Caithness, and of his Sutherland lands to Donald, the Mackay chief. This was exceedingly irritating to Sutherland, but he was unable to prevent it. Caithness took possession of the bishop's seat at Scrabster; Mackay took Skibo by force and placed a garrison in it. In the meantime the Earl of Huntly was made "Lieutenant of the North;" Sutherland being his relative applied to him for assistance. Unable to encompass their wishes by force they resorted to fraud and policy. Huntly advised Sutherland to marry the bishop's sister, who was then a young widow, which he did. The bishop granted to Sutherland and to his son of this marriage all the rents of his lands in Caithness and Sutherland. Mackay would not give up Skibo without an order from the bishop, not even to Huntly, who sent a Captain Cullen to besiege it with some cannon from Leith. Upon the appearance of the big guns the Mackay garrison marched away to Strathnaver.

Huntly, now the "Cock o' the North," summoned Caithness and Mackay to appear before him. They obeyed. Caithness, not having shown any disobedience to Huntly's orders, was set at liberty; Mackay, for his disobeying orders, was confined in Foulis Castle, but Donald Mac-Ian-Mhor Mackay, a Strathnaver man, soon set him at liberty and returned with him to his own country.

Huntly and Sutherland tried all their arts and wiles to injure the Mackay chief by misrepresentations to the Regent and Parliament. They were successful for a time, but a succeeding government redressed the injuries done, and repealed the acts obtained by Huntly and Sutherland in their own favour.

Donald Mackay died about 1550, and was succeeded by his son Iye or Hugh. This young chief, in his father's lifetime, was sent in command of a Mackay contingent to oppose the English raids on the borders. He was in that Highland brigade at the Battle of Pinkie, 1547, who, says Buchanan, "after the Scots army were fleeing, gathered themselves in a round body, kept their ranks and returned safe home. At first they marched through craggy places and inconvenient for the horse, and if they were sometimes obliged to descend into the plain, yet the English horsemen who followed them durst not attack them."

Iye no sooner succeeded his father than his ruin and that of his house and clan, was projected at the instance of Sutherland and Huntly. They represented that his father was illegitimate, and for that and other reasons his estates stood escheated to the Crown. Mackay kept possession. He was summoned before the Queen Regent, but refused to appear, considering it unsafe to place himself in the hands of Huntly and Sutherland, who were with Her Majesty. In consequence of this refusal the Queen Regent granted a commission to the Earl of Sutherland against the Mackay chief and his clan.

Assisted by Huntly, Sutherland raised an overwhelming force, and for the first time an Earl of Sutherland ventured to invade the Reay country. He marched into Strathnaver, "sacking and spoiling in all hostile manner," and besieged the castle of Borve, which after a short siege he took, and hanged the commander, Rory Mac-Ian-Mhor.

Meanwhile the Mackay chief, like a good general, unable to cope with his enemy in the field, made a flank march and invaded Sutherland into its most fertile parts, defeated the Sutherlands who opposed him in the heights of Loth, and burnt the church and all who sought refuge within. The Earl tried to intercept him, but in vain, and the grand campaign ended in no result. Shortly after, dreading Huntly's overpowering influence, the Mackay chief, after placing his country and affairs under the management of John Mor Mackay, his cousin, went away to Edinburgh, voluntarily gave himself up to the Queen Regent, who was much prepossessed in his favour. Several of the noblemen of her court were also favourable to him, such as Lord James, step son of the Queen Regent, Argyll, Huntly's bitter foe, Glencairn and

SITE OF BORVE CASTLE, FARR.

Cassilis. Mackay had disobeyed her commands, and for that act of disobedience he must be made to see the error of his ways. He was imprisoned, therefore, for a short time, but was soon afterwards released, and to please her Majesty he offered her his services in the border warfare then going on, and likely to become more serious. A command was given him, and he acted so gallantly as to acquire some renown, for Sir Robert admits that " he served diverse times in the wars upon the borders against the English, in the which service he behaved himself valiantly."

Meanwhile, John Mor Mackay, nothing daunted by past events, invaded Sutherland, spoiling and raiding, and burnt the chapel of St. Ninian in Navidale. He was surprised in his encampment on Garvary water in the early misty morning, and suffered a reverse.

Iye Mackay now returned, and established a peace with the Earl of Sutherland, which lasted during Earl John's life-time.

HISTORY, Part II. (A.D. 1560-1800),

By Rev. Adam Gunn, M.A., Durness.

A tumult broke out soon after Iye Mackay's return among the MacLeods of Durness. Tormot, their chief, was killed

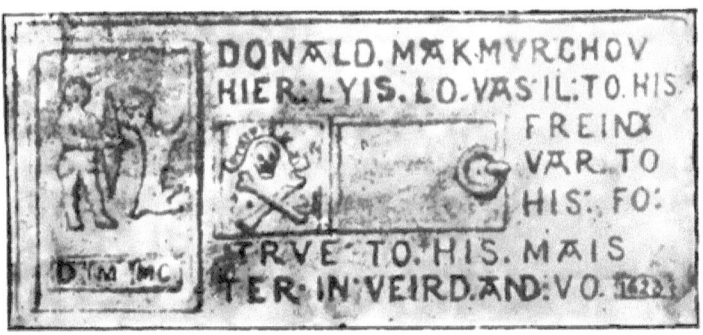

TOMBSTONE ON GRAVE OF MURCHADH MACLEOD.

by Mackay's orders, and out of revenge for this and other insults, they rebelled; but the outbreak was soon quelled, and three of their leaders beheaded. This branch of the MacLeods was known as "sliochd Iain-mhoir," and were a fierce and turbulent race. The Mackays had given Durness to them in consideration of services rendered to the clan by the MacLeods of Assynt on several occasions. They aided the Mackays at the battle of Torran-dubh-riabhach 1517, when Iain-mor-mac-Iain, a son of the MacLeod of

Assynt, barely escaped. This Ian-mor had a son, Murchadh, who was chieftain of the sept in Durness; he was father of Donald, to whom Iye's son, Hugh, life-rented the lands of Westmoin. His grave may be seen in Balnakil Church, Durness; and traditional tales of his boldness and ferocity survive among the inhabitants to the present day.

It was during Iye's chiefship that the Reformation was established by Act of Parliament, 1560. John, Earl of Sutherland, and very probably Iye himself, were unfavourable to the cause. The thoroughness of the Reformation in Scotland was due entirely to the common people; the territorial magnates had no scruples in changing sides, whenever their own interests were in danger. Sutherland, along with Huntly and Caithness, were devoted to Queen Mary and the Popish religion; but the Earl of Murray, who was half-brother to the Queen, and had an eye to the Crown for himself, made the country unsafe for them: so after the defeat at Corrichy, and Huntly's death, the Earl of Sutherland escaped to Flanders, where he remained until 1565, when he was recalled by Mary to take up arms against Murray's faction.

During these troubles, the Mackay chief does not appear to have made himself obnoxious to either party. He repaired to Inverness in 1562, to meet Queen Mary; and for his loyalty on this occasion his crime of 1548 was forgiven him. Now was his opportunity of obtaining a renewal of his father's charters, but he neglected to do this at the time. In less than four years thereafter, young Huntly, cousin of the Earl of Sutherland, was gifted by Queen Mary with Iye Mackay's lands, and parliament ratified this grant. A most unnatural conspiracy seems to have been formed against him by his kinsman, George Earl of Caithness, and his neighbour, the Earl of Sutherland. These two had such influence at Court, that they could pass any measures they liked, and with the aid of Huntly, they very nearly succeeded in ruining the family of Mackay. Providence, however, averted the calamity in a wonderful manner, for hardly had these transactions been concluded when the Earl of Sutherland

RUINS OF HELMSDALE CASTLE.

and his wife were poisoned at Helmsdale, in the house of Isobel Sinclair, a cousin of the Earl of Caithness. The latter was suspected of being instigator of this crime.

Iye Mackay retained possession of his lands, and the successor of Earl John, being yet a minor, fell into the hands of Caithness, his worst enemy.

This gave Iye an opportunity of settling accounts with the House of Sutherland. He invaded Sutherland in 1567, wasted the barony of Skibo, and burnt the town of Dornoch, which was held chiefly by the Murrays. The dissensions of the country both in Church and State, were such that no redress could be had at the time. The protection of Sutherland naturally devolved on Caithness, who had obtained the wardship of Alexander Gordon, the young Earl. He gave the latter Lady Barbara Sinclair, his eldest daughter, to wife. This was an ill match, the lady was thirty-two years, and young Sutherland not fifteen. He subsequently divorced her, on the ground of too much familiarity with Iye Mackay. The Earl gave another of his daughters to the Laird of Duffus, and on his death she married Hugh Mackay, Iye's son, who succeeded his father. Caithness became a great power in the North in this way, both by intrigue and alliances. Huntly began to fear for the safety of his cousin, Earl Alexander. Though the young Earl was kindly treated, fears were entertained by his friends that Earl George coveted Sutherlandshire for himself, and if he could only get Alexander out of the way, his son would marry Lady Margaret Gordon, the young Earl's sister, and succeed to the estates. Rumours reached Huntly of the state of matters. The Earl of Caithness dwelt at Dunrobin now; the Murrays, Gordons, and Gunns had to clear out of the county, as they were ever faithful to the House of Sutherland. But in 1569, the Murrays secured the person of the young Earl, and placed him under Huntly's protection. Earl George, however, clung to the wardship, three years of which had yet to run. It was possible in that time to do material damage to the interests of the House of Sutherland, if no check were placed upon his conduct. Huntly accordingly began to make friends with Mackay, and to stir him up against Caithness in favour of Sutherland. His claims over Mackay's lands were not enforced. He sold Mackay, for £300 Scots money, his heritable right to Strathnaver—retaining only the superiority —which he afterwards granted to the Earl of Sutherland. This was in 1570.

Earl George's plans were thus frustrated. He began to suspect Mackay and his own son John, of plotting against him. The two of them were wiled to Girnigo Castle; John was seized, fettered, and cast into the dungeon, where after many years he was famished to death. Mackay made a hasty retreat into Strathnaver, and in less than four months thereafter, died, leaving his lands to his son Hugh, then only eleven years of age.

Iye was twice married, first to his cousin, daughter of Hugh MacLeod of Assynt, by whom he had two sons, Donald Mackay of Scourie, and John Beg Mackay; and secondly to Christian Sinclair, cousin of George, Earl of Caithness, by whom he had two sons and three daughters, Hugh, who succeeded him, and William Mackay of Big-house; Ellenora, his eldest daughter, married Donald Bane MacLeod of Assynt, the second married Alexander Sutherland of Berriedale, and the third, Alexander, chief of the clan Gunn. The latter was beheaded at Inverness by the Earl of Murray, for his audacity in the town of Aberdeen, when as a follower of the Earl of Caithness, he refused to yield "the top of the street" to Earl Murray and his retainers.

During Hugh Mackay's minority, John More, of the Abrach clan, managed the estate, but this did not suit the Earl of Caithness' designs. The succession belonged to

Donald, Iye's eldest son, and the Abrachs favoured his claim. But Caithness favoured the son of his cousin, and having justiciary power, declared the sons of Iye, by his first wife, bastards, their parents being cousins. Accordingly, he resolved to remove John Mor from his charge. This he accomplished with the aid of the MacLeods of Durness, who seized John and conveyed him to Girnigo Castle, where he soon died. He was succeeded in the management by John Beg Mackay—Donald's brother. He was a wise and peaceable man, and kept on good terms with Earl George, and allowed the heir, Hugh Mackay and his brother William, to remain with Caithness to their no small advantage. About 1578, Hugh married the daughter of Caithness, widow of the Laird of Duffus.

The Clan Abrach resented the interference of Caithness, and were not satisfied that Donald's claims were fairly considered. Neil, their chief, was a man of great personal and mental powers, "bold, crafty, of very good wit, and quick resolution," according to Sir Robert Gordon. He began to oppose the measures of Caithness, and to see justice done to Donald, who was reared by the Abrachs. Caithness thereupon instigated the MacLeods of Durness to invade Neil and spoil his lands, but they were defeated with loss. Neil thereafter attacked the MacLeods of Balnakil, and slew the greater part of them. John Beg, being the nominee of Caithness, came to their assistance, and although Neil had given strict orders to spare him, he was accidently slain. This created a misunderstanding among members of the clan, which continued for a long time, and was injurious to both parties. The Abrachs joined issue with the house of Sutherland, in order to defeat the designs of Caithness on the Reay

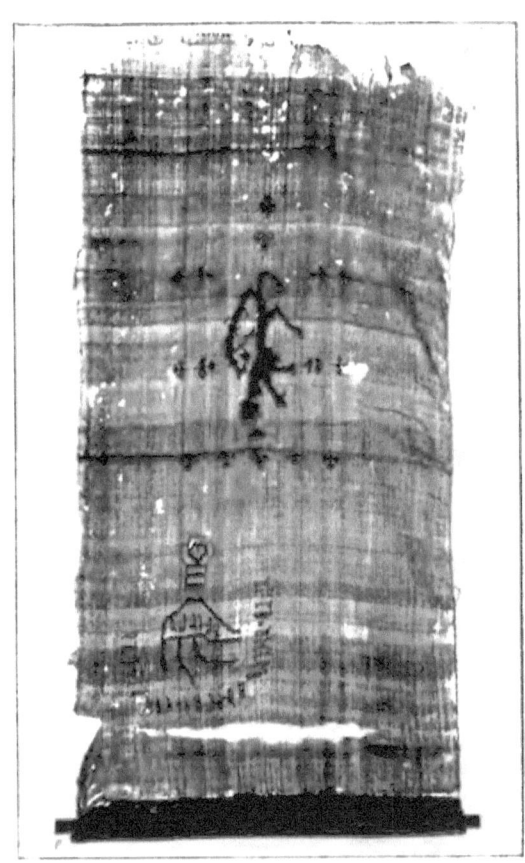

THE WHITE BANNER (AN BHRATACH BHAN) OF THE CLAN MACKAY, CARRIED IN BATTLE BY THE ABRACHS.

Country. The Gunns who had always fought in the past under the banners of Mackay and Sutherland, transferred their allegiance to Caithness, and a deadly feud between them and the clan Abrach ensued, which resulted in the slaughter of the best fighting men in Sutherland and Caithness. So long, so deadly, so inveterate was the feud, that Gordon draws a veil over "the horrible encounters" and bloodshed between these two tribes.

In 1583 George, Earl of Caithness, died, and Hugh Mackay, his son-in-law, took the management of the Reay Country into his own hands. The Earl of Sutherland obtained from Huntly the superiority of Strathnaver, and the heritable sheriffship of Sutherland and Strathnaver. By this transaction he looked upon the Mackay chief as his vassal, but he proved a refractory one. One of his first acts was to go to the assistance of Donald Bane of Assynt, who had married his sister, and was engaged meanwhile in making war upon Neil Houcheonsone, commander in Assynt, and the Earl of Sutherland's follower. The clan Gunn assisted Hugh Mackay in this expedition, and it cost them dear, as the sequel will show. Sutherland prepared at once to invade Strathnaver and Caithness. The now Earl of Caithness was George, grandson of the preceding, and a man equally bold and unscrupulous. The Earl of Sutherland accused him of harbouring the Gunns, and Mackay, of violating his rights as his superior. But by the earnest mediation of friends a meeting was appointed at Elgin, for repairing the alleged wrongs of the Earl of Sutherland. Mackay was not present at the meeting. The Earls were reconciled on the understanding that the Gunns should be exterminated, chiefly such of them as resided in Caithness. No sooner had Caithness returned than he refused to yield them up to the Earl of Sutherland, and Mackay was equally loth to betray the sept of that clan which resided at Strathy. This duplicity of Caithness incensed the Earl of Sutherland. Huntly came north to Dunrobin to effect if possible a settlement. Earl George was sent for, and he arrived duly, but Hugh Mackay refused to put in an appearance, for which he was denounced rebel. Two companies of men were dispatched against the Gunns in Caithness and the Reay Country. The Sutherland men directed their force against the latter, but on their march they fell in with a body of Mackays, under the command of the chief's brother, William of Bighouse, who were carrying away James Macrory's cattle out of Corrie-Kinloch. A fight ensued, and there being only a small contingent of Mackays, the Sutherland men pursued them to the bounds of Caithness. Here the retreating party came upon the Gunns, who had assembled to a man to resist the Caithness force. They resolved to join issues, and live or die together. The Caithness host was in sight of them, led by the Earl's brother, Henry Sinclair. William Mackay's advice was to turn upon the Sutherland men first, who were weary with fighting. But the Gunns preferred to attack the Caithness men, being the stronger force. Although much inferior in numbers, they had the advantage of the hill, and rushing down the slope, and reserving their arrows until they were close upon the enemy, they completely routed the Caithness force, and slew 140 of their number. This is known as the "Conflict of Aldgowne," 1586 A.D. Gordon says that the Sutherland men who were in the neighbourhood, knew nothing of the fight until it was over, and they quietly retreated by night with such booty as they captured. Henry Sinclair, the Earl's brother, was among the slain. Caithness was highly enraged at the issue of this battle, and displeased with the Sutherland men for not coming to the rescue. Out of revenge, he hanged John Mac-Ian-mac-Rob, chief of the Gunns, whom he had allured to Girnigo Castle a short time before the outbreak of hostilities.

Thereupon Huntly sent Sir Patrick Gordon of Achindoun to reconcile the Earls a second time, and to deal with Mackay for harbouring the Gunns. The parties met at Ben Grime; Sutherland agreed to invade them first with two companies, "as the Earl Caithness his forces wer latelie overthrowen by them." He prevailed upon the Abrach branch, and the MacLeods of Durness to assist him. The Sutherland forces were under the leadership of William Sutherland, George Gordon, aud Hugh Murray of Abercross. Hugh Mackay, the chief, recognised the hopelessness of affording the Gunns further shelter, and he discharged them from his country. The Gunns now set out for the Western Isles, but they were overtaken at Leckmeln, Ross-shire, where after a sharp skirmish they were overthrown and mostly all slain. Their captain, George Gunn, brother of MacRob, saved himself for a time by swimming in a loch near by, but being sorely wounded he was finally captured and delivered to the Earl of Caithness. After a time he was released, and the scattered remnants of the clan found their way back to their ancestral homes. Mackay must have restored them to their holdings in Strathnaver, for eight years afterwards we find James Sinclair of Murkle revenging his brother's death, by invading the Strathy Gunns by night and slaying some of them.

Hugh now tried to reconcile the factions of his clan. Without the aid of the Abrachs he could not hold his own in the vicinity of such men as the Earls of Sutherland and Caithness. Therefore to appease them he granted the lands of Eddrachillis to Donald, and Bighouse to William Mackay. It was a wise policy, but not unattended with danger. This Donald quickly invaded Hugh's uncle, the laird of Assynt, and he soon found it necessary to escape to Earl George for protection, in whose forces he fought against the Mackay chief on a subsequent occasion.

In 1587 the Earls of Caithness and Sutherland were again in arms. George Gordon, Garty, intercepted the Earl of Caithness' servants on their way to Edinburgh, and cut off their horses' tails—an indignity which Caithness felt very keenly. He demanded redress of Sutherland, who disclaimed all connection with the offender. War was at once declared. The forces met at Helmsdale. Caithness was accompanied by Hugh Mackay, and John, Earl of Carrick, the Earl of Orkney's brother. Sutherland had on his side the laird of Mackintosh, the MacKenzies of Redcastle, the MacLeods of Assynt, and the Munros. Mackintosh tried hard to prevail on his friend Mackay to desert Caithness, but he failed. By the intervention of friends the Earls were reconciled, but Mackay was left out of the treaty. He went home to his own country grieved at his betrayal by Caithness, but resolved to own no allegiance to Sutherland. His downfall was now plotted between the Earls, but Caithness was not hearty in the matter. The upshot was the marriage of Hugh, who had recently divorced his Caithness wife, with Lady Jane, sister of the Earl of Sutherland, and a fresh combination entered into by Mackay and Sutherland against Caithness.

An occasion was not long wanting for trying issues with Earl George. The notorious Gordon was killed by Sinclair of Mey. Sutherland complained to the King, obtained a commission to apprehend Caithness and imprison him until he gave up the offender. Accompanied by Mackay, Mackintosh, the laird of Fowlis, Assynt and Gilcalm, Rasay, he invaded Caithness, and drew up his camp against Girnigo

COAT OF ARMS OF THE SUTHERLAND FAMILY.

Castle, where he remained twelve days. The inhabitants of Caithness flew in all directions, many were slain, and a great booty secured. The town of Wick was burnt with the exception of the church, and Caithness was forced to come to terms, appointing the Earl of Huntly as oversman. The date of this invasion is February, 1589, and the occasion is remembered as La-na-Creich-mor—the day of the great spoil.

The invasion was followed by a series of mutual raids and skirmishes. The most alarming reprisal was that of the laird of Murkle, who, with 3000 men, entered Strathully. Hugh Mackay happened to be at Dunrobin at the time, and he set out with a party of men to make head against them, until the Earl of Sutherland arrived with more forces. The historian Gordon is loud in the praises of Mackay for his bravery on this occasion, but it is a significant fact that his bravery was never acknowledged by that partial observer until after his alliance with the house of Sutherland.

The Earl of Huntly mediated between the Earls at Elgin and a peace was concluded, but it was of short duration. In 1590 Earl George invaded Sutherland with all the forces he could muster. Fifteen hundred archers were under the command of Donald Mackay of Scourie, who fought on the Caithness side, and was the mainstay of the Caithness army. Night put an end to the conflict, and on the morrow Caithness discovered that Hugh Mackay had invaded his territory, burning and wasting to the gates of Thurso, and carrying off a large booty. A peace was concluded, which lasted until the Earl of Sutherland's death, 1594. He was succeeded by John, then in his eighteenth year.

Earl George was still smarting under his repeated failures, and here was a good opportunity to punish the family of Sutherland while their leader was a mere stripling. But fortunately for the latter the experienced and brave leader of the Clan Mackay remained faithful to the young Earl, who was his wife's nephew. Caithness tried hard to influence Hugh in his own favour, but failed. In 1598 Earl John set out on his travels to the Continent, and during his absence the Earl of Caithness signified a wish to hunt in the Reay forest. Hugh at once declined to give him leave, and the affair ended at that time in some bragging on either side. But in 1601 matters became more serious. Under pretence of hunting, the Earl of Caithness convened his forces at Ben Griam, Sutherlandshire. Earl John returned, and with the aid of his allies encamped within three miles of the Caithness host, and proposed to fight on the morrow. There was a tradition that at this very spot a battle should be fought between the Caithness men and Sutherland and Strathnaver, where Sutherland men should have a great loss, Strathnaver greater, but Caithness greatest of all. This made the Sutherland forces eager for the fray, but the Earl of Caithness thought it safer to retreat by night into his own country. A cairn was erected on the spot to commemorate the event, and it is known as Carn Teichidh—The Flight Cairn.

It is pleasant to turn from these warlike operations to more amicable events. In the August of 1602, we find the Earl of Orkney entertaining a company of the mainland magnates in his island castles. These included the Earl of Sutherland, the Mackay chief, Sir Robert Gordon, Earl John's brother, the laird of Assynt, and others. After a fortnight's stay, they returned to Cromarty whence they had embarked, highly pleased with their splendid reception.

Up to this date it was the custom of the Highland chiefs to settle by force of arms such differences, and they were not few, as occurred among them. But now they adopted the modern fashion of lodging complaints with the Privy Council, and seeking redress by the aid of the law. By this process it happened often that the real offender escaped scatheless if he had influential friends at court. Sir Robert Gordon, who stayed for the most part in England, proved a good friend to the house of Sutherland in this respect, and the house of Mackay as frequently failed to obtain redress. This gave rise to the Gaelic proverbs, "'S feàrr caraid 's a chùirt n' a crùn 's a sporan," and again, "Is direach agus is cam an lagh."

About this time an effort was made by Roderick Murray to secure the lands of Bighouse from William Mackay, brother-german of the chief. This claim was founded on a charter of James I., who granted these lands to Angus Murray. The Privy Council decided in favour of Mackay, and his right was further confirmed by a charter of James VI.

The Earl of Caithness frequently harassed his neighbour, John Sutherland of Berriedale. The latter, with the aid of the Clan Abrach, retaliated, for which he was summoned before the Privy Council at Edinburgh. He spurned the summons, and betook himself to the hills of the interior, whence he made frequent raids on the enemy. Failing to apprehend him Caithness raised an action against Hugh Mackay for harbouring him, and after a long process Mackay judged it prudent to arrest Sutherland, and he handed him over to the Earl of Caithness, who imprisoned him in Girnigo Castle.

Donald Mackay, who was afterwards Sir Donald, and latterly Lord Reay, interested himself in the case, and after spending Christmas with Lord Caithness he secured Berriedale's release. This Donald married first Lady Barbara MacKenzie when he was twenty years of age, and being of an active disposition he began during his father's lifetime to take charge of affairs. He cultivated the friendship of Caithness at an early date, a circumstance which lowered him in the estimation of his astute uncle, Sir Robert Gordon. In 1611 he was commissioned jointly with John Gordon of Embo to arrest Arthur Smith, a maker of counterfeit coin, who fled to Caithness for protection, and carried on his trade in Thurso. Here he was arrested, but not without a scuffle with the neighbouring gentlemen, one of whom, John Sinclair of Stircoke, was slain. Lord Caithness, then in Edinburgh, hearing of his nephew's death, commenced a process against the Earl of Sutherland, Mackay, and Sir Robert Gordon. A counter prosecution against Caithness was instituted by Gordon for seizing Angus Henderson of Golval without a commission and imprisoning him in Girnigo. The reason of this arrest was that he harboured one William Gun, Strathnaver, who was "wanted" by Caithness for cattle-lifting. Gun was arrested in Tain and imprisoned in Fowlis Castle. He tried to make his escape by leaping from the battlement of the tower, but injured his foot and was again captured, and handed to Caithness, who imprisoned and fettered him in Girnigo. He managed to rid himself of his fetters, and leaping into the sea, swam ashore and escaped in the darkness to Golval. Lord Berriedale pursued him there, but failing to apprehend him, he seized Henderson and lodged him in Girnigo Castle. Hence the counter law-suit. Parties were heard for three days by the Privy Council, and opinion was much divided. The King wrote repeatedly to the Council, urging them to advise the parties to come to a mutual agreement. This was at length effected, but Caithness felt so sorely over the matter that an unseemly scuffle took place on the High Street of Edinburgh between himself and Lord Gordon, Sir Robert, and Donald Mackay.

Hugh Mackay died at Tongue in 1614, a man greatly beloved by the clansmen, and esteemed as an honourable man by his peers. He was generous to a fault to his people, yet he managed to preserve the ancient inheritance without encumbrance, and bequeathed it free of debt to his successor.

TONGUE HOUSE, THE ANCIENT SEAT OF THE CHIEFS OF THE CLAN MACKAY.

Lady Jane Gordon, his wife, was equally esteemed for her piety and worth, notwithstanding that she was a Catholic, like her parents before her, who suffered for their adherance to the Romish faith. Hugh's Protestantism was not very pronounced, but he managed to escape censure. The Earl of Sutherland of this date got into trouble with the Privy Council on account of his faith, and he was confined to St. Andrews for a time. But King James VI. was very tolerant towards Catholics and he was soon released.

After Hugh's death Donald Mackay, first Lord Reay, succeeded to the estates, which were at this time not confined to the Reay country. The Mackays had possessions in Sutherland and Caithness from an early period. At one time it would appear that Sir Donald was destined to increase his ancestral estate, and raise the house of Mackay to a position second to none in the north. He bought the estates of Forbes in Caithness, including Isauld, Downreay, Reay, Sandside, etc. About 1624 his possessions extended from the hill of Skaill to Glencoul, on the borders of Assynt—a stretch of about 100 miles. But by the year 1649, when he died, this magnificent estate was sadly curtailed, and hopelessly encumbered with debt. It is true he made the name of Mackay one of European, if not of world-wide reputation, but he secured this distinction at a high price.

His life may be divided into three periods: before, during, and subsequent to his memorable continental service with the Kings of Denmark and Sweden. During the first period, his time, money and patience were exhausted in warding off the encroachments of his wily uncle, Sir Robert Gordon, in whose hands the management of the Sutherland estates lay during Earl John's minority. For Earl John, the sixth of that name, had died in 1615, and left a son, John, only six years old, to succeed him. During the later years of John VI. Donald Mackay interested himself much in regulating the affairs of the house of Sutherland.

But when Sir Robert obtained the management for his nephew, he gradually ousted Mackay from all concern in affairs, and finally succeeded in prevailing upon the latter to renounce all claims to the various properties belonging to him in Sutherland. Sir Robert got himself nominated as arbiter in boundary disputes, secured from Mackay the warrandice of Strathnaver, made him renounce all claims to

ARMS OF DONALD, FIRST LORD REAY, IN TONGUE HOUSE.

the lands of Kinnauld, Over-Skibo, Golspitour, and also the right of jointure given him by the Countess of Sutherland to her own lands. "Thus did Sir Robert wisely shift Mackay out of Sutherland; thus did Mackay's pretences and aims in that country vanish and melt away, piece by piece, not being grounded on godly or good courses." So sayeth Sir Robert himself.

In 1626 Donald Mackay, now Sir Donald, finding himself crossed at home, sought and obtained leave of King Charles to raise a regiment, and go to assist Count Mansfeldt in Germany. He collected a force of 3000 men, and embarked them at Cromarty. He was himself detained by sickness until the following year, when he followed them. Many gentlemen of the north, chiefly out of Sutherland, Ross, and Caithness, went with him in the capacity of officers. These were of the surname of Mackay, Sinclair, Gordon, Munro, and Gunn, and several of them rose to distinction in the service of the King of Sweden. It was a fortunate matter for the peace of the northern shires that an outlet was thus discovered for its warlike and turbulent young gentlemen. They gave a good account of themselves in the continental wars, and some of them returned to take a leading part in the struggles of the home country during the killing times. An account of the heroic conduct of Sir Donald Mackay's regiment appears elsewhere. It will suffice to say here that Sir Donald proved himself an able and skilful commander, and for his distinguished services was raised to the Peerage by King Charles I. in 1628, on his return for fresh recruits. Lord Reay returned to the continent with a fresh contingent of troops, and in 1629 transferred his services to Gustavus Adolphus, King of Sweden, who had now undertaken the defence of the Protestant cause. The Marquis of Hamilton had also obtained leave of His Majesty to raise forces to aid the King of Sweden. He was in much favour with the King, and on the best terms with Lord Reay. But the latter was informed on good authority that Hamilton's real purpose for levying forces was to seize ultimately upon the Kingdom of Scotland.

The loyalty of Reay to the King led him to reveal this plot prematurely to Lord Ochiltree. Reay was summoned before the King, and revealed as much as came to his knowledge of the whole affair. The King had the utmost confidence in Hamilton, and after a very informal inquest passed the matter over. Lord Reay in consequence incurred the hostility of Hamilton and his faction in Scotland. The Privy Council, whose members were mostly favourable to the House of Hamilton, turned against Reay's interests whenever matters concerning his Lordship's affairs were submitted to them. He made himself obnoxious all round, and lost heavily on account of his detention in England, pending this enquiry.

In 1632 the young Earl of Sutherland married Lady Jane Drummond, only child of the Earl of Perth. This was a fortunate alliance in every respect. The lady had means to extricate the house of Sutherland out of its pecuniary embarrassments. She was also a true Protestant, and by her influence the family of Sutherland threw their whole weight on the side of the Covenanters during the ensuing struggle. Mr. Thomas Hog of Kiltearn gives her a high character for piety and ability.

King Charles made a visit to Scotland in 1633—apparently to be crowned, but really to pave the way for Episcopacy in Scotland. Among other acts he disjoined Sutherland and the Reay country from the sheriffdom of Inverness, forming them into one shire; at the same time he erected Dornoch into a royal burgh.

Lord Reay found himself in pecuniary difficulties at this time. He had already received some money from Sir Robert to equip his regiment for continental service, and the latter held the lands of Far, Torrisdale, and others in wadset for this consideration. He now threatened Reay with law-suits about the lands of Durness, and as the latter had few friends in the Privy Council he deemed it prudent to accept the terms offered. A contract was entered into in 1633, whereby Lord Reay accepted the lands of Durness from the Earl in feu for service, and bound himself to attend the Earl at Parliaments and Conventions. Various other articles injurious to Reay were agreed to.

The aggressions of the Episcopacy in Scotland came to a head in 1637 when the Dean attempted to introduce the liturgy into the High Church of Edinburgh, which produced the well-known tumult in which Jenny Geddes played a conspicuous part. The alarmed Privy Council warned the King of serious disturbances if Episcopacy were to be forced on the Scottish people, but he was inexorable. Thereupon the great bulk of the people of Scotland resolved to maintain their civil and religious liberty at all hazards. The Covenant was renewed—the National Covenant entered into in 1580, and was subscribed by multitudes of all ranks throughout the nation. The Earl of Sutherland and Lord Reay both signed the Covenant, but the latter was suspected by the Covenanters, as he was well known to be loyal to the King. Huntly, who was the chief enemy of the Covenanters in the north, tried hard to gain Sutherland and Lord Reay to his side, but he failed. Lord Reay's son, John, did indeed go to Elgin to confer with Huntly, where both were apprehended and lodged in Edinburgh Castle. The Master of Reay was soon liberated, and subscribed the Covenant, and promised to deal with his father to adhere to that party.

General Leslie was appointed commander of the Covenanters' forces in Scotland, and the Viscount of Aboyne

A CORNER IN TONGUE HOUSE GARDENS.

of the King's forces. The latter, however, devolved the command on Colonel Gunn, who had lately come out of Germany, whither he had gone with Lord Reay. He was an experienced officer, and does not seem to have much relished the work of fighting against old friends like Reay, Sutherland, and the Northern Covenanters. These latter erred greatly in giving the command of the Northern Counties to Seaforth instead of appointing Reay to the post, for undoubtedly he had more military experience than any man on the Covenanters' side. His loyalty to Charles was likely the reason of passing him over. The consequence was that he was never hearty in the service, and latterly went to Denmark to command a regiment there, to be outside the reach of both parties. He was, however, recalled, when the troubles of Charles increased, and was captured at the taking of Newcastle, and sent prisoner to the Tolbooth, Edinburgh, 1644. In 1645 the victorious Montrose liberated the State prisoners, and Lord Reay among the rest. After this he came north, and found his eldest son, John, Master of Reay, harbouring the Earl of Huntly, and with him preventing the men of the Reay country and Caithness from taking part with the Covenanters. This half-hearted support of the Covenant on the part of Mackay, and harbouring of Huntly, was used by Sir Robert afterwards against Lord Reay.

In 1639 Lord Reay found it necessary to obtain a loan of money from Mr. John Gray, Dean of Caithness, as he was unwilling to put himself in the hands of Sutherland, who was thirsting for his lands, and particularly Strathnaver. It transpired that this Gray was only a tool in the hands of the Earl. In this way the mortgaged lands of Durness fell ultimately into the hands of the Earl of Sutherland. Strathnaver also fell into the same hands, and for similar reasons. But in selling Strathnaver, in 1642, neither Reay nor Sutherland took into account that the upper portion was the property of the clan Abrach, (Mackays), by the gift of Neil Wasse, the chief, and that it was in their possession for two centuries. This bred trouble when Sutherland sent officers to collect the rents. A company of regular troops had to be stationed on the strath for preserving order and enforcing payment.

Lord Reay's affairs were thus far from prosperous. He was unfortunately involved in matrimonial difficulties, having divorced Rachel Winterfield, his second wife, a decree which the Privy Council reversed, and found him liable in all expenses and aliment. He sailed for Denmark for the last time in 1648, after making such arrangements as he could with the Earl of Sutherland, regarding the money due to the latter, and the lands mortgaged. Strathnaver was now lost to the Mackays, although Neil Abrach made a stout resistance to the nefarious arrangement. Lord Reay's losses in the Protestant cause abroad, and by his loyalty to his King at home, were never refunded. On his death in the following year he left his curtailed and burdened estate to the Master, now John, Lord Reay. His body was brought to Tongue, and laid in the family vault at Kirkiboll. He was the most distinguished of the Mackay chiefs, a good soldier, and a brave general, but too liberal in proportion to his income. The historian of the clan Mackay says, "he was not improperly called Donald Duaghal, for he was indeed a man of troubles."

About this period Sir Robert Gordon, tutor of Sutherland, and historian of the family, was the most influential man in the north. Notwithstanding the unsettled times, he managed to preserve the interests of the family unimpaired. He re-

KIRKIBOLL CHURCHYARD, TONGUE.

mained mostly in England, but made frequent visits to the north to quell disturbances, and make peace between his friends. He was unquestionably the preserver of the house of Sutherland at a time when other estates often changed hands by reason of the changes in the State. He was the first to build and repair churches in Sutherland, after the Reformation, a work in which he was greatly assisted by Dean Gray, minister of Dornoch. He did much also in the way of providing maintenance to the ministers of the various parishes. On the occasion of one of his visits to the north, he was instrumental in bringing to justice several robbers who made the Ord of Caithness their habitat. Some of them were hanged on a gibbet erected on the Ord, as an example to evil doers. The history which he compiled of affairs in the north, will always remain the chief authority, notwithstanding a natural bias in favour of the house of Sutherland. He handed over the estate on a sound financial basis to Earl John the seventh, in the year 1630. He became Sheriff of Inverness, and Vice-Chamberlain of Scotland, in the same year, in room of James Stuart, Duke of Lennox, who, with the King's authority, resolved to travel abroad for a time.

It was after the death of the first Lord Reay, 1649, that the struggles of the Covenanters became really intense. The Earl of Sutherland proved a faithful friend to the cause, but John, Lord Reay, was prevailed upon by his uncles, Seaforth and Pluscardin, to join the Royalists. Lord Reay came with three hundred able men to join Huntly, but he was captured by the Covenanting force at Balvainy, 8th May, 1649, and sent as a prisoner to Edinburgh. Many of the Mackays were slain, and the remainder sent back under Hugh Mackay of Scourie to their own country.

Next year Montrose landed in Caithness in favour of the King, and raised the Caithness men, forcing ministers and laymen to sign a bond in his favour. Reay was in prison, but Mackay of Scourie, and Mackay of Dirlet and Strathy, repaired to the Marquis with assistance. They advised him to keep to the interior of the country while passing through Sutherland, where cavalry could not act with advantage. But he would not be prevailed upon to alter his route. They foresaw the result of such rashness, and returned apparently for more forces, but they did not interest themselves further in the matter. In the course of the year Mackay of Scourie was Colonel of his countrymen, fighting on the Covenanters' side. Montrose was defeated by Strachan on the borders of Sutherland, and being captured by MacLeod of Assynt, into whose lands he wandered, he was taken to Edinburgh and executed. The MacLeods of Assynt have been greatly blamed for this act, but without much reason. It was one of the causes which led to the loss of their estates subsequently. It is quite probable that MacLeod, without any promise of reward from the Government, would have acted as he did, seeing that his superior, the Earl of Sutherland, and his cousin, Munro, were both in pursuit of the Marquis.

In 1651 Charles II. was crowned King at Scone amidst great rejoicing. Another regiment of 1000 men from Sutherland and Strathnaver—the first in 1650—was sent to the King to Stirling. But Cromwell soon entered Scotland at the head of his sectarians, overthrew the Scottish army, released the State prisoners with the exception of Lord Reay, whom for a time he kept in durance, but latterly he was released by the efforts of his lady, the daughter of Hugh Mackay of Scourie.

In 1655 an effort was made by the Earl of Glencairn to liberate the nation of the English sectaries, in which he was joined by Reay—which ended in the capture of Glencairn by General Monk. Reay escaped, but his house of Tongue was burnt.

Things had gone into confusion in England on the death of Cromwell. The nation was heartily sick of the new order of things under Cromwell, and in a fit of revived loyalty the King was recalled. The first Scots Parliament was held in 1661. So glad was the nation to escape from the anarchy of the past that they were ready to yield everything to the King's creatures. In this famous Parliament the Presbyterian Government and discipline were overturned, the Covenants declared unlawful and seditious, the Marquis of Argyle, the best patriot in the State, and Mr. Guthrie, the best in the church, were condemned to death. The infamous rescissory act was passed, which has been called the "gravestone of the Reformation."

Caithness, Sutherland, and Reay, were present at this Parliament. Sutherland, by taking the oath of allegiance, lost in a great measure the credit he gained for his former appearances on behalf of Presbyterian liberty. He died in 1663, and was succeeded by his son, Earl George.

The Scottish Parliament was commanded by the King to make up the losses of the family of Mackay in the recent troubles on account of their loyalty to the King. The commission appointed valued these losses of father and son at 60,000 pounds Scots money, but he was never refunded in any part of them. It is perhaps not too much to say that no family suffered so much for their loyalty as the Mackays did. After this date neither the Earl of Sutherland nor Lord

Reay took much interest in public affairs during the reigns of Charles II. and James II. Accordingly their names are not to be met with during the fierce persecution of the Presbyterians. In the Highland host which was let loose on the Covenanters of the south and west of Scotland, there were none from Sutherland or the Reay country. On the contrary, the county provided shelter to scores of eminent persons escaping from the fury of the dragoons. In this way, the people of the district were early imbued with the principles of religious freedom and piety. Seaforth and Duffus were empowered to put down conventicles in the north, but neither of them seems to have been very harsh. The Earl of Caithness, however, did not have the same scruples in suppressing them within his bounds, the bond which he compelled the principal persons in that shire to sign being still preserved.

The Revolution of 1688 added fresh lustre to the name of Mackay, and brought that family into a greater prominence than they had ever secured. When the Prince of Orange came to the rescue of the country against the tyranny of the Stuarts in the person of James II., he devolved the command of his forces in Scotland on General Hugh Mackay of Scourie—an officer who had gained great experience in the continental wars. The career of this brave and pious general suffered a partial eclipse at Killiecrankie, but four days after this reverse he turned the tide of victory in his favour. The Privy Council hampered his movements and thwarted his plan of compaign, but William had unbounded confidence in his ability. In a very short time, by moderation, diplomacy, and clemency to the vanquished, General Mackay pacified the Highland clans, and was afterwards sent to Ireland, where he acquired further renown as an able and brave officer. As was natural, the Mackays flocked to his standard. Five hundred of their best men took the field during this period, the Earl of Sutherland furnished some men likewise, as also the Munros and Grants. Among the Mackays who held commissions under him were his brother James, killed at Killiecrankie, George and Robert, sons of Lord Reay, and his own nephews, Captains William Mackay, Kinloch, and Hugh Mackay, Borley.

The next occasion on which the Sutherland men and Mackays rendered service to the Government was during the rebellion of 1715. Many in Caithness favoured the Pretender, but John, Earl of Sutherland, and George, Lord Reay, were faithful to the house of Hanover. Sutherland was in England when the rebellion broke out, but he sailed north with all speed, directing arms and ammunition to be sent after him. This was done, but the rebels intercepted the vessel at Burntisland. Assisted by Lord Reay and others, Sutherland pushed on towards Inverness, where he was joined by Lovat, who deserted the Pretender. They numbered about 1800 in all. Seaforth's army was, however, 4000 strong, and the Earl of Sutherland judged it hazardous to try issues with him with such a small and not well-equipped force. Retiring northwards before Seaforth he accomplished his object without striking a blow, which object was to prevent the junction of the forces of Seaforth with the Earl of Mar. Before this was accomplished the Duke of Argyle engaged with Mar at Sheriffmuir. Seaforth was too late to be of assistance, so he turned northwards to attack the Earl of Sutherland. The latter hearing this marched at the head of 800 men, including Mackays, Grants, and

CLANS SUTHERLAND AND MACKAY.
From "Highlanders of Scotland," by Kenneth Macleay, R.S.A., (*The Queen's book of the Clans*).
(1). Sergeant James Sutherland, Doll, Brora. (2). Adam Sutherland, Knockarthur, Rogart. (3). Neil Mackay, Ferryman at Hope, parish of Durness.

Munros, to within four miles of his camp. Seaforth thereupon laid down his arms, and dissolved his forces, requesting these friends of the Government to use their influence to secure his pardon. The Sutherland men and Mackays remained at Inverness for some time to disperse bands of desperados which committed robberies and other acts of violence on the outbreak of hostilities. Captain Hugh Mackay was in command of the Reay countrymen.

The next Jacobite attempt was made in 1745. At this time also the loyalists of the north were of great service to the Government in overawing the malcontents of Caithness, and preventing them, the MacKenzies of Ross, and a large party from Orkney, and others from joining the rebel army. It was at this time that the Hazard, sloop of war, was sent from France with £20,000 to help Prince Charlie. Being discovered in the Moray Firth by the Sheerness man-of-war she sailed northward to the Pentland Firth, and along the coast to Tongue, where she ran aground on the Melness sands. They all landed safely to the number of 200 men, William Mackay of Melness* receiving them kindly. But old Lord Reay heard of the arrival, notice was given to a company of Loudon's troops at Lairg, and Daniel Forbes, Lord Reay's factor, with a handful of men captured them, not, however, before breaking the boxes containing the gold, and throwing it into a lake close by. The prisoners were put on board the Sheerness man-of-war, which had come so far in pursuit of the French frigate.

In this rebellion Lovat and Cromarty both joined the Pretender—notwithstanding the efforts of Lord President

---

* A different version of this incident is given by Colonel Kerr in *Lyon in Mourning*, Vol. I., page 358. See also chapter on "Regiments," by Mr. John Mackay *(Ben Reay)*.

Forbes to prevail upon the Highland clans to remain loyal. Caithness was full of rebels, who organised themselves into companies, but they failed to move out of the county. Cromarty attempted to effect a junction with them, but was captured by the Sutherlanders and Mackays in the castle of Dunrobin, where he threw himself upon the clemency of the

DUNROBIN CASTLE.

Duchess. Through Sutherland's influence his offence was pardoned.

George, Lord Reay, died in 1748, and was succeeded by his son Donald, who died in 1760. The Earl of Sutherland, William, who took an active part in putting down the rebellion of '45 died in France in 1748, and was succeeded by his son William, in 1750. He raised a fencible regiment in 1756, during the French scare, of which regiment Hugh

Mackay of Bighouse was Lieutenant-Colonel. It was disbanded in 1763. The Earl and Countess died at Bath in 1766, leaving a daughter, Elizabeth, to succeed. She married in 1760, George Granville Leveson Gower, Viscount Trentham. By this time the spirit of feudalism and chivalry had subsided, and the clan system came to an end.

Donald, Lord Reay, was a pious and benevolent nobleman, and so was George, fifth Lord Reay, who succeeded him in 1761. He died in 1768, and was buried in Holyrood. His brother Hugh succeeded, for whom the Lords of Session found it necessary to appoint a tutor to manage his estates. Lord Hugh lodged with James Mackay of Skerray, and the Mackays of Bighouse managed the Reay estates. He died in 1797 and his cousin-german Eric, seventh Lord Reay, succeeded. In his time the Reay Fencibles, who distinguished themselves in Ireland, were raised. This regiment was commanded successively by Colonel Mackay Hugh Baillie (grandson of Hugh Mackay, Bighouse), Major John Scobie, Lieutenant-Colonels Ross and Colin Campbell. It was disbanded, after earning much renown for bravery in the field, and good behaviour in camp, in 1802. It was of this regiment that General Lake spoke when he was defeated at Castlebar, "If I had my brave and honest Reays here, this would not have happened."

Eric, Lord Reay, was the last to own his ancestral estates. The property fell into the hands of the Sutherland family, as Assynt also did, so that at the present time, practically the whole of the county of Sutherland belongs to the noble family which bears the name. The title, however, was preserved, and the present Lord Reay is not the least illustrious of that long line of chiefs which shed lustre on the name of Mackay.

A SHORT TREATISE ON HOMESPUN,

CHIEFLY IN ITS RELATION TO

SUTHERLAND.

BY

HER GRACE THE DUCHESS OF SUTHERLAND.

EVER since this dying century has passed its prime, and the discoveries of the wonderful power of steam, and of electricity, have become part of its existence, we have learned to associate the centres of the great industries of the world with the hideousness, the squalor, the restlessness, the crime, which are the natural result of human ascendency, in a world that was planned to be Divine.

Heavily hangs the smoke of countless chimneys over the brick and mortar erections that do penance for the woods and hilly fields of long ago: pitilessly revolve, madly, unceasingly, the countless wheels of a machinery which in its iron grasp crushes the art of dead centuries, flinging it out to a self-satisfied generation, that to its own crude fancy moulds the shapeless wreck, crying "see, see"—triumphant as the gutter child over its first mud pie.

Mr. Arnold White in his volume on "English Democracy" says, "the folly and wickedness of those who destroyed the spinning jennies, the engines, and the printing machines, at the time of their introduction, have been denounced with so unanimous a voice that it would be futile to suggest that the ignorant peasants, or delirious mechanics, who obeyed the first instincts of their nature, were animated by a true sense of self-preservation, however careless they may have been of the future of the human race." Mr. White reluctantly makes an admission. It was the prophetic spirit of self-preservation that had inspired those men, in the intuitive knowledge that not all the advantages of affluence and power to the minority—not the rise of a few poor to riches, a few rich to millionaires—not the undeniable freer circulation of gold—could compensate for the sufferings of thousands, who, tumbling pell mell into our great cities, thirsting for the employment scattered broadcast by these marvellous inventions, had found, all too late, among the curses of their half-starved children, the bitter results of such impetuosity far out-weighing its blessings.

Whilst the larger portion of the world looks on in sullen indifference at this tottering state of things, there are others, tired of cackling speculation over quack remedies, who in real earnest have attempted to rescue some of the spoils of better days, as they are borne along on the flood of time. Perhaps foremost in importance among these poor little rescues comes the Hand-Spinning and Hand-Loom Weaving Industry of the United Kingdom. In England it exists only in the tiny oasis which men like John Ruskin, steeped in artistic feeling, and thirsting after the old order, have established under personal supervision, but in Ireland and Scotland the last decade has seen an extraordinary reaction, bringing the hand made tweeds and linens again into the world of demand, and likely to produce lasting benefit to the peasantry of each country.

The general processes connected with the manufacture of cloth are well known, but a few remarks may be permitted as to specialities of method, and the following extracts from a paper written by the Rev. Dr. Joass of Golspie for the Chicago Exhibition will prove of undeniable interest.

"The wool packets being opened out and roughly sorted or stapled according to quality and length of fibre, of which there is considerable variety in the same fleece, the wool is cleansed from the grease derived from contact with the sheep (and the various protective 'dipping' or 'bathing' processes to which that animal is in autumn subjected) by steeping in a hot liquid. Dried and shaken up and still further 'sorted' the wool is then passed through the process of carding and combing, to lay its fibres in the same direction. This is effected by means of a pair of implements like hair-brushes, with the handles at the sides, and set with metal teeth. It is now nearly ready to be spun into thread. The distaff and spindle were, from very early times, used for this purpose. The former is a staff, about four feet long, fixed in the waist-belt on the left side, or, more commonly, in the up-turned outer skirt, which thus forms a pocket in front for carrying the clews or balls of thread. To the projecting head of the distaff, the wool, previously cross-carded into inch-thick cylinders, (in which the fibre has now assumed a sort of spiral arrangement) is tied in an open bunch or bundle. From this it is fed out by the left hand of the spinster to the spindle, held at starting in (and afterwards swinging from) the right. This is a rounded piece of wood, about a foot long and half an inch in diameter, loaded at the lower end by the whorl, which acts as 'fly-wheel,' and is generally made of stone, often a disc of steatite, about the diameter of a bronze penny, and weighing over an ounce and a half. Some wool, drawn out from the store on the distaff, to which it still remains attached, is twisted into a kind of thread and tied to the middle of the spindle, from which it passes upwards and is fastened by a simple hitch to a notch near the spindle-head. This is then twirled by the right hand, and as it spins it twists (as it is allowed to drop slowly towards the ground) all the wool up to the distaff, the hands regulating the speed and further supply, and thus determining the thickness of the thread. From time to time the thread is coiled around the shaft of the spindle into a ball, and a new hitch made till the clew is large enough to be slipped off and a new one begun.

From the number of whorls found in connection with prehistoric remains in Sutherland their use must be very ancient, yet the spindle is still to be seen at work on the hillsides of Assynt, in the north west of this county, employed for its original purpose of spinning. On the east coast it is used occasionally for twining together different colours of thread, all the spinning being done by the well known spinning wheel.

The next process is dyeing, and whether this is done 'in the wool' or 'in the thread' there is a final treatment in an ammoniacal liquid, called by the Highlanders 'fual,' which removes the last traces of oleaginous matter and prepares the wool for receiving and retaining the dye. The securing of uniformity of tint or shade has hitherto presented some difficulty, and this is partly due to the imperfection of the apparatus in common use, and to the usual habit of measuring the dyeing material merely by the handful.

Mineral dyes are now mostly used instead of those of vegetable origin. A list of the latter, some of which are in local use, is here given as collected from various sources of information.

COLOUR.	DYES.	BOTANICAL NAME.	NATIVE NAME. (Gaelic).
BLACK	Alder-tree bark	Alnus glutinosa	Cairt an Fheàrna
	Dock-root	Rumex obtusifolius	Bun-na-copaig
BLUE	Bilberry (with alum)	Vaccinium myrtillus	Dearcan-Fraoich
BROWN	Elder (with alum)	Sambucus niger	Droman
	Stone lichen	Parmelia saxatilis	Crotal
	Dulse	Halymenia edulis	Duileasg
,, (yellowish)	Currant (with alum)	Ribes	Preas dhearc
CRIMSON (bright)	Wall lichen	Parmelia parietina	Crotal-builhe
,, (dark)	Corcar-lichen	Lecanora tartarea	Crotal-corcuir
FLESH-COLOUR	White lichen	Lecanora palescens	Crotal-geal
GREY	Dark lichen	Parmelia ceratophylla	Crotal-dubh
GREEN	Willow bark	Salix viminalis	Cairt an t-Seilich
	Iris root	Iris pseud acorus	Bun-an t-Seilisteir
	Broom	Genista tinctoria	Bealaidh
MAGENTA	Furze bark	Ulex Europacus	Cairt a' Chonuisg
ORANGE (drk)	Heather (with alum)	Erica cinerea	Fraoch
PURPLE	Dandelion	Leontodon taraxacum	Beàrnan-Bride
RED (dark)	Bramble	Rubus fructicosus	Preas-Smeur
,, (bright)	Sundew	Drosera	Lus-na-feàrnaich
SCARLET	Rock-lichen	Ramalina scopulorum	Crotal-nan-creag
VIOLET	Rue-root	Galium verum	Bun an-Ruidh
	Limestone-lichen	Urceolaria calcarea	Crotal clach-aoil
YELLOW	Tormentil	Tormentilla officinalis	Leanartach
	Water-cress	Nasturtium officinalis	Biolaire
	Bitter vetch	Orobus tuberosus	Carmeal.[—uinnsinn
	Ash-tree root	Fraxinus excelsior	Freumh na craoibh
	Bracken-root	Pteris aquilina	Bun-na-Rainich
	St. John's Wort	Hypericum perforatum	Lus Chaluim Chille
(bright)	Sundew (with ammonia)	Drosera	Lus na-feàrnaich
	Bog-myrtle	Myrica gale	Roid

The dyed thread, washed in salt water if blue, or in fresh if of any other colour, is next woven into a web either at the cottage hand-loom or a small cloth mill driven by water power. The next process is that of 'felting' or thickening, called 'waulking' in the north, probably from its being chiefly effected by the feet. The microscopic projections on the fibre interlock when the web is beaten wet, and as the 'waulk-mill' is apt to overdo the work, turning out a texture hard, stiff and heavy, the old process is still preserved in the west Highlands of Inverness and Ross, and in some parts of Sutherland, and secures a fabric soft, supple, and sufficiently dense to be wind and weather proof. The following description by A. Ross, LL.D., late Provost of Inverness, is taken from a paper read before the Gaelic Society there in 1885.

"In the Highland districts women make use of their feet to produce the same result, (felting), and a picturesque sight it is to see a dozen or more Highland lassies set around in two rows facing each other. The web of cloth is passed round in a damp state, each one pressing it and pitching it with a dash to her next neighbour, and so the cloth is handled (? footed), pushed, crushed, and welded as to become close and even in texture. The process is slow and tedious, but the ladies know how to beguile the time, and the song is passed round, each one taking up the verse in turn, and all joining in the chorus. The effect is very peculiar and often very pleasing, and the waulking songs are very popular in all the collections.

"I have on various occasions" he continues, "watched the waulking process, but seldom in recent years. It is often the occasion of a little boisterous merriment and practical joking, for, should a member of the male sex be found prowling near by, he is, if caught, unceremoniously thrust into the centre of the circle and tossed with the web till, bruised with the rough usage and blackened with the dye, he is glad to make his escape from the hands of the furies."

While to this method of 'felting' the web, something of the softness of the genuine 'homespun' is due, it is also worthy of mention that the longer stapled wools are less liable to become matted and hard under the thickening process, of whatever kind, than those which are of shorter fibre. Now it is only with the longer fibred wool that the Highland wheel can work. Its very imperfection then as an implement, or rather machine, becomes of advantage as a guarantee of durability as well as of comfort in connexion with the work which it turns out, for whereas the mill can use up almost any sort of wool, however short in the fibre and inferior in quality, the wheel can only use the best and this is, in the end, the cheapest."

A transition time, through which several of the northern counties had already passed, fell upon Sutherland about the first quarter of this century. For a long time previous the people were content to be clothed in their native homespun, and the demand occupied the time of the thrifty housewife and the female members of the household, when the closing year brought relief from the more pressing labours of the croft or the farm. The opening up of the county by roads and the influx of apparently cheaper and finer fabrics introduced a change of taste and the old home-industries flagged.

There was reason to fear that this would come to be regarded as but an eddy which attended the stream of progress, and that the check to fireside winter-work, though sad, was inevitable, and must be endured because of compensating advantages. It also seemed not improbable that it might be set aside as only a woman's question.

This indeed it has eventually become in the widest sense, mainly on account of the kind of sympathetic impulse required to initiate a remedial domestic movement, and the special skill and careful personal supervision, which, from the nature of the work, is needed to encourage and direct it. As good, that has once been personally experienced, rises again to the surface, even after a tempestuous lifetime of evil, so, notwithstanding the contamination of southern influence, every year increased appreciation of the artistic merits and practical usefulness of their hand-made tweeds, is returning to the northern people. The thatched, chimneyless roof of the cabin, once the only dwelling of the industrious weaver, now more often than not shelters his sleek cow; the weaver himself sitting snugly between slates above and white-washed walls around, and it is not too optimistic to assert that the webs of moss-green, heather-red, and sky-blue, peacefully rolled out from his purring loom, could, if correct in quantity, and perfect in quality, be sold trebly over, even were the number of weavers doubled throughout the county.

From parish to parish busy committees are forming themselves, for encouragement and communication with the market, and while there is no idea of competing with the great woollen factories of Bradford, Huddersfield, etc., either in pattern or in price, the orders from London tradesmen for genuine homespun goes on, like the mountain stream, torrential in the proper season, and silent at others.

In common with men—women cyclists and women pedestrians, have discovered its advantage for comfort and durability, but is it fantastic to add, that in the touch and smell of these tweeds there is a quality that enslaves them, by its appeal to the nobler sensation of sentiment? In their close proximity, imagination conjures up the scent of autumn heather, mingling with the peat smoke from the scattered homesteads, curling out to the wide swell of the Atlantic; the mind's eye pictures the wild hill-tops bathed in the mist of a passing shower—the covey of grouse whirring to the hollow by the deep swift salmon river—and beyond, in the glorious rainbow light of the August sunset, the startled listening hinds, motionless against the sky line. Surely under such conditions, the Scottish Highlands reveal in effect the enchanted summer-land of the world.

Rev. ROBERT MUNRO, M.A., B.D.

THE ANTIQUITIES OF SUTHERLAND,

BY THE

Rev. ROBERT MUNRO, B.D., F.R.S.E., F.S.A., SCOT.

IF Sutherlandshire may be regarded as geologically representing an epitome of the entire formation of the earth's structure, so from the view-point of the antiquary it may be taken as embracing every sphere of the field covered by Scottish archaeology. It is rich, perhaps beyond any county, in monuments and remains of prehistoric times. Its naturally mountainous and isolated position has in great measure preserved the memorials and ruins of its past civilization, if not from the ravages of time, at least from the more destructive agency of human hands. Strongholds and forts, cairns and tumuli, monoliths and rude stone circles have been invariably respected and left unmolested during all the years. Generation after generation has looked upon them as part of the soil, has prided itself in them and viewed them with more or less veneration, so that to-day, not less than a hundred years ago, it is esteemed a kind of sacrilege to disturb a primitive grave or to excavate an ancient stronghold.

Since the time of the great northern archaeologist Thomsen it is usual to study the antiquities of any land as passing through the three distinct stages of stone, of bronze, and of iron. These stages or periods indicate the successive steps in the rise from rudeness to civilization, from a lower type of culture to a higher; and may generally be accepted as outlining the course of development through which all the higher races have passed. In the antiquities of Sutherland examples of the three periods are abundant. As far back as history can go we have proof that the use of iron was universal in Scotland. The old Caledonian warriors had their iron chariots and weapons, and were able to make a formidable stand even against the legions of Rome itself. But, further back than this remote age, there is evidence of a time more remote still when iron was altogether unknown, and when the only metal used in making instruments and weapons was bronze. And again, even more distant than the bronze period, in the prehistoric distances, there existed an era when man had no knowledge of either bronze or iron, and when all his tools and weapons were constructed of natural materials, such as stone and horn, bone and wood. Each of these ages—pointing to successive conditions of culture and civilization—must not however be considered as in every instance absolutely marked off and defined. The stone age may, for example, overlap—in some cases it does overlap—the bronze and iron ages, and the bronze age may run down far into and alongside of the iron age. These exceptions may be admitted; yet in its widest application the "three-age system" has proved itself to be a safe principle of classification in archaeology.

I.—The Stone Age.

The tools and weapons belonging to the stone age are of two kinds: there are those that are rude and unpolished, brought to the desired shape by a few rough strokes, and showing no marks of smoothing or grinding; and there are others that manifest great skill in the workmanship, being beautifully executed, ground, and polished. The rough unpolished implements are found in the older deposits along with the bones of extinct animals, and are called Palæolithic; the smooth and more highly polished ones, belonging to a more advanced stage and co-eval with the age of bronze, are known as Neolithic.

Mr. Samuel Laing has tried to prove, in his *Prehistoric Remains of Caithness*, that an aboriginal tribe of savage cannibals, as little advanced as the men of Abbeville and Les Eyzies, lingered on for many centuries in that county. They were too rude to have known anything of the later Stone or Bronze Periods of Britain, or to have superseded an earlier or less civilized race of prior aborigines. If Mr. Laing had been able to prove his theory—which he utterly fails to do— we might also reasonably look for Palæolithic man and his remains in Sutherland. But, as it is, there is not a single trace of him there; and for that part of it, as far as has yet been scientifically ascertained, not a trace of him or of his works in the whole of Scotland.

Naturally then we must begin not with the earlier epoch of the Stone age, but with the later or Neolithic epoch.

The implements of the later Stone Age are almost the same in all lands. They consist of axes, hammers, spear-heads, knives, daggers, arrow-heads, saws, chisels, borers, and the like, made of polished stone or flint. The implements found by Mr. Stevenson on Golspie links, and now deposited in the Antiquarian Museum, Edinburgh, give a good representation of the Sutherland Stone Age weapons. The axes and hammers are of the usual type. The arrow-heads—beautiful in form and execution—are of the types known as barbed and tanged, lozenge and leaf-shaped, and a few are of the Irish type, barbed without tang. Yellow and brown flint, but more frequently the chert associated with the Jurassic deposits on the Golspie coast, which takes a fine edge and has the conchoidal fracture of flint, is the material used.

Scattered throughout the county there are several sites where stone implements were manufactured. There is one near Golspie, where scrapers, saws, knives, and fashioned flakes used to be found plentifully. Similar sites are at Badanloch in Kildonan, at Lairg, near the churchyard, at Rogart, near the Dalmore rock, and at Dornoch, close to the Meikle Ferry.

Arrow heads are called by the natives "elf-darts," and are popularly believed to be hurled by the fairies in their efforts to injure man and beast. Flint hammers and axes are not popularly recognised as such : they are supposed to be thunderbolts "that have fallen with the lightning from heaven." Various healing and supernatural virtues are attributed to them, and it is thought that a house in which they are kept cannot be struck by lightning. It is curious that these old-world notions, still credited in Sutherland, should be current not only in the British Isles, but in almost every part of the world that has passed through a Stone Age.

The erections of the Stone Age that have escaped the hand of time are principally commemorative or sepultural. Of these perhaps the most distinctive are the huge chambered cairns, of which there are such good examples in the parish of Farr.

At Rhinavie, about a mile from Bettyhill, there is a group of three of these cairns lying in line due north and

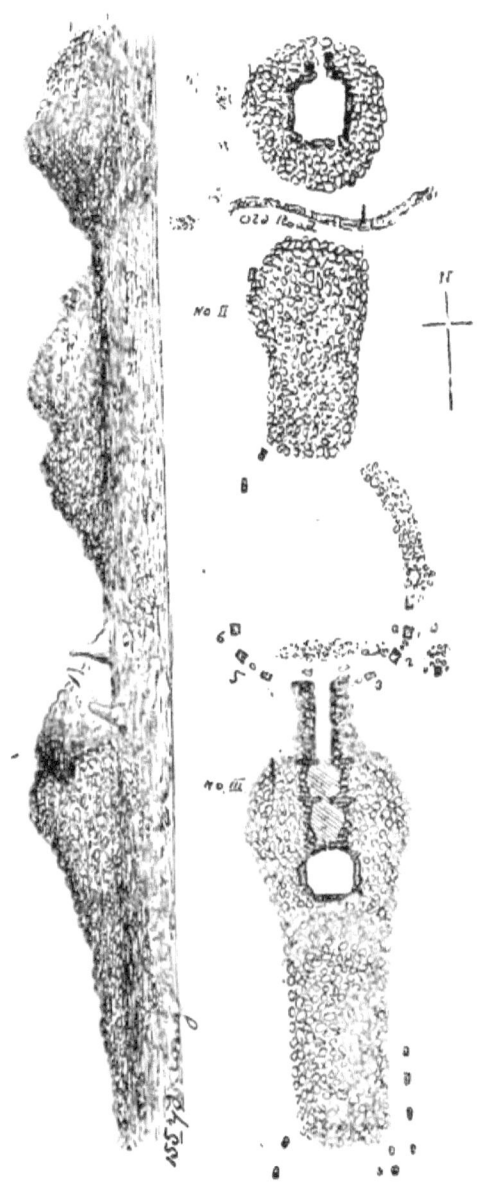

VIEW AND PLAN OF RHINAVIE CAIRNS.

south. The largest is 230 ft. long, 80 ft. wide at the north end, and narrowing to about 50 ft. at the other end. It is furnished with a tricellular chamber reached by a solidly built passage 17 ft. in length, and 2 ft. in height and in

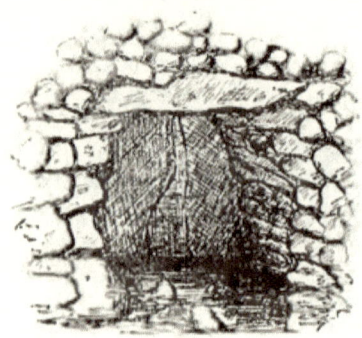

DOORWAY FROM 1st TO 2nd CHAMBER OF LONG CAIRN.

width. The largest cell is the end one, or that which is furthest in. It is 7 ft. in diameter and 8 ft. in height. Divided from this by upright stones are two other cells built of rude masonry and covered over with large slabs, one of which measures 6½ ft. by 3 ft. The middle cell is 5 ft. in length, nearly the same measurement in breadth, and originally 6 ft. 10 in. in height. The cell next the entrance is scarcely as large as the middle one, but this may be due to the fact that the walls have bulged in considerably. Fronting the entrance to this tripartile chamber is an arc of a circle composed of large stones varying in height from 3 ft. to 7 ft. 10 in., and placed at distances ranging from 10 to 16 ft.

NORTH END OF CAIRN No. 3.

The second cairn in the group is an oblong heap 100 ft. in length. It has not been excavated, but it is evidently of the same chambered character as the above.

The third, or northermost cairn is circular in form, 60 ft. in diameter, with a vertical height of about 12 ft. It has a chamber in the centre, whose walls are fine granite slabs set on end, the spaces between being built with uncemented masonry. The chamber is about 7 ft. in diameter, with a height of 8 ft.

A cairn of the same type as the above is situated further south, on the other side of Skelpick burn. Its length is 220 ft. and its breadth from 20 to 30 ft. It contains two chambers, the first being 8 ft. by 10 ft., the second 10 ft. by 12 ft., each being apparently about 8 ft. in height.

At Fiscary, on a hill near Swordly, are four large cairns which, though differing somewhat in external appearance from those mentioned, have the same well-marked internal structure of passages and separate chambers.

These cairns are in every way analogous to the celebrated chambered cairns of Caithness, which have been so fully investigated by Dr. Joseph Anderson. They are places of sepulture for the dead, who were laid in the cells in a recumbent or sitting posture. Sometimes a succession of such interments took place in the same cairn, so that it is not uncommon to find several skeletons in a single chamber. Along with the dead were buried their personal weapons and ornaments, evidently in the pathetic hope that they might be of service in a future world. Earthenware vessels are occasionally found in the graves, filled now with earth, but originally containing food which it was supposed the dead might require in the life beyond. On the floor of some of the chambers the bones of the dog, the horse, the ox, the swine, and the deer, have been dug up, as if they, the companions of man's earthly existence, could keep him company in his tenancy of the tomb.

The semi-circle of standing stones at Rhinavie is of

interest as showing that as far back as the Stone Age circles of this kind were set up to distinguish sepulchral sites. Whether originally they served any other purpose we know not. At a later time they came to be regarded with superstitious reverence, and religious rites were practiced in connection with them. The remarkable chambered cairns at Clava, on the Nairn—similar in structure to the Farr cairns—are surrounded by circles of erect stones, on some of which are cup-markings. These mysterious sculpturings—hollow basins carved out of the rock, with sometimes one or more incised concentric rings—are common in Sutherland, though they have not yet been discovered in connection with its chambered cairns. What they are, archaeology has in vain tried to solve. They are found not only in Great Britain and Ireland, but in different parts of Europe, in Palestine, and the Sinaitic Peninsula, in India, North Africa, and America. They have been regarded as the blood basins of Druidic altars, as emblems of the sun-god, as astronomical devices, as symbols of the old Lingam worship, and some have been prosaic enough to hazard the conjecture that they are the maps of a prehistoric civilization, or the marks cut out by Neolithic man as he polished his tools and weapons on exposed rock-surfaces. All that is indisputable is that they are as old as the Stone Age, and that their use has been prolonged into Christian times. They are found on isolated slabs and earth-fast rocks, on monoliths and megalithic circles, dolmens and chambered tumuli, on the lids of cist-vaens, and the stone coverings of burial urns, carved on the walls of Christian churches, and adorning headstones in rural churchyards. Wherever they exist they are held in veneration. In Scandinavia, Switzerland, and Scotland—where they are called "elf-stones," or "stones of the dead"—needles, buttons, eggs, and milk are placed in the cups as offerings to the souls of the dead. In many lands they are supposed to have the power of warding off disease and of counteracting sterility.

Interesting it is, too, in this connection, to notice that some of the Sutherlandshire rocks possess carvings which are evidently designed to represent human foot-prints. Delineations of the naked human foot, scooped out of, or incised in the rock are not confined to the British Isles: they are of frequent occurrence in Scandinavia, and they are known to exist in France and Germany. Herodotus states that an impression of the foot of Hercules, two cubits in length, existed on a rock beyond the river Tyres in Scythia. The sacred foot-print of Buddha, on Adam's Peak in Ceylon, is well-known, and need only be mentioned. In Scotland and Ireland rocks on which such impressions are carved are supposed to be coronation or inauguration stones, on which Kings and Chieftains took the oath of loyalty to the laws and customs of the nation or the clan. To what age these notable sculpturings must be assigned cannot yet be made out with certainty. They may have an origin dating back to Neolithic times, or they may be comparatively recent. Dr. Joass, when excavating one of the Sutherland brochs, found the impression of two foot-prints on a stone in the entrance passage.

It would seem as if already in the Stone Age the people of Sutherland had attained to some measure of culture and civilization. They used weapons of stone and urns of clay which manifest skilful workmanship and aesthetic taste. They possessed the same domestic animals that we possess, they pursued the chase, and they fished in the lakes and rivers. It is more than likely, too, that they had fixed places of abode, or tribal villages ; for it is scarcely possible that the people who reared such splendid dwellings for the dead should themselves lead a purely nomadic life, without any permanent shelter but that of the caves and the rocks. The chambered cairns of Strathnaver clearly point not only to high religious instincts, and reverence for ancestry, they also presuppose an organized society or fellowship which is the first necessary step towards civilization. Hard, perhaps, the lot of the men of the Stone Age might at times be, but on the whole it need have been neither so miserable nor so savage as it is sometimes pictured. Their existence was free and natural, in no way cramped or confined. They had the hills and the valleys, the rivers and the forests, - they lived a many-sided, active life,—finding their own food, making their own clothes, and weapons and houses,—having also, all the while, to hold their own against wild beasts and human foes—and from the very exigencies of their environment they must physically and mentally have occupied no mean place. Higher, to say the least of it, they certainly were, both in nature and endowment, than the multitudes in our large cities who toil in badly ventilated rooms, who seldom enjoy the beneficent light of the sun, or behold the glories of earth and sea and sky, and who spend their whole lifetime in the doing of one little monotonous task that paralyses the mind and arrests the true growth of manhood.

II.—The Bronze Age.

Bronze finds in Sutherland are much less abundant than those of stone, yet they are sufficiently numerous and widely

98 SUTHERLAND AND THE REAY COUNTRY.

distributed to suggest the existence of such an age here as elsewhere in Scotland. Bronze celts of the early type—

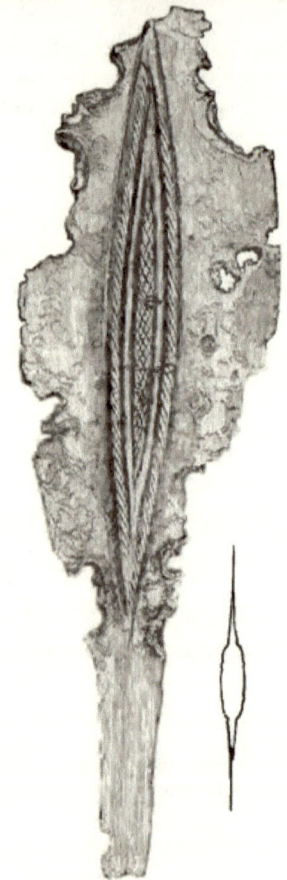

BALBLAIR BLADE.

almost identical in shape with the stone ones—have been found at Rogart. Palstaves, or winged celts—so called because the sides project into wings or flanges so as to form grooves for the insertion of the cleft handles—evidently an advance on the early type—have been found there also, and at Strath-halladale, and on the eastern shore of Loch Hope. At Lierabol, Kildonan, a plain oval blade of bronze, with fractured tang, was discovered in a tumulus amongst incinerated bones under an inverted urn. A similar blade, but ornamented along the centre by lozenge-shaped spaces, alternately plain and filled with fine lines crossing obliquely, formed part of the contents of a cist that was opened at Rogart in 1834. Some years later another blade, oval and ornamented, was found at Balblair, Creich, in connection with a cremated burial. Dr. Anderson, speaking of the ornamented blades, says, "that they are the rarest of all the forms of these bronze implements." An anvil of bronze, found near the Kyle of Oykel, is the only one of the

BRONZE ANVIL.

kind that has yet been met with in Scotland. Like the Continental examples it is comparatively small in size, being about 4 in. in length, and weighing only 10½ oz. It can be used in two positions according as either of the pointed ends is fixed in the stock. In 1868, during the construction of the railway, a hoard of seven bronze vessels, one packed inside another, was unearthed near Helmsdale, behind a boulder, one foot under the present surface. They have been described by Dr. Joass in the *Proceedings of the Society of Antiquaries*, vol. viii., (new series, p. 214). Two of them are perforated in tasteful design, by small clean-cut holes, and the rim of one is ornamented in chevron pattern. The

BRONZE VESSELS FOUND NEAR HELMSDALE.

BRONZE VESSELS FOUND NEAR HELMSDALE.

whole appear to have been beaten into form and lathe-dressed. In the same neighbourhood a stone ball of the Bronze Age was also picked up. From Kintradwell—a district full of many antiquities—we have clippings, waste-jets, and crucibles, pointing to the presence here at one time of artificers in bronze.

Among the personal ornaments of this period are shale beads, bronze pins and buttons, necklaces of jet and bronze armlets. Beads, pins, and buttons often constitute part of the "grave goods" in bronze burials. Dr. Joass found in a cist at Torish, near Helmsdale, a necklace of jet in an almost

TORISH NECKLACE

perfect condition. Fragments of charcoal, an arrow-head of chert, and a spear-head of yellow flint, were also found among the ejected material. At Uppat armlets of bronze were got in connection with cremated burials.

The Bronze Age, like the Stone Age, affords no indication of the kind of dwellings in which the people lived. They had, no doubt, houses built of turf or of stone, but all trace of them has long since vanished. The only structures belonging to this far away time are the dwelling-places of the dead. Strangely enough these do not manifest such architectural skill as the great cairn chambers of the Stone period, nor are they, like those, uniform in shape and character. Some of them—the earliest, as they are the rarest—consist of a moderately large cist made of rough slabs or flags in which the body was laid unburnt; others—and these constitute the largest number—consist of a smaller cist in which was placed an urn holding the ashes of the cremated body; while a third kind of interment was that of the simple urn, with a lid, containing the ashes of the dead, but not enclosed by a cist. The cists again were sometimes covered over with large heaps of stone, so as to form considerable cairns; but as frequently they are found in earth mounds, and hillocks of gravel and sand. On the other hand, in many cases of the humbler urn burial, the urn was merely laid in a hole in the earth. The grave deposits associated with these different forms of Bronze Age burial are of the same peculiar type. They consist of thin oval blades with tangs, rivetted triangular blades, rings and pins, beads and necklaces of jet, polished stone weapons, arrow-heads and flint knives.

The external characteristics of the burials of the Bronze Age are as well defined as their contents. Their distinctive feature is not the cairn, the mound, the cist, or the urn; it is the enclosure of stones encircling the grave, and marking it off from the surrounding area. These enclosures, or stone circles, occasionally assume large and impressive proportions, as at Stennis and Callernish; more rarely they formed many lines of small stones arranged in parallel or irregular rows, like those at Clyth and Latheron, in Caithness; but wherever they exist, unless in conjunction with chambered cairns, they constitute the most distinguishing mark of a Bronze Age burial. Of the larger type of stone circles there are several interesting examples in Sutherland, as at Dal-Harald in Strathnaver, at Abercross, near Morvich, at Rosehall and Bonar Bridge. The only instance of the many lines and circles of small stones is at Lierabol, Kildonan, where they are associated with a group of Bronze Age tumuli.

Monoliths—single pillar stones—the oldest, as well as the most recent of stone monuments—are not very numerous. One stands in the centre of the Lierabol tumuli, another near the Crask road from Loth mill to Kilearnan, and a third at Lochan Treathail, Dornoch. Near the two last are several hut circles. Monoliths also occur at Strathnaver and at Creich, and are said to mark the spot where Scandinavian warriors lie buried. At Farr, near the Fiscary cairns, there is a long recumbent stone which at one time, in all likelihood, occupied the erect position.

Scattered throughout the county are several groups of megaliths, or large stones. From their position and character they seem to be the ruins of the tripartite chambers of the Stone Age cairns, stripped long ago of their smaller stones for building and other purposes.

The people of the Bronze Age in Sutherland must have reached a comparatively high level of culture and civilization

Although no querns or whorls have been found in deposits of this period we need have no hesitation in believing that agriculture and the art of spinning were then well known. The possession of bronze—an alloy of copper and tin, present in the proportion of nine parts of copper to one of tin—shows that the natives had a system of commerce which brought them into contact with the products and enlightenment of other peoples and nations. The beauty, too, with which they fashioned their implements, and the ornamentation with which they decorated their personal effects, their weapons, adornments, vessels, and burial urns, indicate that they not only mastered the mechanical details of the material they worked upon, but that they also possessed feelings of culture and refinement of an advanced kind. There are, indeed, many facts and indications that go to prove that they had more of the comforts, and even luxuries, of life than we could think possible at so remote a period.

III.—The Iron Age.

Iron, the true beginning of civilization in Europe, must have been known in Sutherland at least 150 years before the Christian era. Sites of ancient iron furnaces are found at Loch Unes, Loch Merkland, Lairg, Golspie Links, Suisgil Burn, Durcha, and Altasbeg, near Durcha. Some of these may have been in use as far back as the close of the Bronze Age. At first the process of manufacture must have been primitive enough, and may have been carried on without the aid of an artificial blast—the ore being simply calcined or roasted in a wood fire exposed to the force of the breeze.

Implements of iron belonging to the earlier iron period are exceedingly rare, owing to the destruction of the metal by oxidation. Dagger blades, dirks, spear-heads, and socketed chisels form part of the contents of the Kintradwell and Cairn-liath brochs. In the Cairn-liath broch were also found two plates of brass, hammer-marked in lines across the surface, and a silver fibula of the bow-shaped and cruciform type—really Celtic in character, though associated with the late Roman period. Objects belonging to the later Iron Age, which may be said to coincide with the time of the Vikings, are not unfrequent. Swords and fragments of swords and other weapons have been found at Strathhalladale, Strathy, Kildonan, and Farr. A curious bronze swivel, apparently of the Viking age, has just been reported by Dr. Joass. It is a beautiful and solid piece of workmanship, and was possibly used in helmet decoration or in connection with falconry.

Of more interest, however, than the few relics that have come down from the Iron Age are the structures belonging to this period—the brochs, the vitrified forts and eirdehouses.

BROCHS are very abundant, there being not fewer than sixty throughout the county. Commanding, as they usually do, elevated positions along the sides of straths and valleys they form attractive and picturesque objects in the landscape. Dun Dornadilla and Castle Cole are the most remarkable in the Sutherlandshire group. Dornadilla is 24 feet high, and the part of it still standing is built of undressed stones without cement or mortar. The outer circumference measures 150 feet, the diameter of the inner court is 29 feet, and that of the wall 8 feet 8 inches. In the centre of the wall, and really dividing it into two concentric walls, there is a series of small chambers, like the dingy rooms in a Feudal

Castle. On the outside there are no windows, and there is but one doorway which leads through the breadth of the wall to an inner court, or area, exposed to the sky. From this court there is access to the chambers on the ground floor; and above these are the remains of a second gallery reached by a rough stairway. Cordiner, who visited the fort in 1780, mentions that three distinct rows of galleries could be traced within the walls, and that he walked up and down different stairs from the first to the second storey, but that the third storey was partially filled up owing to the displacement of the stones. The different rows of apartments in the heart of the wall are lighted by slits or apertures looking into the interior area. Castle Cole, in Strathbrora, is even more striking than Dun Dornadilla. It is built on a steep eminence, guarded on three sides by hills, and defended at the weakest parts by a double row of fortifications made of rude stone masonry. Like the common type it also had several galleries in the centre of the wall, separated from each other by a flooring of flags or smooth stones fitting into the wall. Portions of this fort are still about 15 ft. in height.

These singular erections—which are peculiar to Scotland, and may have been built as centres of defence against the Norsemen—have been carefully investigated by archaeologists. Querns, stone lamps, whetstones and pounders; combs, pins, and bone buttons; several instruments of bronze, oxidized fragments of iron, and ornaments of silver and gold, are among the objects that have been found. Besides these manufactured articles there have also been discovered parts of the human skeleton, bones of the lower animals, and the horns of the rein-deer, then common in the north of Scotland. Traces of charred grain have likewise been detected, indicating that the occupants of the buildings were not ignorant of agriculture.

VITRIFIED FORTS. This is the name given to certain stone enclosures whose walls bear traces of having been subjected to the action of fire. They are generally situated on the flat summits of hills which occupy strong and easily defended positions. No lime or cement has been found in any of these structures, but all of them present the peculiarity of being more or less consolidated by the fusion of the rocks of which they are built. At one time they were supposed to be limited in their range to Scotland: they are now known to exist in Ireland, in Upper Lusatia, Bohemia, Silesia and Thuringia, in the provinces on the upper banks of the Rhine, and in several parts of France.

A fairly good example of this unique kind of ancient stronghold is Dun Creich. The Dun has a conical top approached only from the west side. The east side slopes steeply to the sea, and the south is also precipitous seaward. The west side is the most open and exposed, and has a low rampart, partly laid open where it shows considerable vitrifaction—the rocks being solidly fused together. All the other sides are naturally protected more or less by their steepness. There are traces of a low rampart across the east end, a few yards inwards from the edge of the Dun, which is also apparently vitrified. In the centre of the Dun is a circular hollow, which used to be a well, but which is now filled with stones to prevent cattle from falling into it. The rock of which the vitrified rampart is built is the ordinary mica-schist, a rock which could be readily fused in the open air by means of a wood fire, the alkali of the wood serving in some measure as a flux.

EARTH-HOUSES, or underground dwellings—primitive in structure as anything in the Stone Age—are comparatively modern, being later than the Roman occupation. The Earth-house at Erribol, though smaller than the usual type, is 33 ft. in length, 4 ft. in height, and for the greater part of its length only 2 ft. wide, expanding to 3½ ft. for some distance at the extreme end. The sides are built and the top roofed over with stones. These singular structures,

EIRDE HOUSE, ERRIBOL. (CROSS SECTION).

known in some districts as "fairy houses," were no doubt used by the natives, in times of stress, as places of concealment for their wives and children and goods. The range of the type stretches from the south of Scotland to the Shetland Isles. There is also an Irish and a Cornish group with some distinct peculiarities of their own.

IV.—HISTORICAL AGE.

Passing from purely Pagan times, and coming down to the Christian or historical era, we find many objects of deep archaeological interest.

In the Duke of Sutherland's museum, at Dunrobin, there is a stone on the one side of which is a highly finished Celtic cross extending the whole length of the stone. The limbs and the margin are filled with panels of varied and artistically interlaced decoration. As a work of ornamental skill this cross is very beautiful. Yet on the reverse side there is incised in the centre a representation of a rudely dressed man in the act of slaying a bull—possibly for sacrifice. In his right hand is an uplifted axe, in his left a knife. On the same side there are also the double disc, the crescent with the rod bent like the letter V, the serpent and other well known symbols of Paganism. This Stone, called the Golspie Stone, has an Ogam inscription in the Pictish language, written along a moulding on the right hand margin of the stone, and continued over the top towards the left. Professor Rhys, one of the most recent who has tried to decipher it, gives the reading *allhallor edd Mac Nuuvva rreirng*, which he translates provisionally "Beast and Mac-Nuva's conflict." In the County there are not fewer than thirteen sculptured stones, many of them like the cross at Farr Churchyard, being exceedingly fine. All of these are older than A.D. 1100, and some of them belong to a much earlier date.

To the same period—the period of the highest expression of Celtic art—also belong the three exquisitely designed and decorated brooches found at Rogart in 1868, and which formed part of a hoard of similar brooches discovered by a workman, who no doubt had the rest melted as bullion.

Of buildings and ruins which can lay claim to a more or less remote antiquity, the more important can only be noticed.

DUNROBIN, supposed to have been founded in 1098 by Robert, Earl of Sutherland, is reputed to be the oldest inhabited house in the kingdom. It is first mentioned in charters in 1401. The greater part of this magnificent pile

ANCIENT GRAVESTONE IN FARR CHURCHYARD.

is modern, being built by the second Duke between 1845 and 1851.

CASTLE BORVE must have been at one time a formidable stronghold, (for picture see page 41). It is built on a promontory joined to the land by a narrow pass a few feet in breadth, which had been guarded by a draw bridge. Beyond the pass there is a large space of ground where the ruins of the castle and the guard's houses, and the remains of a trench and wall can still be traced. Beneath the castle in the rock below there is a natural passage 200 ft. in length, like a grand arch, which can be traversed by a rowboat. The castle was a stronghold of the Norse during the time of their supremacy. There is a tradition that it was built by Thorkel, who agreed to receive no payment if any flaw could be found in the work on its completion. When the castle was finished the Viking and his lady expressed themselves as satisfied with it, but the north outer wall could only be examined properly from the sea in a boat. Meantime the lady contrived to let a black thread hang down the wall from the principal window. When Thorkel detected what he took to be a crack in the wall he demanded to be lowered by a rope that he might examine the nature of the defect. This was done, but the rope was dropped from above, and the unfortunate architect was drowned. Thorkel is reputed to have lived about the 11th century.

With the decadence of the Norse power the castle became the property of the Mackays of Farr. It was destroyed by the Earl of Sutherland in 1551. Iye Mackay —against whom there were several charges, one being treason —was summoned to appear before Queen Mary at Inverness, but he, not feeling sure of his head, disregarded the command. John, Earl of Sutherland, was thereupon commissioned to invade Mackay's territory. This he did, and after a short siege took Castle Borve, and hanged Rory Mac Ian Mhor, its captain. Iye in the interval invaded Sutherland, and later on distinguished himself in the Border wars against the English.

CAISTEAL BHARRUICH—an old square tower of considerable strength placed on an eminence on the east side of the Kyle of Tongue (see page 27)—is stated in the *Origines Parochiales* to have been on one occasion the residence of Kali Hundason, who made an effort to conquer Scotland on the death of Malcolm II. The invasion in which King Kali acted a part, and which proved so disastrous to the Northmen, took place in the year 1033. It is suggested by others that the castle was built in the 11th century by Bishop Bar, who was the founder of Bar's church, at Dornoch, demolished in 1570.

Not far from Castle Bharruich, on an islet in Loch Hacon, are the remains of a building about 30 ft. square, with walls nearly 6 ft. in breadth. There is no door or window, although the parts of the walls still standing are over 6 ft. in height. Tradition says it was built by the wife of a Viking as a retreat where she could meet with her favoured lover during her husband's absence on the North Sea. More probably it was built by Hacon, Earl of Orkney, who lived in the beginning of the 12th century, and was intended as a shooting rendezvous. This curious and nteresting erection is called *Grianan*, or summer-house.

HELMSDALE CASTLE, (see page 45) now in ruins, was built by the 7th Countess of Sutherland in 1488. It is noted as the scene of the murder of the 11th Earl of Sutherland

and his Countess in 1567. The Earl's aunt, Isobel, poisoned them while at supper, and would also have poisoned heir son, but the draught intended for him was taken by her own son, who died two days afterwards. The instigator of this horrible crime was George, Earl of Caithness, who soon after became guardian of the young Earl that so narrowly escaped the fate of his parents. It was while acting in the capacity of guardian that this unscrupulous man is said to have destroyed all the Sutherland Charters and Papers he could find—an irreparable loss not only to the noble house of Sutherland, but also to the history of the nation.

ARDVRECK CASTLE, the ancient seat of the MacLeods of Assynt, occupies a beautifully picturesque position at the end of a long rocky peninsula near the head of Loch Assynt. It was built about 1590, and is memorable as the place where the great Marquis of Montrose was detained on his capture in this district. After the fatal rout of Invercharron he and the Earl of Kinnoull betook themselves for safety to the heights of Assynt. Here they wandered for some time, until the Earl, faint and footsore, was not able to travel any further, and was left among the mountains to perish. Montrose would have also followed his example were it not that he chanced to come upon a hut in the hills where he was supplied with bread and milk. Meantime Neil MacLeod, Laird of Assynt, got a hint of the situation, and sent out search-parties everywhere in hope of capturing the fugitives. Some of them met with the unfortunate Marquis and brought him to Ardvreck. Montrose tried hard to obtain his liberty by making all kinds of promises, but MacLeod would not be bribed, and handed him over to the authorities. He was executed at Edinburgh on the 21st May, 1650. Close to Ardvreck, on the opposite shore, is Calda House, erected about 1660, by Kenneth MacKenzie, 3rd Earl of Seaforth, and destroyed by fire towards the middle of last century.

FOLK LORE,

BY

A. POLSON, J.P., C.C., DUNBEATH.

To the Folk-lorist the county of Sutherland is peculiarly rich. This is partly accounted for by its immense area, which on the west borders the stormy Minch, across which must have been carried to it many of the West Highland Tales, that here found fitting environment, and therefore took root. On the north its harbours afforded a shelter for the Vikings and their descendants, some of whom, after they had harried Orkney and Shetland, came to this county, and with them brought their Norse notions; while the east coast was the home of a people of somewhat different origin, who, when they first came, could not leave their superstitions behind. Again, the inhabitants of the interior who knew little of the then more numerous dangers of the surrounding seas must have had notions of their own.

But whatever outside influences may have furnished the ancient Sutherlanders with their beliefs, the proverbial and peculiarly lively imagination of the Celt, always much influenced by natural vicissitudes, must have cast its weird glamour over the whole. Little wonder it therefore is that to them the low-lying brooding mists, the numerous dark sullen tarns, the dreary moorland across which flitted the "will o' the wisp," should be peopled by creatures having peculiar powers, whose favour they would do well to court; and these supposed powers, it has been asserted, not without reason, are the remains of a religion anterior to Christianity, and which Christianity has not yet rooted out. They are now, however, disappearing more quickly with the decadence of the *cèilidh*, which has in great measure been supplanted by the newspapers and books which Sutherlanders use so abundantly.

The superstitions of the various parts of the county differ widely, and it is not to be supposed that what follows is believed in by all the people, or that any native of the county, however superstitious, reckons a tithe of them among his beliefs. They are, it must be understood, merely the summary of a collection which the writer has been making for quite a number of years.

To all who have given the subject of folk-lore any attention it has become apparent that superstitions cling round every stage of life, and that nearly all of them are connected with a desire to peer into the unknown and unknowable future. They begin with a person's birth and end only after his death.

Following this order we find that the belief is entertained in Sutherlandshire, as elsewhere, that a child born on a Sabbath will be more fortunate than one born on any of the other six days of the week. Although one does not here think of 'chime hours,' the child born at midnight will grow up to 'see things' hidden from others—to have, in short, the gift of second sight. It would be curious to ascertain if those who in the Highlands claim this gift were born at this hour 'when churchyards yawn.' If the little one have a caul or thin membrane on the head when born, it will be especially lucky, and cannot be drowned while the fortunate hood is preserved. At least one Highland clergyman—a Catach—now alive, had one such, and his career is eagerly watched by those who know of this circumstance in connection with his birth. This caul also prevented fairies or evil spirits secretly taking the little child away and leaving one of their own in its place. Much more firmly believed in is 'the evil eye,' to the sinister influence of which unbaptised children are much exposed. For this, baptism is, of course, reckoned a cure, but if for any reason, that is not available for a smitten child, then water has to be carried from a running stream over which the living and the dead pass (from under a bridge), gold and silver coins placed in it, after which it is sprinkled on the child in the name of the Trinity. To be effectual, the water carrier must speak neither going nor returning—must, in witch-doctors' parlance, 'carry it dumb.' It is also considered lucky and a precursor of rising in the world, that a child, after leaving its mother's room for the first time, should go *up* stairs rather than down. History has made this good in the case of many Sutherlanders born in one storeyed lowly crofters' houses, in which were no stairs to descend, and who, in after life, climbed well up into the world. It is still believed that it is unsafe to leave a cat in the room in which a baby is sleeping, as pussy is thought to be able to choke it. If the child be discontented and frequently puts out its tongue, it can only be soothed by something which the mother longed for but did not get.

The rite of baptism to which much importance is attached, is, it is to be regretted, still entwined with many superstitions. Thus, only a 'lucky person' is allowed to accompany the parents to the church or rendezvous, carrying with her a piece of bread and cheese, which is given by her, as from the child, to the first person met, after the performance of the ceremony. When children of different sexes are to be baptized at the same time, care is taken that the boy is baptized first, for it is thought that if this order be reversed the lad will grow up beardless, and the girl on arriving at womanhood will, to her grief, be possessed of the hair he lacked. To be lucky the child ought to cry when the ceremony is being performed, and it is conjectured that this has originated in the fact that unclean spirits cried aloud when driven out by our Saviour.

The water sprinkled on the forehead is seldom wiped off, and to get something on which the baptismal water has fallen is to be possessed of a charm, and a mother sometimes puts pins in the baby's breast before baptism, so that she may have something holy to give away to her friends, though even to them she will on no account divulge the child's name before baptism. As the child grows up, a gum-stick of juniper wood ought to be given it, as that will prevent its having toothache at a later age. From this time forward until the period has arrived when marriage is to be thought of, the youth is liable to no special danger from 'evil eye,' witches, or fairies, and attention is paid only to those precautions which it is necessary all should take.

MARRIAGE.

Marriage, though certainly regarded as a most important step, does not seem in Sutherlandshire to be surrounded by the very numerous notions which hold in the southern part of the kingdom. Sutherland *nigheans* have few love "charms" and fewer means of ascertaining the form, features, and fortunes of their future partners. They are on the whole content to wait. Of the few "charms" there are, most belong, it is strange to say, to the vegetable kingdom. Thus they know that if the leaves of the elder tree be variegated, a wedding is sure to pass that way, and on Hallowe'en maidens sometimes still sow hemp as they did in the days of Burns, and repeat the words :—

> " Hemp seed I sow thee,
> My love I do not know thee,
> Whether by land or whether by sea,
> Pray come and harrow this for me,"

and expect to see the future partner come to do the harrowing. Much more faith is placed in dreams, and the favourite and quickest method of having these is to eat a salt herring before going to bed, and if one is to have a lover at all he is sure to appear with a drink of water to quench the consequent thirst. The years during which a girl still has to remain single are best known by counting the cuckoo's notes in Spring. When, however, the 'contract' or formal betrothal is celebrated, the three weeks which intervene before the wedding is a time when young men and women may be similarly smitten by rubbing shoulders with the bride or bridegroom. They attend church on alternate Sabbaths, and on the night previous to the wedding there is much hilarity, but little forecasting of futurity at the feet washing, only when that is over they ought to sleep on different sides of running water, and next day it is best that they should not meet until they do so before the minister, and it is even better to get drenched with rain than to meet a funeral procession either going or coming. On leaving the church after the ceremony they should be preceded by a married luck-insuring couple. When the house is reached bread is thrown over the bride's head, and for this there is a scramble, as there also is for the small silver coin which she on that day wore in her stocking, and which is always thrown among the company after she has retired. The finder of the coin is reckoned as pretty sure to be the first of that company to give cause for another similar happy gathering. When the bride and bridegroom leave home for the first time they should not, if possible, go out by the same door. After this, they with wonderful quietness and quickness settle down to their new life, and while health, wealth and prosperity continue, pay less and less heed to auguries and charms.

Death.

But by and by, the dark messenger comes to them as to all, and its advent Sutherlanders have, in common with nearly all Highlanders, invested with peculiarly painful premonitions, for they certainly are mindful of their latter end, and many are the tokens which recall it to their memories. Unusual sights or sounds are readily construed as meaning that they are to be "called." Animals, generally, are assigned a sharper vision than human beings in this respect. Thus, a cock which persists in crowing more than usual, and more especially if it does so at night, is deemed so sure a precursor of news of death that it is usual to go to the roost to look in what way its head is pointing, for from that direction will come the sad news. The unusual howling of dogs is another pretty sure omen, and sometimes a dog is said to howl with its head pointing in the direction of the dying one. When, at night, horses shy without apparent cause, they are believed to see something which human eyes cannot, and which is thought to be a phantom of a funeral which will soon pass that way. Birds—even innocent robins, tapping at a window on a winter's morning—denote death, no less surely than the demoniacal laughter of an owl in the neighbourhood. The sight of a Will o' the Wisp is a sure forerunner of death, and the direction in which it goes is eagerly watched by the seer. "Corpse candles" are, however, a warning to the persons who see them that their time has come. Phantom funeral processions were often seen, and it was always considered best for the seer to stand aside, and let them pass, which they quietly did, but if relief were offered, the seer might expect to be remorselessly trampled on by the cortège. In his life of "The Petty Seer," Mr. Maclennan tells the story of Janet Melville, Doll of Brora, who once accompanied such a cortège from Greenhill to Loth, a distance of about five miles. It seems that Janet, who while serving with the minister of Loth, was visiting home at The Doll, and returning somewhat late at night saw the procession going forward in front of her, and walking quickly, caught it. She knew and spoke to several of those in it, but received no answer. She heard the man in charge give the order for 'relief,' when those who bore it on their shoulders were changed. She, little thinking what it was, accompanied it to the churchyard, saw the coffin lowered into the grave, which was duly filled up, and then the whole vanished out of her sight. She now became thoroughly frightened, and hastened into the manse. A few days afterwards, a funeral cortège, composed of the very people she mentioned as having seen on that night, reached Loth churchyard, and buried a person in the very spot where she had seen the spectre burial take place. Other 'foregangs' are numerous and awe-inspiring enough, such as the village joiners hearing at the dead hour of night phantom joiners at coffin-making, or even in broad daylight seeing pieces of wood, usually laid aside for coffins, being moved by no human hands, but by what can only be the ghost of the person about to need it.

MEDICAL.

The journey from birth to death is very seldom accomplished without much intervening physical suffering, and the mass of medical folk lore which preceded the modern book lore and 'first aids' is believable only when it is remembered that for each of the many ills which flesh is heir to there are many remedies. For every ill, Sutherlanders believed something ought to be *done*, that applications of something externally or internally had to be made—just as not long ago a woman who scalded her foot, and not knowing exactly what to do, besmeared it with marmalade.

Half a cure is to get the physician to understand the disease; and the method of arriving at the *locale* and nature of a disease varies; but two samples of doctoring lately practised in the county must be sufficient. Take on three consecutive mornings from a place over which the living and the dead pass three pebbles which have been covered by running water, mark them head, heart, and limbs respectively, put them into the fire until hot, let them next be placed in a basin of cold water, of which a few mouthfuls taken for several mornings will work a cure, no matter whether the disease be located in head, heart, or heels. But even the superstitious seem to believe in specific rather than universal remedies, and as there are separate cures for separate diseases, it is necessary to be certain of the exact ailment before applying the remedy. This is done as follows: Take a worsted thread, wind it round a spoon—preferably a horn one—name the disease the person is supposed to be suffering from, and then pass it three times round the crook, watching meanwhile if the thread comes off in the operation. If it does, the patient does not suffer from the disease named, but if the thread stays on, he does, and as the doctors' books say, 'then apply the usual remedies.'

For toothache, which surely bears the bell among diseases, no diagnosis is necessary, and, if persistent, it is oftenest charmed away by far more gentle means than the dentists' forceps. One of these charmers was, until removed by death, a weaver who, Silas Marner-like, lived in a lonely cottage, and alone, save for the converse he held with some weekly sensational newspapers, and visitors who found him an interesting retailer of old world ways. When a sufferer asked if he could cure toothache, he replied with characteristic caution " Indeed, some people are saying that I can, but perhaps yours is not of the kind that I can cure." On being assured that his cure would be tried, he without more ado went to an inner sanctum, and in about a quarter of an hour emerged with a folded piece of paper, which he said was to be worn for seven days underneath the waistcoat and over the heart, but if when relief came, the patient told the means by which it came, the pain would return. On the paper being opened, the following was found written in a very very shaky hand :—

"Petter was sitting on a marable stone, weping. Jesus came by and said, " What els (ails) ye. Petter answered and said, "tuaack (toothache). Jesus answered and said, " be ye weel from that, Petter, and not ye only, but everyone that believe on me, Petter, may the Lord Jesus Christ bless his own words, and to him be all the praze (praise), Amen."

Evidently, it was long long ago known to dwellers in the north that a strong faith is about as powerful as any drug in the pharmacopœia. A small piece of broom—and this savours strongly of witchcraft—kept in the mouth for som time after a charm has been muttered over it, is also a cure. Perhaps chemists can tell whether there be any curative substance in it which would make it equally efficacious before being thus charmed. Another specific which is known to cure toothache is to take a common earthworm, carry it in the mouth "dumb" to the next parish, and there bury it. This is perhaps a little difficult to do in the Highlands, where everybody knows everybody else, and where, if you do not pass a remark regarding the weather to everyone you meet, you are thought to be very proud, or to entertain them a grudge. My informer tells me that she knows of several persons who were cured in this way, and among them, herself; only, in order to be unseen, she left home at 3 a.m. One scarcely knows, in a case like this, whether to pity most the poor worm or the poor patient.

The belief that the seventh son who is also the seventh child of the same father and mother, is a "born doctor," is common all over the country, but in the north of Scotland the poor fellow is not allowed to *prescribe* his cures, he must *act* them. And of the many which he is able to perform the two following may be taken as fair examples. Anyone suffering from a sore back has only to lie prone while this doctor walks seven times up and down on it. Should the sufferer be unable to bear this trampling it will suffice that the doctor step across the patient the same number of times.

But it is in the case of " King's Evil " that he is most useful. To effect a cure the following procedure is necessary :—

Take before sunrise some water from a well opening towards the north. Carry it dumb to the patient's house, and with this, the seventh son must in the forenoon, and before tasting any food, bathe the diseased part, say a short prayer, and spit on the water. This treatment must be continued for seven whole weeks, and for all this the poor doctor is to expect no fee. But this hydropathic treatment is humane when compared with that for fits, which is that a live cock of which every feather is black and the legs and beak yellow, be buried in the very spot where the fit first came on.

When it is considered that so much good arises from the using of the mineral waters of the home and continental spas, it is not to be wondered at that sometimes the superstitious should ascribe supernatural powers to them. But strangely enough though there are hundreds of lakes in Sutherlandshire, only one or two are regarded as possessing healing virtues. The most celebrated of these is Loch Monar in Strathnaver, which may work a cure on any morning, but is particularly effective on the first day of May. Many stories are told as to how this lake acquired its power, but the one most generally accepted is as follows :—

On its banks lived a woman who was possessed of a talisman, which, on the payment of a silver coin to its owner, gave a sure and speedy recovery to the donor, no matter what his or her disease might be. It must have been rather an ugly loss to the poor woman that she persistently refused to let the talisman do its good work if the donation were given by proxy, and to the sceptical this ought to be proof enough that she performed no cure for love of gain. But the maxim about the powerful being always envied by the powerless found no exception in this case, and the poor woman was attacked by a veritable scoundrel of the name of Gordon, who "burglariously and feloniously" attempted to lighten her of her cherished talisman, and so hard was she "put to" that she actually threw it into the lake crying "Mo nàr, mo nàr" (Anglicè "for shame, for shame") and from that time to this the lake bears the name of Loch Monar. Though the talisman was thus lost to sight it became to memory dear, for it was soon found that the lake would now under rather peculiar conditions do the work of the talisman to all, save persons of the name of Gordon! How his clansmen must have execrated him for being foiled by a woman. Now for the conditions. The believing patient has to come to the lake, bathe, dress, deposit a piece of silver and be out of sight of it ere sunrise. Though the coins thus deposited were protected by the threat that whosoever took them away also took the depositor's disease, very very few coins are now to be seen within its margin.

It is the speciality of at least one woman in Sutherlandshire to extract any dust or specks which may have accidentally got into a person's eye. She tells that she requires to know into which eye the speck has got and what the sufferer's name is, that then she proceeds alone either before sunrise or after sunset, to a well opening to the north, utters a few words of Gaelic, takes a mouthful of the water in which when she puts it out again she invariably finds the troublesome speck. When asked as to how she got such peculiar power, she quite willingly tells that the Gaelic words which seem to constitute the charm were told her by her father who was an elder in the kirk, and that he got them from an aged woman on her death-bed. This power can only be possessed by one person at a time, and to propagate it she repeats the charm to one person in her lifetime, and he in his life-time to one woman to whom the power comes after its former possessor's demise. "Many," she always adds, when she has told how it is done, "would not like to be able to do this because I must not take any money for doing it, for when my father gave it me, he said, "Freely ye have received, freely give."

It is a pity, that it has to be added that although only such specialists have the power of giving good health, yet it is believed to be in the power of most malevolent persons to give ill-health by means of the *corp-creadh* (clay body). For this purpose a clay effigy of the doomed one is made, pins are stuck all over it, and then it is placed under falling water which, as it washes the clay away, will in some sympathetic way as surely sap away the health and means of the condemned person.

Though the methods of effecting cures are legion, few of them, such as the wearing of earrings for sore eyes, are practised openly, most of them are nowadays preferably practised in secret—if possible without the knowledge of a second person, as when one suffering from a "sty" secretly pulls a single hair from a black cat and rubs it nine times over the pustule.

DIVINATIONS.

The examination of a people's folk-lore must be more interesting than relics having an antiquarian value only, for these beliefs have a double meaning. They not only in some measure throw a light on how people lived and built up their beliefs in the past, but also on the means by which they thought, and have managed to get others to think after them, that they can divine the future. A few of these common in the county may be given. If it be found that any of our neighbours have meeting eye-brows they had better be avoided as unlucky, whereas if they have closely set teeth they may be regarded as greedy, but if they be possessed of teeth set widely apart their friendship ought to be cultivated as they are sure to be generous and prosperous. To dream about teeth, however, is to foreknow that sorrow of some kind is at hand. For oneself coming events cast their shadows before in a variety of ways. An itch in the nose, usually called a "mermain," betokens the early arrival of a letter or a stranger; the turning hot of the left ear shows that some one is speaking well of us, while a similar heating of the right denotes the reverse, and a loud tingling in the ear is warning enough that the sufferer will soon hear of the death of an acquaintance. An itching of the right eye betokens joy, an itching of the right palm denotes that money will soon be placed in it, while an itching of the foot plainly foretells that a journey must soon be undertaken. The white specks on our finger nails are supposed to have a meaning quite apart from the cause which gave rise to them. The explanation in Sutherlandshire is :—

Thumb,	...	...	a gift.
Forefinger,	...	...	a beau.
Middle,	...	...	a friend.
Third,	...	...	a foe.
Fourth,	...	...	a journey.

Luck.

The methods by which what short sighted people call luck are insured, can only be remnants of the means used to propitiate the gods before the advent of Christianity, and those most ready to resort to superstition are generally the people who obtain their livelihood precariously; thus it is well known that elsewhere mendicants find that those flocking to a horse race give them extravagantly, hoping, no doubt, for a thousand fold return. In this respect the most superstitious class in Sutherlandshire is the fishermen, who cannot explain why, on some occasions, certain crews return with a good fishing, while others who fish beside them all night get nothing, when to all human appearance the circumstances are exactly alike. There are few others in the county who take anything like the same pains as they do to induce, they know neither what nor whom, to give them more abundantly than could reasonably be expected from the antecedent efforts put forth.

Most of the superstitions practised by Sutherland fishermen are those which obtain among the same class in other Highland counties. When a new boat is got it is desirable to put some of the plenishings from the old into the new, especially if good fishings were got in the old one, for thereby the good luck is transferred to the new. It is told that a Golspie fisherman, a few years ago, had a small boat with which he had an extraordinary run of luck in the prosecution of his calling. Inside the stem was nailed an entire horse's shoe given him by a 'wise person.' As he prospered, his ambition grew till he purchased a larger boat, and he sold the smaller one and its belongings to a neighbour. From the first day he went to sea with his new boat luck forsook him, nor would fickle fortune be wooed. He bethought him of his horse shoe and went to his neighbour to demand restitution. This was denied, the new owner contending successfully that he had purchased the boat and its gear. Although fishermen believe that it is extremely unlucky to give a minister a passage in their boat or even to have a minister's blessing when going to sea, yet when they find that luck has completely forsaken them, they try to get one of "the men" to hold a service on board so that the unfriendly influence may be exorcised.

Other means of getting fickle fortune to favour them is to deposit a small piece of silver, with a hole in it, in the boat on the first day of the year. Others believe that it is best to secure this coin in the strands of a rope. Fishermen believe that the first person met, as they set out for their boat, is a lucky or unlucky person. If they be successful on that night their 'first foot' gets a share of the fish, but if success has not followed, then it appears to be demonstrated to them that the first foot is an enemy. It is considered extremely unlucky to talk of a hare at sea, and if one of the crew does so, the only antidote is to touch cold iron. Whistling aboard the vessel at any time is also forbidden, as certain to cause a storm of wind. Other Sutherlanders pin their faith to other methods which are regarded by them as the most effectual of getting luck to step their way; thus all the old folk tried to get something new to wear on New Year's day. It is considered next best to wear any new article of clothing for the first time to church or on Sunday. Some time ago the Bible was, on the last day of the year, placed above the door, so that the evil one could not come in next morning with any unlucky first foot, of whom the most undesirable was a flat-footed, red-haired woman. Even the cattle were not forgotten on New Year's day, as a good extra sheaf of unthrashed corn given to them was supposed to insure plenty throughout the coming year. Besides attaching importance to the first person met, when beginning a journey, it was considered advisable to ask and get a pin from the first person met, whereas it was extremely unlucky to turn back for anything forgotten. When servants set out for another situation, it is the proper thing to throw a shoe after them, quite as much as to do the same to a newly married couple. Perhaps one of the worst superstitions, and one which, for the sake of the people, were better dead, is the belief that it is extremely unlucky to report a thief, as he might, in consequence, become mad, but if the thief, being penitent, should wish to return the stolen goods, it is safest not to accept them. A story is told of a pig, once stolen, of which a part was afterwards restored to its owner, with the result that his daughter was choked while eating the first piece of it which was cooked. As a contrast to this, it is believed that whoever perjures himself commits an unpardonable sin, and that a suicide is not expected to go to heaven. Of other lost articles it is considered lucky to find a pin, and the person who lifts it lifts luck, whereas the finding of a knife, however valuable, betokens future ill.

Many other superstitions must have been brought into the country at a comparatively recent date, as the ground on which they proceed had no existence in the Highlands until lately; thus, the breaking of a looking glass is thought to forebode misfortunes, and should a child notice its own reflection before it is one year old, it will die before reaching its prime. Similarly, the divinations of fortunes in tea-cups must be another recent superstition. Again, some very widely believed superstitions do not hold in this county. Very few attribute any importance to the spilling of salt, else it would woe betide the women who work at herring curing. Recently, however, it has come to the writer's notice that one woman spilt salt at an enemy's door, in the hope of doing harm, and harm was done, for a row not yet patched up was the result. The beliefs regarding thirteen sitting down at a meal, or of crossing one's knife and fork are very seldom heard, and few, if any, think anything of passing under a ladder.

Regarding the moon, the most widely accepted superstition here, as elsewhere, is that a change of weather is to be anticipated at each quarter, and that it is lucky to have a piece of woollen cloth or a silver coin in the hand, when first the new moon is seen. A later addition to this is that it is unlucky to see the moon through glass.

WITCHCRAFT.

Though the belief in the power of witches seems at present to be dying fast, it is as yet by no means dead. At all times savage and semi-civilized peoples appear to have believed in it, and among African tribes it is still rampant in all its horrors. In Bible times, summary measures were adopted towards those who professed to have this power, and pretended to use it to terrify those who were weak-minded, and in Mosaic times they were silenced only by the injunction in Exodus xxii. 18, "Thou shalt not suffer a witch to live." Since the Roman Catholic Church, four hundred years ago, laid down in its *Malleus Maleficarum* (Hammer of witches), the procedure against witches, until 1772, when the last witch was burned at Dornoch for transforming her daughter into a pony, and getting her shod by the devil, it is estimated that no fewer than thirty thousand persons were put to death for this crime in Great Britain. Witches are now, however, by a statue of George IV. prosecuted only as rogues and vagabonds, and very very seldom as such. As elsewhere, those who in Sutherland had occult powers attributed to them, generally have some peculiarity. If a woman is of a masuline type, with say enough hair on her face to make a schoolboy envious, and particularly if she lives alone, and preferably in a lonely house, or is dumb or dwarfed, and perhaps cunning and malevolent, and has prophesied some evil to some unfriendly person which has actually come to pass, her character as a witch is soon firmly established. Rev. Mr. MacDonald, Reay, tells of a woman who asked a coach driver for a 'lift.' He refused, and she simply said, "Very well, I will be in Thurso before you." A mile further on one of his horses fell dead, and he had the mortification of seeing the professed witch pass him in triumph. No one since then will willingly refuse her a drive.

Witches are reputed to take the form of various animals. Sometime ago they were supposed to take the form chiefly of black cats. Pennant, in his first *Tour to Scotland*, published in 1771, says that at that time the belief in witches was dying out, and tells that there lived in Thurso a young man who was tormented by them in this form. After some time he resolved to give them battle, and got ready his sword. When next he was attacked he slashed right and left, and cut off what he believed to be a cat's leg. Next day a woman appeared who begged him to return her her leg. This he did, and he told that he never afterwards was troubled by witches. To show the absurdity of the man's story, he was asked to say in what part the woman would have been wounded if the cat's tail had been cut off. The form they are now believed oftenest to assume is that of a hare, and their chief avocation seems to be to interfere with cows and their produce, and many are the means used to guard against their malign influence. They were supposed to have a special aversion to the rowan tree, and in many a part of Sutherlandshire, where a green spot and a ruined house show that once a family lived there, may still be seen standing a solitary old rowan, which had doubtless been planted for the purpose of keeping witches at a safe distance. They also hated iron, and the horse shoe—now an emblem of luck —was nailed behind many a byre door to keep them outside. But if the owners were shy to show their superstition so openly, it was deemed quite as efficacious to keep in the house a hare's stomach, as none of them that assumed the form of that animal would then come near. If these precautions have been taken, and the cows are still found to be without milk in the morning, the next most effectual plan is to put a crooked silver coin—for other shot is of no avail—into a gun and try to shoot the hare. If it is not seen while the gun is thus loaded, the bewitched cow should be bled, and in less than three months the cow belonging to the witch who milked the bled cow will die. Modern dairy teachers explain scientifically how it happens that 'butter will not come,' but in Sutherlandshire they sometimes placed a silver coin in the bottom of the churn to make it come quickly, as well as to prevent the substance being taken away from the cream by any sinister influence. Others prefer to let no reputed witch have a taste of their milk, as it seems to be necessary that ere any witchery can be practised, such a taste is necessary. Others again, whose cattle have to be out during the summer nights, draw a hair tether all round the field in which the cows are grazing, and no hare will then venture into it.

Fairies.

Fairies are still believed in, and though the means of inter-communication between this county and the rest of the world must have been for ages limited enough, yet the fairy tales current in Sutherland and the Reay country are those common to almost the whole race, so that it would seem that the tales which originally have been the delight of men in the childhood of the world, are now because of their simple charm become the delight of childhood. Fairies are represented as little men and women dressed in green, living a life of jollity in the chamber of the 'tullochs,' 'brochs' or green knolls, of which there are so many in this county. They do little harm beyond exchanging their own children for those of any of the people around them, though even their own do not take kindly to the change, as they continually cry in their new homes, and depart only when fire is applied to them. As they are represented as already possessing all things most desired for comfort in this world, it is conjectured that it is possible that they, like the Peris of the East, may be the descendants of fallen angels, and wish to get united to mankind in the hope of retrieving their position. One of them is said to have asked a good man, whom she saw reading the Bible, whether there was any hope for the like of her, to which he replied that he knew of hope being held out to all the sons of Adam, and to them only. Another, who was asked who she was, is said to have replied, " I am not of the seed of Adam or Abraham." This conjecture regarding their origin is strengthened by the belief that they are unable to steal a baptized child, and 'God bless you' said to an unbaptized one is sufficient to save it from them. This expression seems to be able to terrify them at any time. The story goes that the fairies were long ago tired of crossing the Dornoch Frith in their cockle-shell boats, and resolved to build a bridge across it. This bridge was to be a work of great magnificence, the piers and posts and all the piles were to be mounted with pure gold. Unfortunately, a passer by lifted up his hands and blessed the workmen. When they heard this they disappeared beneath the waves, the sand accumulated, and there remains to this day the dangerous bar and quicksands of the Gizzen Briggs or *Drochaid na Fuath.* Notwithstanding their supposed descent, all the Sutherland fairy tales go to show that time was never felt to be passing by those who joined the fairy revels in their own homes, and a story told by Campbell in his *Popular Tales of the West Highlands* is an excellent specimen of those most commonly retailed. It is as follows :—

A man, who had just become a father, set off for Lairg to have his child's name entered in the session books, and to buy a cask of whisky for the christening fête. As they returned, weary with their day's walk, they sat down to rest at the foot of a hill, near a large hole, from which they were, ere long, astonished to hear a sound of piping and dancing. The father, feeling very curious, went a few steps into the cavern, and disappeared. The story of his fate sounded less improbable then than it would now ; but his companion was severely animadverted on, and when a week elapsed and the baptism was over, and still no signs of the lost one's return, he was accused of having murdered his friend. He denied it, and again and again repeated the tale of his friend's disappearance down the cavern's mouth. He begged a year and a day's law to vindicate himself, if possible; and used to repair to the fatal spot and call and pray. The term allowed him had but one more day to run, and as usual he sat in the gloaming by the cavern, when what seemed his friend's *shadow*, passed within it. He went down, heard reel tunes and pipes, and suddenly descried the missing man tripping merrily with the fairies. He caught him by the sleeve, stopped him and pulled him out. "Bless me! why could you not let me finish my reel, Sandy?" "Bless me," rejoined Sandy, "have you not had enough of reeling this last twelve month?" "Last twelvemonth," cried the other in amazement; nor would he believe the truth concerning himself, till he found his wife sitting by the door with a yearling child in her arms.

Though generally harmless, they can also on occasion take vengeance, and they are said to have chased a man belonging to Rosehall into the sea, and destroyed a new mill because the earth for the embankment of the mill dam had been dug from the side of their hill. Nothing according to common belief seems to annoy them more than interference with their houses, and perhaps it is the dread of their vengeance that makes so many labourers diffident to work at the opening of any of the brochs, when an antiquarian determines to examine one. It is related that a land improver once began to demolish a broch which stood in his fields. The work had been carried on only for a couple of days when the cattle began to die, the plague spread, and the demolition of the broch was meanwhile stopped. In the course of a week the farmer's wife had a visit from a little woman, who said she wanted a warming. Inquiry as to who she was revealed that she was a resident in the neighbouring broch for ages, and that the cattle plague was sent on them as a punishment for the destruction of her home. Restitution of the stones taken away was promised, and the good graces of the little wise people could again be won only by the lighting of the *teine eigin* (fire of necessity). Ere this could be effectually lighted, every fire in the district must be extinguished, and the hearths allowed to grow quite cold. The whole population must then congregate on a small island in the river, for water must necessarily be all around them. There, by means of two dried sticks, and a considerable amount of elbow grease, they managed to get a light. From this, the household fires were rekindled, the plague stayed, and gladness reigned once more in that district.

Theories galore to account for the origin of the belief in fairies have been advanced, but the following is quite as plausible as any, and is the one most commonly accepted here. Before the Christian era, when the Celts came to Scotland, they found a very small limbed section of the Picts settled in the north. These, they gradually drove further and further into the wilds, where they built the numerous underground dwellings which are still in existence. But the Picts had greater intelligence than the large limbed Celts and gave them so much trouble that the belief soon gained ground that they were of supernatural origin. There still, indeed, lingers a belief in the deadly efficacy of the fairy arrow *(saighead sithich)*, the flint heads of which are still embedded in the moorlands. If a Celt or any of his animate possessions fell dead pierced by such an arrow, and the hand that sent it on its way was nowhere to be seen, what more natural than to attribute it to fairies? If the Celt lost himself in the depths of the forest, it is quite likely that by choice he would have lain down on the dry grassy knoll, above an underground dwelling, to await morning, and while there might have heard the sounds of music and revelry, which could only be inspired by uisgebaigh, which word, though now the accepted Gaelic for whisky, really means the juice of the birch or heather, from which they are reputed to have known how to make a delicious stimulant.

Other fairy tales there are, ghost stories, many of them gruesome enough, abound, methods by which witches might be met are told, explanations are numerous as to how cures could be wrought, but we now-a-days can see that whatever went beyond the work-a-day world of this ancient people, whatever was beyond their immediate ken was relegated to what to them was a region of philosophy and theology, at which we can afford to smile. It is all the same interesting and sometimes exciting to have a run back into the dark, and there dimly to understand the primitive thought of our far away ancestors, as well as what Ossian sings of as

> "Gathan gréine nan làithean a dh'aom
> Sòlas banail nan daoine a bh'ann."

> "Sunbeams of the days that were
> Social joys of men of yore."

TOPOGRAPHY,

BY

Rev. ADAM GUNN, M.A.

The subject of this chapter—the place-names of the county—is full of interest, not only to natives, but to antiquarians generally. The topographical record of Scotland is being slowly deciphered, notwithstanding the difficulties of the task. Of late years a good deal of light has been thrown upon the place-names of the Highlands by the labours of Captain Thomas, Professor MacKinnon, Mr. Alexander MacBain, Inverness, and Mr. John Mackay, Hereford. In order to arrive at a satisfactory solution of a place-name, the following requisites are necessary :—*(a)* access to the oldest written form of the word, in maps and manuscripts. In some instances this alone suffices to give a clue to its meaning: *(b)* acquaintance with the physical features of the locality is almost indispensable. Without this, all attempts are little better than guess-work : *(c)* a knowledge of Gaelic and Norse, and of the dialectic varieties of the former. A good ear, to distinguish the nicer shades of pronunciation, according as a consonant happens to be flanked by a broad or small vowel, is also necessary. This, of course, pre-supposes some acquaintance with Gaelic phonetics : *(d)* last, but not least in importance, is some knowledge of the history of the locality, as preserved often in the native traditions. In the matter of maps and manuscripts we are fairly well off in Sutherland; and quite recently the student of place-names has received substantial aid by the printing of the Sutherland Charters by Sir William Fraser, in The Sutherland Book.

The oldest map is Ptolemy's, who flourished in the second century of our era. His map of Scotland, as a whole, is unsatisfactory, for his initial error of placing it at right angles to England, produces an element of confusion. The tribes occupying Sutherland at this early period are the Caereni to the west, the Logi in the south, while the Cornavü occupy the northern shores and Caithness. Not a trace of these tribes can be discovered in the topographical record. Three capes and two rivers are also mentioned; but critics are not agreed as to their locality. The headlands are Verubium, Virvedrum, Tarvedum; the rivers, Ila, and Nabarus.

The cape-names probably denote the headlands of Caithness, but the rivers are recognised as the original of Illigh and Naver—the Helmsdale river, being in Gaelic *Avon-Illigh*. Nabarus is in some MS.S. Nabaeus; but almost all critics are agreed that the Naver is meant. The root seems to be *nav*—swim; Lat. *nav-is*; and Gaelic *snàmh*. Skene considers *Ila* a pre-Celtic word, and points out that *il* is common in Basque topography. An examination of Ptolemy's map of Scotland does not yield much information. We may gather from its names, however, the fact that a Celtic population occupied Sutherland at the beginning of the Christian era, and for some centuries previous to it. These Celts were Picts, and formed part of the ancient Caledonians who opposed the Roman eagles at a later date. An Iberian or Basque population may have preceded them, and were probably the aborigines.

The Norse occupation of Sutherland for some 400 years (800-1200 A.D.) is very clearly stamped on the topographical record. Nearly one-half of our coast names are Norse; and they are by no means confined to the coast, although more frequent there. In the *Orkneyinga Saga* we meet with the original form of many of these. Sometimes the Norse scribes make use of the Celtic name; but as a rule they gave names to the localities they visited, generally describing their physical characteristics. As these songs were written during the Norse occupation, or shortly thereafter, we may claim a very respectable antiquity for many of our Sutherland place-names.

In Bleau's maps, we meet with the spelling of the word as it was 200 years ago; but, unfortunately, the Rev. Timothy Pont, minister of Canisby, Caithness, who contributed the Sutherland portion, knew no Gaelic, and very little reliance can be placed upon his phonetic spelling. This energetic clergyman occasionally deviated into the etymology of place-names on his own account. About the middle of Strathnaver was a small hamlet called *Saghair*, Englished into *Syre*. *Saor* is the Gaelic for a wright or carpenter, and of course has no connection with the place-name; but it appears on the map as "the wright's field."

Perhaps the most valuable repository of the ancient spelling of Sutherland place-names is to be found in the Sutherland book, recently printed by Sir William Fraser, containing the Sutherland Charters from the twelfth century onwards. The large bulk of the names met with here belong to the south-eastern portion of the county; only a very few of the names of Assynt and the Reay country occur in ancient manuscripts.

It may be well at the outset to state the different classes of place-names which are to be met with in our county. We may conveniently range them under five heads—

1. Remnants of the pre-Celtic speech. That there was a race of non-Celtic origin in North Britain is clear, and that some traces of these should be preserved in place-names is natural. We have already referred to *Ila*, in *Bun-illigh*; the probability is that remnants of this pre-Celtic speech enter more largely into our topography than is generally admitted.

2. Old Gaelic words now obsolete. A good example of this class is found in *Elphin* in Assynt. This is a compound word, *ail* (stone), and *fionn* (white), and neither word is now in use. *Fionn*, white, occurs frequently in compound words, and is often placed before its noun. *Foinaven* in Durness, is probably *fionn-bheinn*, white-hill, so called from its appearance when the sun shines on the huge masses of rock on its summit.

3. Norse words. This class is a large one, and they are mainly descriptive of physical features.

4. Well known Gaelic names, which may be easily explained by the aid of a dictionary, and some knowledge of Gaelic. In the following paper, these will be passed over where they present no difficulty.

5. Double names for the same locality—generally a Gaelic and a Norse name. Some of these are interesting. *Tongue*, for example, may be designated in three ways, (1) Gaelic *Ceann-t-sàile*, Kintail i. e. head of the salt-water. To distinguish it from another Kintail in a neighbouring county, it was called of old "Kintail a' Mhic-Aoidh." (2) Kirkiboll, Norse, the Kirk-town. (3) *Tonga*, Norse *Tongue*—from the slip of land running into the sea at Tongue Ferry. Now all

of these are applied to the village of Tongue; but the parish name is invariably in the mouths of the older inhabitants "*Sgìre Chinn-tàile.*"

To this class also belongs the county name. Sutherland comes from *Sudrland*, Norse, Southern land. It is curious to find this name given to a county which for sixty miles borders on the north sea. But we must remember, that when it was so called by the Norsemen, it embraced only what is now the south-eastern portion of Sutherland—a district which is still distinguished by its Gaelic name *Cataobh*. Katanes—Caithness—was the name applied to the north coast from Cape Wrath to Duncansbay Head.

The Celtic *Cataobh* is an older term, and comes from Catti—probably an oblique case of it. This must have been a pretty numerous tribe in pre-historic times—having given names to Caithness and Sutherland. On Celtic ground the root is common. It occurs in Caturiges (cath righrean) warlike Kings, and in Catu-slogi (Cath sluagh) warlike people, and in the proper names Catullus, Cassivellaunus, and Cathel. The root is *cath*, war, and its prevalence among all branches of the Celtic race is significant.

There is no Gaelic name for what is now known as Sutherland. *Cataobh* designates only the south-eastern portion. Lord Reay's Country, (Gaelic *Duthaich-Mhic-Aoidh*—Mackay's land) and Assynt, G.—*Asint*, were included in Sutherland about 1630, when John, XIII. Earl of Sutherland surrendered to the King the heritable offices of sheriff and coroner of Sutherland for £1000 stg., and the King added Strathnaver, Strath-halladale, Eddrachillis, Durness, and Assynt to the district called Sutherland, and erected the whole into a free and separate sheriffdom. This is how the old

K

Norse *Sudr-land* was extended to include the north and western portions of the county. When first applied, it exactly described its position—south of Caithness, which in Norse times extended along the sea-coast to Cape Wrath. This extensive county belongs now almost wholly to the Duke of Sutherland. The Macleods of Assynt never prospered after the betrayal of Montrose, and the litigation that ensued. The property passed for a time into the hands of the Seaforth family, but finally came into the possession of the Earl of Sutherland. The other district, which did not originally form part of Sutherland, was the Reay country, and it too passed into the hands of the Sutherland family in 1829, being bought by Lord Gower for the sum of £300,000.

In a paper like this it will be impossible to examine all the place-names on the survey maps; and it would be unprofitable. Notice will be taken only of such words as present some difficulty to an ordinary Gaelic scholar. Beginning with the parish of Farr, which now includes the Sutherland part of the parish of Reay, we shall work our way westwards along the north coast, deviating now and then into the interior of the county, along the water courses. We may follow the coast as far as Assynt, where we shall turn eastwards by the parish of Creich, and strike the sea again at the Kyle of Sutherland. From that point we may turn northwards by the coast, and complete the circuit.

Parish of Farr.

This extensive parish of 267,040 acres is, like ancient Gaul, "divided into three parts" by the rivers Halladale, Strathy, and Naver. In olden times, the bulk of the population lived in these three valleys. In the *Orkneyinga Saga* they are called the "Dales of Catanes." Of easy access from the Orkney islands, we may infer an earlier and a more complete Norse occupation, and the topography bears this theory out.

Strath-halladale comes first in order—a beautiful valley, about 14 miles long. Halladale is Norse, *helgadale* (holy dale). *Strath* (Gaelic) was prefixed, when the meaning of Norse *dale* was forgotten. This often happens in place-names. *Maenstone* in Cornwall is "stone-stone"; the latter *stone* being added when the natives forgot the meaning of Cornish *maen*-stone. So Gaelic *Dal-hall a dale*. The first *dal* is Gaelic, and we can always distinguish the Celtic *dal* from its cognate Norse *dale* by its position. In Gaelic, the generic term comes first, thus, Dalmore is Gaelic *dal*, and *mòr* large ; but Langdale is Norse *dale*, long dale, and comes last. *Helga* may very likely have been a proper name.

Forsinard and *Forsinain*. These are made up of Gaelic and Norse. *Fors* is N. a waterfall : *ard* is G. high, and *ain* G. low, *àine* (from *fhàine*, comp. of *fan* down, now obsolete). Rob Donn has

"An rum is *fhaine* tha 'san tir"
(The *lowest* room in the land).

Trantle-mòr and *Trantle-beg*. N. here is euphonic, and is not heard in Gaelic *Trau-dal*. The word is Norse. "Trow" is the lower ground through which a river runs, and dale, Norse *dalr* (trow-dale). We now come to some half-a-dozen Gaelic names lower down the strath, viz :—

Croick—G. *cròg*, the hand, from the natural configuration.
Dalhalvaig—G. *dal*, dale, and *sealbhag*, sorrel.
Kealsey—G. *caol, caolas*, narrow, and *i* or *uidh*, stream.

Ardachy—G. *ard*, high, *achadh*, field.
Achumore—G. *achadh*, field, *mòr*, big.
Cuilfearn—G. *Coille*, wood, *fearn*, alder.
Kirkton—G. *Baile-na-h-eaglaise*, was the most important township on the Halladale. There was a church here in Norse times—doubtless of Culdee origin. Here also was the consecrated burying-ground for the lower parts of the strath, and still used as such. The site of the church may yet be seen.

Golval. G. *Gall*, stranger, and *baile*, township.

The "strangers" were no doubt Norse. Caithness, where the foreigner came to settle permanently, is *Gallaobh* to the present day.

Achredigill. Norse, with the exception of *ach*, *achadh*. This is the first instance of Norse, *gill*, a ravine, which is very common in Sutherland; as a terminal suffix it occurs as frequently as dale. Sometimes it is apt to be confounded with the oblique case of Gaelic, *geal*, white. *Smigel*—the name of a burn higher up the strath, shows the same termination.

Bighouse. Gaelic *an Torr*, Norse *big hus*. There are two places of this name on the strath; and they are interesting as showing the part which the sinking of the accent plays in Gaelic phonetics. In the case of upper *Big-house*, the first syllable is accented, and with the accent thus sunk upon it, it ceases to be used as a compound word, and appears on the map as *Begas*. Its origin forgotten, it is used as a Gaelic word. But the lower *Bighouse* still remains a compound word, and it is never called Bighouse in Gaelic, but *an Torr*, the heap or fortified place, where of old a castle stood to defend the entrance to the bay.

Before quitting Strath-halladale, it may be mentioned that there are remains of two Pictish towers on opposite sides of the river, half-way up the strath, and also at *Cnoc-an-fhreaca-dain* or watchhill. These, with the fortification at the mouth of the water, were its military defences. From Theiner's *Monumenta*—a Vatican MS. we learn that the church of "Haludal" in 1274 contributed 9/4 to the Crusades, and a similar sum in 1275, this time "Helwedale."

We now come to the north coast, where Norse names prevail. *Melvich* is from N. *melr*, sand-bank or links, and N. *vik*, a bay, a creek. *Portskerra* N., *port*, harbour, and *sker*, a skerry. Gaelic *sgeir* is borrowed from this word, and enters largely into place-names.

Baligill, G. *baile*, township, and N. *gill*, a ravine. The burn to the east of the village answers Norse *gill* ideally. There was a castle on the edge of the cliff here, separated from the mainland by a narrow neck of land; but there are no traditions preserved. *Strathy* is Gaelic, strath. The termination *y* is probably Gaelic *i*, water, stream. This forms the second of the dales opening from the north coast. It is about 12 miles in length; but it was not so densely populated as the valleys of the Halladale and Naver. Its place-names are partly Celtic and partly Norse.

Dal-bhaite is the submerged dale, Gaelic *baite*, drowned, seen in Badenoch.

Rhi-ruadh, Gaelic, red burn. *Rhi* may be a flowing stream, or a declivity. It is very common in the diminutive form *Rhian*. It is cognate with Greek *reo*.

Dal-ting, Norse *thing*, where the parliament met. This word on the map appears as Daltine, and the latter part is easily mistaken for *teine*, fire. But the phonetics of the

Gaelic forbid this derivation. Half-way up the glen, it was the meeting place of the Norse settlers (compare Dingwall for *Thing-vollr*).

Bowset, Norse, *bo* and *settr* : "sheiling dwellings." This *settr* occurs frequently in Lewis as shader. In Sutherland, it takes the forms *set* and *saite*.

Dalangdale—Norse *Lang*-dale-langdale.

Bra-rathy—G. *Braigh-rathie*, upper Strathy.

An t-Seilach—G. *seilach*, willow.

An uair. This is a name given to one of the tributaries of the Strathy river. Its meaning is not quite clear, although it has something to do with water. In the native dialect *an uair* is often used for a sudden storm of wind and rain; also for a water-spout. Allowing for the dipthongisation, the original form should be *ur*; and *ura* is Basque for river, water. This is probably a pre-Celtic remnant.

Returning again to the coast, and proceeding westwards, we come to *Brawl*, G. *braigh-bhaile*. *Leadnaguillean*, G. *Leathad*, slope. The last part is difficult, probably a Gaelicised plural of N. *gills*. This would suit the natural scenery well; at its south end are numerous *gills* and *gullies*.

Armadale, Norse *armr*, arm of sea and dale.

Pillaoriscaig, is a sea-side hamlet at the back of Armadale.

Poll, is G. *poll* or N. *pool*, which are cognates. *Aoriscaig* appears again as *Overscaig* on Loch Shin. In both places there is a stream and small bay. *Aig* is a remnant of *vik*. We are left thus with *aoris* or *overs* to account for; and *aross* means a river mouth in Norse (cp. Arisaig, *aros-vik*).

Kirtomy, in Gaelic *Ciurstamaidh*, accented on first syllable, Norse *Kjors*, copse-wood, and Icelandic *hwam-r*, a little valley. Norse words beginning with h, require a *t* in Gaelic phonetics. Out of *holmr* and *hor-gr* arise such forms as Dun-*t*ulm and *T*orga-bost.

Swordly, Norse *Svardr* and *dale*, sward, dale.

Farr. There is a village of Farr, and Farr Point. The parish took its name from these. Gaelic and Norse claim the word. Norse *faer*, a ship (Faroe Islands), and Gaelic *faire*, watching. Although *a* of Farr is long in English, the Gaelic is short, fắr. In ancient MS.S. it is always spelled Far. On the whole a Gaelic derivation is more probable.

Crask, G. cross-way. All the Crasks in Sutherland agree in this respect that they denote a short pass leading from one village to another, or from one parish into another.

Bettyhill. A modern name, so called from Countess Elizabeth, who built an inn there. The Gaelic name is *Blaran-odhar*, the dun field.

Achinà, G. *achadh*, and *àth a* ford.

Inver-Naver, G. mouth of the Naver.

Strathnaver. If we accept Ptolemy's *Nabarus*, as indicating the river Naver, the matter is finally settled. In old MS.S. it is sometimes Strathnavernia, and often Strathnavern. The Norsemen took possession of it early, as was likely from its large extent and valuable arable lands, but the old name was probably retained. This, no doubt, is one of the dales of which the Norse poet sings when he tells of the extension of Earl Sigurd's power "over Scotland, Ross, and Moray, *Sudrland* and the *Dales*." This would be about 980 A.D.; and as Caithness "dales" were occupied 200 years earlier, the reference must be to the dales of modern Sutherland. It is not likely that they secured possession without a struggle. On this beautiful strath are several remains of circular towers, and so situated for 24 miles inland, that intelligence could be quickly conveyed by signals from the coast to the interior. But there was no resisting of the foreign invader, and the valley of the Naver records the subjugation of the Celt on its tell-tale topographical face.

STRATHNAVER PLACE-NAMES :

Achnabourin, G. *achadh* and *buirghean*, *bvrgs*, field of fortifications.

Apigill, Norse *gill*, a deep ravine, is evident. *Ap*, uncertain.

Achcheargarry, G. *achadh*, field. Kergarry, N. *Kjarr*, brushwood, and *garthr*, field.

Skelpick, G. *sgeilpeach*, shelvy, terraces.

Rhifail, G. *rhi*, declivity, *fàl*, an enclosure.

Skail, N. *shieling*.

Dalvina, G. *Dal*, dale, *mìne*, smooth, Dalmhine.

Syre (doubtful), Gaelic *Saghair*, probably N. *settr*.

Dalharold, N., Harold's dale. Some standing stones are found here which tradition connects with a conflict fought between Harold (Maddadson), and Reginald of the Isles (circa 1198). One of the standing stones is called *Clach-an-righ*, the King's stone.

Achness, G., the waterfall on the Mallart gives name to the place ; *achadh-an-eas*, field of the cascade.

Achool, G. *achadh-choille*, field of the wood.

Grumbeg and *grumbmore*, sometimes called in Gaelic *na grumbaichean*, are probably of Gaelic origin. *Grum* is a variant of *drum*, a ridge, whence Drumbeg in Assynt. Initial *g* and *d* are apt to change places, for the reason that in the aspirated and oblique cases, they are pronounced similarly, *dhruim, ghruim.*

Altnaharra, N. and G. *alt*, burn. *Harra*, Norse for heights—compare Harris, so called from its hills. We have several such burns in Sutherland, and this derivation suits very well their character.

Mudale, N. muir, dale.

Bad-an-t-seobhag, G. *bad*, clump, collection, place, and *seobhag*, hawk.

Parish of Tongue.

Its Gaelic name, Kintail, (head of the sea), was the district name until 1724, when a separate parish was formed, parish of Tongue (N. *tung*, a tongue), out of the original extensive parish of Durness. The place-names of Tongue are a mixture of Norse and Gaelic, the former prevailing.

Torrisdale, N. *Thor's*, dale, cp. Thurso.

Achtoitidh, G. *achadh*, field, *tobhta*, a Gaelic loan-word from N. *toft*, tuft, hillock.

Skerray, N. *skerja*, borrowed as Gaelic *sgeir*. Almost all words beginning with *sg, sc*, are loan-words in Gaelic. The Celt disliked initial *sg*. The Welshman gets over the difficulty by prefixing *y*.

Scullomie, N. *skol* (cup-shaped), *hwamr*, village.

Lamigo, N. *lamb's goe*.

Colbacky, N. *kyle* and *bakki*, sand-banks, so named from the sand-banks at the mouth of the Kyle. Norse *Kyle* becomes *Keol* in Gaelic, cp. Keoldale (Kyle dale).

Ribigill, N. *rygar-bol*, ladies' township. Old spelling Rigaboll, by metathesis Ribigill.

Tongue, N. *tonga*, tongue.

Kirkiboll, N. *Kirkja-böll*, church town.

Melness, N. *melr*, sand-bank, *ness*, point.

Skianaid, G. *sgiath*, wing, and *aite*, place ; "the wing of the place" is fully descriptive.

Talmin, G. *talamh*, earth and soil, and *mine*, smooth.?

Port Vasco. On the ordinance survey maps it is etymologised into G. *port an fhasgaidh*, port of shelter. The word is more probably Norse, the final *goe*, creek, proving its Norse origin.

Achaninver, achadh-an-inbhir, G. *inbhir*, river-mouth.

Moine, G. *am moine*, the moss or peat-moss.

Beinn Thūtaig, a hill 1340 feet high. Removing the aspiration, the original form is *Tuit-aig*. *Aig* is of frequent occurrence as a place ending, and generally means small. *Tuit* is from N. *toft*, knoll.

Lettermore, G. *leitir*, hillside, *mor*, great.

Hysbackie, N. *hûs*, house, *bakki*, bank, ridge.

Ben Loyal, G. *leamh* and *choill*, elm-tree.?

Parish of Durness.

Until 1724 this parish extended from Kyle Sku on the west to the water of Borgie, thus including modern Tongue, Durness, and Eddrachillis. It is divided by arms of the sea into three sections, the Moine district, including Eriboll; Durness proper, between the Kyle of Durness and Loch Eriboll; and the Parph district, between the Kyle of Durness and the Atlantic. Its place-names are mainly of Scandinavian origin.

Durness, N. *deer* and *nes* point; point of the deer. Various other derivations have been given, but none suits the phonetics but the above. In old MSS. and the Sagas, it is always *Dyrnes*.

There is a small village, *Durin*, which some suppose has given name to the parish, but the Gaelic of Durin is *an Dùrinn* : *d* is flanked by a broad vowel, and not by a small as in Diuirineas. Besides, the parish name is very old, and Durin, only a modern township, comes from G. *dubh*, black, and *rinn*, point, or *raon*, field. The soil of Durin is different from the sandy soil of the neighbouring district.

Eriboll, N. *eyrr*, pebbly-beach, and *boll*, township.

Hope, river, loch, and ben; comes from N. *hòp*, a bay, inlet.

Arnaboll, N. township of the eagle.

Heilim, N. *holmr*, an islet, often a rock detached from the mainland.

Fresgill, N. *gill*, a ravine, *fraes-a*, noisy. The name may have been given from the noise of the sea in the caves in its face. One of these is said to extend half a mile inland.

Polla, G. *poll*, and *à*, ford.

Laid, G. *Leathad*, slope.

Rispond, N. *rhis*, copsewood, and G. *beinn*.

Sangobeg and *Sangomore*. N. *sand*, and *goe*, bay.

Durine, see above, under Durness.

Balnakil, G. *baile*, and *cill*, church. There was a Culdee monastery here. From Theiner's *monumenta*—a Vatican MS.—we gather that the church here contributed fourteen shillings and eight pence for the crusades, in the year 1274.

Keoldale, N. Kyle and dale.

Farrid Head. Ordnance survey map etymologises this into *far-out-head!* The Gaelic is *an fhairid, am faire aite*, the watch-place.

Parph. N. *hvarf*, receding, a turning away.

Achimore, G. *achadh*, field, *mòr*, large.

Dall, G. *dal*, dale.

Kerwick. Here there is a small bay — *wick*, which probably is the last part of the word. On the maps it is *Cearbhag*. The Gaelic pronunciation is *ceathramh-ág. Car* is a common prefix, signifying a fortified place, from Gaelic *caithir*, a city. We have it in this district in *Car-breac*, where there does not appear any trace of a fortification.

Cape Wrath. This it entirely the map-maker's name, taken from the Gaelic *parbh*, N. *hvarf. P.* as an initial sound is not Celtic; hence the Lewisman calls it not *am Parbh*, but *an Cairbh*. The hill on which the light-house stands is called *an dunan*, the small fort. If we agree with many that *Tarvedunum* on Ptolemy's map represents Cape Wrath, and not a Caithness headland, we might connect *tarve* with modern *parbh*, the Greek letters p and t being easily confounded in the MSS. On this theory, *parbh* would be a pre-Celtic word.

Parish of Eddrachillis.

Eddrachillis once formed part of the parish of Durness. It was erected into a separate parish in 1724, when Kinlochbervie district was added to ancient *Eddrachillis, eadar-da-chaolas*, between two Kyles — Kyles Sku and Laxford.

It now comprises about 175 square miles. The western portion once formed part of the barony of Skelbo, and was included in the church lands assigned by Hugh Freskyn, ancestor of the Sutherland family, to Gilbert, the Bishop, 1200 A.D. He again bequeathed it to his brother, Richard Moray, of Culbyn; but the church maintained its claim in subsequent times. About 1440, it passed into the family of Kinnaird, of Kinnaird, by whom it was disposed in 1515 to

John Mackay of Eddrachillis, son of Mackay of Strathnaver, the superiority remaining with the Earl of Sutherland. The purchase of the Reay Estates restored it to the House of Sutherland, after a lapse of 650 years.

Kinlochbervie, G. *Ceann-loch-buirbhidh*, head of Loch Buirve. There is no such loch now as Bervie. But there are remains of a *burg* or fort, on an arm of Loch Inchard, whence the name.

Ashare, on the maps, Oldshores. There are two Oldshores. The old spelling in Privy Seal Record is Aslarmore, Aslarbeg, 1551. The Gaelic pronunciation is Ashar, the first *a* being long. This gave rise to the conjecture that it is *fàs-thire*, as opposed to the sterile district of *Ceathramh-garbh*, rough quarter.

Sandwood, G. *Seannabhat* from Norse *sand*, sand, *vat*, lake, the sandy lake.

Sinairidh, G. *seann, àiridh*, old shieling.

Badcall, G. *bad*, clump, *coille*, wood.

Achreisgilll, G. *ach, field*, N. *rhis*, copse-wood, and *gill*, a ravine.

Rhiconich, G. *rhi*, declivity or running stream, and *coineach*, mossy.

Achlighness, G. *achadh-luidh-an-uisge*, wet field.

Inchard, an arm of sea; the last part is N *fiord*, the *inch*, suggests G. *innis*, an island or peninsula, but is more likely Norse; cp. Icelandic *Innes*, resting houses. Inchard is one of the best harbours on the coast.

Laxford, N. *lax*, salmon, and *fiord*, loch. The Gaelic is *Luisard*, a corruption of the Norse.

Scourie. There is a Scouroe in Arran, which is explained by Lytteil as a Norse term meaning Robbers' Hold, or Buccaneers' Fort.

Handa Island, N. sandy isle.

Fanag-more, G. *Feannag*, an agricultural term, Eng. lazy bed.

Tarbat, a common place-name all over the Highlands. G. *An Tairbeart*. The old derivation *tarruing-bhàt*, drawing-boats, must be given up. The characteristic of Scottish Tarbats is, that they mostly all form peninsulas. This suggests a Norse derivation from *bhat, vatn*, water.

Badcall-scourie (given above). There are many small islands in Badcall bay, all bearing Gaelic names.

Duart-more, G. *dubh, àrd*, height.

Kylestrome, N. *Kyle, and stròm*, stream.

THE PRINCIPAL HILLS OF EDDRACHILLIS ARE :—

Beinne-Leothaid, G. *leathad*, slope.
Beinn-stac, N. *stakkr*, abrupt hill.
Beinn-strom, N. as above.
Beinn-Arkle, N., the latter part being *fell*, Norse for hill. The first part of the word is possibly N. *ark*, from its level top.

Meall Horn, G. *meall*, eminence, N. *horn*, oblique case of *arn-r*, eagle.

Meall, Rinidh, and *Altan-rinidh*, G. *rinn*, point.

Sabhal, beag, and *mòr*, G. *sabhal*, barn.

PARISH OF ASSYNT.

The parish of Assynt forms the western portion of Sutherland. Its extreme length is 36 miles. Tradition has it that it once formed the hunting grounds of the Thanes of Sutherland, for which it was well adapted from its mountainous character. From the middle of the 14th century to the close of the 17th, it belonged to a sept of the Macleods of Lewis. The last baron, Neil, the betrayer of Montrose, lost the property after a protracted litigation, when it passed into the hands of the Seaforth family. In 1715, the Seaforth estates were forfeited to the Crown; and in 1758, Assynt was sold to the Earl of Sutherland, with which family it has remained to the present day.

ASSYNT PLACE-NAMES:

Assynt. No satisfactory derivation has been given of this name. The Norse *a-synt*, seen from afar, in reference to its mountains, has been suggested; but the probability lies in favour of a Gaelic origin. *Ais* is an obsolete Gaelic word for *hill*; we have it in *aisridh*, a hill, a path. Duncan Ban uses *àsainn* in reference to the habitat of the deer :—

"'S i 'n *àsainn* a mhuime
Tha cumail na ciche
Ris na laoigh, bhreac bhallach."

A very large proportion of Assynt names are Gaelic, and easily recognisable. The following explain themselves readily to the Gaelic student—Inchnadamph (stags' pasture), Culkin (back of the head), Badnaban (nun's place), Balchladich (sea-side village), Clachtoll (*clach*, stone, *toll*, opening, hole), Clashnessie (waterfall), Drumbeg (small ridge), Knockan, Culag (small wood, recess), Strathan. The following present more difficulty :—

Elphin, G. *ail*, stone, and *fionn*, white (both obsolete).

Ach-melvich, *melvich* is Norse, *mel*, sand-bank and *vik*, bay.

Oldaney, N. *ey*, island.

Raffin, G. *rath*, a circle, and *fionn*, white

Brackloch, G. *breac*, trout and loch.

Soyea, sheep isle, N. *saudhr*, sheep, cp. *Soa* and *Hoan*, the latter, in Durness, an oblique case.

Felin, G. *Feith* and *linn*, marshy, pool.

Unapool, N. *bol* often takes this form of *pool*. *Una* may be a proper name (cp. Ullapool, Olave's town).

Ardvar, G. *àrd*, *high*. There is a river, glen, or loch of this name. *Var* may stand for *mhara*, sea, or *bharr*, a top. The latter is more likely. *Bar*, in Sutherland, mean crops.

Nedd, G. a nest, from its appearance.

Stoer, G. *stòr*, a high steep cliff.

Letteressie, G. *leitir*, countryside, *eas*, cascade.

Kirkaig, N. church land. There is a village, bay, and river of the name. A Culdee establishment was here; not far off is Badinaban, the nun's place.

Clachtoll, G. opening in a rock. Here, until quite recently, were two large boulders, with another on the top of them, forming an opening. One piece of the upper stone gave way at the French Revolution. It was predicted that the structure would entirely collapse on the arrival of some other important event; and the Disruption of the Church in 1843 saw the prophecy fulfilled!

Tralagill, N. *Troll's gill*, giant's ravine.

Stronchrubie, G. *stron*, nose, *chrubie* from *crubadh*, crouching, bent. *Crubie* enters largely into place-names, cp. *Crubin*, *Cruboge*, *Slievecroof*, etc.

THE MOST IMPORTANT OF THE ASSYNT HILLS ARE:—

Benmore, G. large hill, 3230 feet high.

Cuinag, a lofty ridge, extending from Unapool and terminating in a peak above Loch Assynt. It derives its name from the minute peak in which it terminates. G. *cuinneag*, a narrow-mouthed bucket.

Suilven (English Sugar-loaf), N. *sulr*, stack, cp. *Sulasgeir*, a rock, about 30 miles off the north coast.

Canisp. This hill rises to a height of 2780 feet. *Can* is old Gaelic for white; but the latter part is doubtful.

THE MOST IMPORTANT LAKES ARE:
Loch Assynt, the largest in the parish.
Cam Loch, G. *càm*, irregular.
Loch *Vattie*, N. *vatn*, water.
Skinashink, G. *sgiathanach*, winged loch.
Urigill, N. *Utri-gill*, further *gill*.

PARISH OF CREICH.

This parish, for thirty-five miles, forms the southern boundary of Sutherland, hence the name G. *crich*, boundary. Norse names are not quite so common here as on the coast, but a few do occur, as Spinningdale, Swordale, Migdale, which prove the occupancy of the district by the Norseman.

Migdale, N. moist, dale, N. *mokkr*.
Swordale, in old charter, *Suardell*, N. sward, dale.
Achiemore, G. large field.
Rhiancoup, rhian and *rian* are frequent in place-names. The root meaning is *reo*, to flow, hence a slope, declivity, or running stream. *Cop* is G. foam, and *copag* (Scotch) docken.
Linnside, G. *lion*, flax, or N. *linn*, waterside.
Achinduich, achadh, field, and *davoch*, a measure of land.
Inveran, G. *Inver*, mouth of river.
Balblair, G. *baile*, town, *blàr*, field.
Portnalick, G. *port* and *leac, gen*) *lic*, rock.
Drimlea, G. *druim*, ridge, *liath*, grey.

L

Loubcroy, G. *lub*, bend, *croy*, an enclosure, horse-shoe.
Ospisdale, N. dale, and *Ospis*, a proper name.
Ardens, G. *àrd*, high.
Rosshall, Glen Rossal, etc. G. *ros*, a peninsula.
Altass, G. *ault*, a stream, *ass* may be a corruption of *uisge*, water.
Badfliuch, G. wet place.
Pulrossie, G. *poll*, pool, *ros*, isthmus, *il*, water.
Tulloch, G. *tulach*, a hillock.
Larachan, G. *larach*, habitation; gorge.
Bonar, G. *A' bhann-a*. G. *bun-àtha*, the foot of the ford.
Bosset, N. *bo-settr*, dwelling-place.
Caslie, River, G. *cas*, swift, *lighe*, flood.

Parish of Lairg.

Lairg is an inland parish, about twenty miles from the sea, and mountainous in character. There are a great many remains of the ancient "dunes" in the district, which point to a considerable population in olden times. Its place-names are nearly all Celtic, as might have been expected. The Norsemen did not care to make locations at any great distance from the sea.

Lairg, G. *learg*, a sloping ground, an eminence.
Achadhphris, G. field of the bush, *preas*, a shrub.
Balcharn, G. the township of the cairn.
Balindialish, G. *dialuis*, a weed, a kind of cabbage.
Culbuie, G. *cùl, a recess*, or *coille*, wood, *buie*, yellow.
Balloan, G. marshy township, *lòn*, a marsh.
The *rhians* are numerous (from *rhi*, slope), Rhianbreck, Rhianmuir, Rhimarscaig, Rhinamain, Shinness, N. *sunnan, nos*, southern point.

Torresboll and Collaboll are also Norse; but the remaining are clearly Gaelic, and present no difficulty to a Gaelic scholar. Examples—*Dalchork, Tomich, Saval*, etc.

Strath Tirry, G. *tior*, dry, good soil.

River *Shin*, Shinness is said to be *sunnan-nos*, Norse for southernmost point of Sutherland. *Shin* would thus mean *south*, which is the direction taken by the river.

River *Oykel.* We meet with this river in the Saga as *Ekkial, Ekkialsbakki*; possibly, however, the Norsemen used the Gaelic name. The root meaning, if Celtic, is *high*: the river has its source in Benmore, Assynt. W. *achel*, high, cp. Ochill Hills.

PARISH OF DORNOCH.

This parish is the most important in the county, from a civil and ecclesiastical point of view. The town of Dornoch is the only Royal Burgh in the county, being erected in 1628, by a charter of Charles I. It was formerly the seat of the Bishops of Dornoch, whose See dates from the 12th century. The parish, however is not a large one : its extreme length and breadh being fifteen and nine miles respectively.

A Celtic origin has been assigned to the name Dornoch, *dorn-eich*, horse's hoof. There is a tradition to the effect that a certain Earl of Sutherland, about the middle of the 13th century, signalised himself in battle against the Danes, armed with the leg of a horse. The arms of the burgh, which contain the horse-shoe gives countenance to this derivation; but it must be given up. In old charters the form Durunach is frequent. Dur or Dor from *dobar*, water, is common in place-names; *n* belongs to the article, *àrd*, *ach*, *achadh*, a field. The fact that the parish is a kind of peninsula favours the Celtic origin.

A new element enters into the topography of East Sutherland—the Pictish or Brythonic. All along the north and west coasts there is no trace of any dialect of Celtic, save the Goidelic; but it is clear the south-east formed part of Pictland. Here we meet with *pit*, the Pictish equivalent of *baile*, township; also *aber* for *inver*, river-mouth. Initial *p* enters more frequently into place-names on the east coast, another sign of Pictish occupation.

Pitfour, Pictish, *pit*, township, or *portion* and Welsh *paur*, pasture. The Pictish language is more nearly allied to the Welsh than to the Gaelic. There are two *Prouncies*, an upper and lower; initial *p*, suggests a Pictish origin. There is a Welsh word, *Pren*, meaning wood, which may be connected with the root-meaning.

Achavandra, G. Andrew's field. There was a Bishop Andrew at Dornoch, who had his *floruit* about 1150 A.D.

Achosnich, G. *ach, oisneach* ; cornered, field.

Astle, N. *ash*, dale.

Balvraid, G. *baile, bhraighead*, height.

Caamore, G. *catha*, a steep ascent, *mòr*, large.

Clasnagrave, G. *clash*, hollow, *nan craoibh*, of trees.

Clashmore, G. large hollow.

Embo, N. *bo* for *boll*, township. The natives pronounce it *Eriboll* in Gaelic, which comes from Norse *eyrr*, pebbly-beach, and *boll*, town.

Skelbo, N. shell-town.

Lednabirichen, G. slope of heights, *bir* is a point.

Fleucharey, G. *Fliuch*, wet ; *airidh* sheiling.

Rearquhar, G. *rhi*, declivity ; the last part may be a proper name.

Strathtollie, G. strath, and *toll*, hole, a fissure.

Torboll. Norse or Gaelic; *torr*, a heap, and *baile* ; or from Norse *boll*, township.

Pitgrudy, Pit, place, and *grudie*, a common place-name in all parts of Sutherland. Grudie is a river in Durness, a a place-name in Lairg, N. *grjot*, stones.

Parish of Golspie.

Golspie is a small parish, being only eight miles in length, and six in breadth. Here is the residence of the Earls of Sutherland, Dunrobin Castle. The ancient name of the parish was Culmaily, but in 1619 the church was transferred to Golspie.

The parish name is Norse, *Gill's-bie*, the township of the glen. The glen of Golspie is the most striking feature in the scenery ; and although *l* is not pronounced in Gaelic *Goisbec*, that is a feature of the Sutherlandshire dialect ; *l* goes out before *s* ; *soillse* becomes *soise* ; *feallsa, feasa*, etc.

Backies, N. *bakki*, banks.

Badan, G. a small location. Balblair, G. *blàr*, plain.

Clayside, G. *cladh*, a raised fence, an enclosure : the name, however, may be a rubbed-down form of N. *Kleiff settr*, cliff hamlet.

Drummuie, G. *drum*, ridge, and *màgh*, a plain.

Culmailie, G. *cill*, church, and Maluag, a Culdee saint.

Morvich. Of frequent occurrence in the Highlands. The common feature is an extensive plain by the sea-side. The word is probably Pictish ; W. *mor*, sea. G. *mòr-achadh*, large field, has also been suggested.

Rhives, an Englished form of Gaelic, *rhidhe*, a slope.

Uppat, pronounced *oopaid*. N. *upp*, high place.

Dunrobin, G. *Dùn*, a fort or mote; and *Robin* is probably a personal name; who he was is by no means certain. Sir Robert Gordon's Earl Robert is proved to be mythical, and Gaelic phonetics forbid any connection with Rafu, a Norse ruler of considerable influence in Caithness and Sutherland in the 12th century.

Aberscross. This word shows the Brythonic or Pictish element in *aber*, for Gaelic river, river mouth. Its old spelling varies from Aberschoir to Hibberscor and Abbirscross. The natives pronounce it Aberscaig; *escaig* is from *uisge*, water.

Ben, *Vraggie*, G. *bràigh*, each, high lands. Some church names are also met with here, as *Loch-a'-vicar*, vicar's loch, Kirktown, church town, and *Uamh-ghill-Aindreas*, Gillander's cave.

Salachie Burn, G. *salach*, muddy.
Ben Horn, N. hill of the eagle, N. *arn-r*.
Loch Lundie, G. *lòn*, *dubh*, black morass.
Farralarrie, G. *Fuar-laraich*, cold habitations.

Parish of Rogart.

This inland parish forms a square of about ten miles. Norse names are few, and there is evidence of a Pictish occupation. The parish name presents some difficulty. Its Gaelic pronunciation is *Raoird*, which seems to point to a Gaelic origin, *Rhi-àrd*, high slope. But the early charters give *Roth-gorthe*; and both are well known in Highland topography; *roth*, a circle, and *garth*, cultivated land. Care, however, must be taken not to confound the Gaelic *gart* with Norse *gardr*, also meaning an enclosure (Eng. yard). When *gart* is prefixed, as *Gartymore*, it is the Gaelic word; but when it comes last as in Rogart, it should be Norse.

Fleet, N. *fljot*, flooding ; *fleet-water* is water which overflows ground, in broad Scotch.

Rossal, G. *ros*, a promontory, and *ail*, rock.

Langwell, N. *langdal*, has been suggested ; but as it is not a dale name, so much as a district name, its root is probably Norse, *lyng*, heather ; which agrees with the native pronunciation *Langal*.

Blarich, G. *blàr*, plain ; the *ich* is an affix.

Milnafua, G. *meall-na-fuadh*, hill of the spectre. *Fuadh* is common in place-names, *altan-na-fuadh* in Durness.

Davoch-beg, G. *davoch*, a measure of land.

Eden, G. *aodan*, face.

Pitfure, Pictish *pit*, Gaelic *baile-phiuthair*, W. *pawr*, pasture.

Rovie, Treasady, Toskary contain doubtful elements, but the majority of Rogart names are easily explained with the aid of a Gaelic dictionary. The following present no difficulty : — *Achcork* (oat-field), *Achadhnacaillich* (nun's field), *Achinluachrach* (rushy field), *Achnagarron* (gelding's field), *Achooan* (bothy field), *Achvrail* (high field), *Balchlaggin* (skull place), *Blairmore* (large marshy field), *Culdrain* (bramble-wood), *Druimanairgeid* (silver ridge), *Dalrevoch* (spotted dale), *Inchomney* (meeting field), *Inchoraig* (shamrock field) *Kinnauld* (burn head), *Lettie* (half-side), *Muie* (plain), *Morness* (large plain), *Rhelin* (running stream), *Rhemusaig* (primrose slope), *Rhicalmie* (Colum's slope), *Shenval* (old town), *Shenlone* (old meadow), *Skiag* (winged), *Tulloch* (eminence).

There are some place-names here which have been explained before, as *Grudie* (N. *grjot*, stony), *Grumbie, Dalnessie*, etc.

Parish of Clyne.

The low-lying grounds of this parish along the coast, which are extensive and well-cultivated, gave name to the district. *Clyne* comes from G. *cluain*, a meadow, and the oldest written form is *Clun* in Bishop Gilbert's MS. *Brora*, the principal village, is in a fair way of supplanting the old name. It is of Norse origin, probably, and means bridge. There is also another Norse term *brù*, ridge, which occurs in Lewis *Brue* : and Brora may be from *Bru—shrath*, which agrees with the Gaelic pronunciation. Coal was worked at this place for three centuries, Lady Jane Gordon, Countess of Sutherland, interesting herself in the matter as early as 1573. The Norse names are comparatively few ; and the Pictish or Brythonic element disappears. The following are easily recognisable in Gaelic : *Ardochie* (high field), *Aultcraggie* (rocky burn), *Badnellan* (island clump), *Cavaig* (variant of *camhan*, (a hollow plain) *Clynelish* (*cluain-lios*, meadow-garden), *Dalchalm* (Colum's dale), *Doll* (dale), *Brechin* (*breac-achadh*, spotted field), *Kilcolmkil* (Columba's cell), *Fascoille* (in old maps *Ascoil*, now Faskally), *coille* is wood : the first part doubtful ; it may mean the near wood, the sheltered wood, or wood on the hill, from old Gaelic *ais*, hill. *Gordonbush* is modern English, and the Norse element appears in the latter parts of Achrimsdale, and Strathskinsdale. The parish terminates in the interior of the county in Ben Armin—often Ormin in the maps, for which there is no authority. *Armunn* is Gaelic for a hero ; it is about 2500 feet high. At Kilcalmkill, there is an ancient cemetery which, with the name, marks it as an ecclesiastical residence ; another *cell*, or church, is preserved in Killean (John's cell). On the south side of Loch Brora is Craig Bar, a saint to whom the church at Dornoch was first dedicated. Kilcalmkil belonged for 300 years to the Gordon branch of the Sutherland family, the Gordons of Carrol, from obsolete Gaelic *ail*, a rock, and *carr*, stone. The Gaelic for a quarry-face is *caoireall*. A very good specimen of the Pictish tower is in this parish, situated on the Black-Water. It is called Castle Cole ; and part of the walls is still standing, 11 feet thick. It was doubtless the residence of a Celtic *maormòr*, and subsequently of a Norse chieftain ; and the line of watch-towers to the coast may still be traced.

Parish of Loth.

This place-name is of doubtful origin. Ptolemy, a Greek writer, who flourished in the last quarter of the second century, places the *Logi* in south-east Sutherland, and some connect *Loth* with this tribal name. Others, again, look upon it as a rubbed down form of *loch*, a lake. Within historical times, a large part of the low-lying grounds of the parish was under water, until about the beginning of the 17th century. A direct course was cut out of the solid rock, for the river of Glen Loth, and the bed of the lakes was turned into rich arable land. The Gaelic pronunciation is Lo.

Kintradwell, Gaelic *Ceann-Trolla* is from *Trollhena*, otherwise *Triduana*, a female saint, whose memory is preserved also in Orkney.

Culgower. G. goat's wood, or goat's recess, *cùl*, nook.

Crakaig (occurs also in Strathnaver), G. *cràic* and *croic*, means deer's horns ; thus anything extensive or branching, as the hand.

Kilmote, G. *cill*, church, *mote* is either a personal name, or more probably *mòd*, assembly.

Garty occurs in many combinations, East Garty, Mid Garty, and Gartymore, G. *gart*, arable land.

Portgower, G. *port*, harbour, *gabhar*, goats.

Parish of Kildonan.

This parish is wholly inland; its extreme length is 24 miles, and it varies in breadth from 5 to 17 miles. The old statistical account compares it "to a tree stretching out at the top or height of the parish into branches." Viewing Kildonan Strath as the trunk, the branches are formed by the Tilny, Free, and Achnahow burns on the west side; and the Suisgill and Kinbrace burns on the east. A great many ecclesiastical names occur here, such as—

Kildonan (oldest form, Kilduranach, in Gilbert's MS.), Donan's cell, Donan being a well known Culdee saint.

Kilpheder, Peter's cell, church dedicated to St. Peter.

Kilearnan, St. Earnan's cell or church.

Loch-an-abb, Abbot's loch.

The Norsemen have also left their foot-prints here, this strath forming, doubtless, one of the dales so often referred to as "the Dales of Caithness" in the Orkneyinga Saga.

Ben Griam. Two hills are so called, big and little Ben Griam. The word is Norse *grim*, dark and massive.

Helmsdale, N. *Hjalmundal*; this is the name in the sagas; *munndal*, means the dale at the mouth; *hjal* either stands for the older Ila, the name of the river in Ptolemy's map; or is N. *hyjalli*, shelf, terrace, with reference to the aspect of the hill behind the village.

Navidale. N. the first syllable, of doubtful origin; possibly N. *naefr*, birch (Mackay); more likely, Ninian's dale.

Suisgill, N. *susi* (soss Scotch), roaring, burn.

Marrel, N. *mar-dale*, sea-side dale.

Learable, N. *leir*, muddy, and *bol*, township.

Borrobol, N. *bor*, *bur*, habitation, and *bol*, township.

Eldrabol, N. *eldr*, beacon.

Diobal, N. *dy*, bog.

The following are clearly Gaelic :—*Dalhalmy* (Colum's dale), *Gailval* (*gall-bhaile*, stranger's township), *Preschoin* (Dog's bush), *Seanachadh* (old field), *Tomich* (hillocks), *Torrghortan* (*torr*, hill, *gortan*, dim. of *gort*, field), *Kinbrace* (*ceann-bhraigh-uisge*, head of water-source), *Garvault* (rough burn), *Badanloch* (loch villa), *Torrish* (*torr-uisge*, fortification by the water), *Achintoul* (barn-field), *Claggan* (skull).

LANGUAGE.

By Rev. Adam Gunn, M.A.

The natives of Sutherland and the Reay Country are bi-lingual. English is spoken very well all over the county; and strangers give us credit for a more pleasing accent than our Teutonic neighbours in Caithness. A Sutherlandshire youth finds less difficulty in adapting his tongue to English sounds than his cousins of Wester Ross and Lewis; while the natives of Sutherland proper are not prepared to yield the palm, even to Inverness, in the purity of their English diction.

So much, however, cannot be advanced in behalf of our Gaelic. It is by no means so pure as our geographical position might lead one to suppose. Every year sees the foreign element in it on the increase, and the area in which it is habitually spoken becoming more and more limited. Assynt alone can claim to hold its own in regard to purity: and even there, corruption has set in. Such a greeting as "Tha'n latha *beautiful*," is common all over the Highlands; and various reasons may be assigned for the greater amount of foreign material in the dialect of Sutherland.

(1) The Norse occupation, from 900—1200, is account-able for a good deal of this foreign element. Of course all the Gaelic-speaking area of Scotland, with the exception of Perthshire, and the heights of Inverness, came more or

less under this influence ; but a deeper impression has been made upon Sutherland by them, than upon any other Highland county. The topographical record makes it very manifest that the whole county was over-run by them ; and weight of numbers alone prevented Sutherland from being an English-speaking county like its neighbour, Caithness. As it is, the Norse influence is very marked in the dialect, and quite a host of words, in every day use as Gaelic, owe their introduction to the Norse occupation.

(2) The near proximity of Caithness, where the Scandinavian came to stay, explains in some measure, the number of Teutonic words in use in our dialect. This is more evident on the east and north coasts, where the intercourse between Teuton and Celt was close and continuous. It is true that hostile feelings between the two races existed until recent times ; but the proximity was bound to tell on the purity of the Gaelic speech.

(3) Two more recent causes may also be mentioned as contributing to this result. The army was the natural destination of Sutherland youths in the good old times ; and every encouragement was given to enlist in one or other of the Highland Regiments, the Reay Fencibles, and latterly in the 93rd Sutherland Highlanders. After long service, and mixing with English speaking peoples, these men found their way back to their native glens, and brought with them a knowledge of English. In this way, such words as " Kisseag " for *pòg* (kiss) and *comrad* from comrade, which are now looked upon as pure Gaelic, came into use. The economic changes which took place in the early years of this century also had some share in this detereorating process. Large tracts of land were placed under the management of English

speaking farmers, who brought their shepherds from the borders; so that in the very heart of Sutherlandshire, where a hundred years ago not a word of English was spoken, there is to-day a congregation of worshippers so entirely English, that the native language is but rarely used in the pulpit.

There are two main dialects of Scottish Gaelic, a northern and a southern; and it used to be matter of keen debate in Celtic Societies—where was the best Gaelic spoken, at Inverness or Inveraray. Probably no solution satisfactory to both parties was ever offered to this problem. But from a variety of causes, which need not be enumerated here, Argyleshire, or the southern dialect, came to be recognised as a sort of standard to which the literary efforts of northern authors must conform when they venture into print. In this way, there is no good specimen of the northern dialect to be seen in print; and the labours of such poets as Rob Donn suffer immensely from a well-meaning desire on the part of editors and publishers to conform his dialect to a supposed literary standard. The dialect of the Reay Country bard was far too pronounced to admit of this accommodating process; and the consequence is that his songs have lost in print a great deal of the smoothness and rhythm which they possess in their native garb. It is too late in the day to alter matters now, for the rendering of the Bible into the southern dialect has stereotyped the standard, and Argyllshire peculiarities must be borne with, notwithstanding the fact that a considerable portion of them is not of native, but of Irish origin. As a set off to this hardship, the north countryman has the advantage of knowing the southern dialect in print; he has, therefore, no difficulty in understanding the southern; while a native of Argyll will find it next to impossible to follow with intelligence the conversation of north countrymen.

There are three test-sounds by means of which we classify Gaelic dialects into northern and southern—one main and two subordinate. (1) The main peculiarity of the northern district is a change of *eu* into *ia*; thus *beul, ceud, breug, meud, deug, feur* of the south becomes *bial, ciad, miad, diag, fiar* of the northern counties. It should be observed, however, that, to begin with, this *eu* is long by compensation ; *ceud* compensates for a lost n by lengthening the vowel (compare Lat. centum). This divergence does not take place in the case of *eu* when it is not arrived at by compensation ; it stands *eu* in the north and south, and is pronounced similarly, except perhaps in half-a-dozen monosyllables, which have become *ia* in the north by the force of analogy. (2) The northern dialect dislikes a long vowel, preferring the use of the dipthongs. Thus, Argyllshire *trom*, heavy, becomes Sutherland *troum*. Professor Rhys calls this habit *diphthongisation*, and thinks it is due to a more musical ear. (3) The diphthong *ao* is opener in the south ; the *saoghal* of Argyllshire is quite different from the attenuated *seevil* of the north. By one or other of these test-sounds, the question of a Highlander's residence on either side the Grampians is easily settled.

Sutherlandshire Gaelic belongs of course to the northern dialect. But with regard to the main test, *eu* into *ia*, the Reay country proves an exception. It agrees rather with the south, or more properly speaking, introduces a new diphthong. Thus, *eu*, which ought to become *ia*, becomes *ea* ; and the following scheme shows how we stand comparatively :—

SOUTH, OR LITERARY.	NORTH.	REAY COUNTRY.
beul	*bial*	*beal*
sgeul	*sgial*	*sgeal*
neul	*nial*	*neal*

I. In words where the dipthong is not flanked by *l*, as the above examples, we follow the southern dialect: *breug, feur, meud,* is pronounced in Sutherland exactly as in Argyle, with the exception of Assynt and the south-east.

II. Another peculiarity of our dialect is our partiality for the broad *a*. Southern *o* becomes *a* in numberless instances. Of course it must be remembered that *o* appears in print often in deference to Irish orthography, where it is never used, even in Argyle; thus, *focal, cos,* is nowhere on Scottish soil so pronounced; they are *facal, cas*. Sutherlandshire Gaelic, however, changes southern *o* into *a* in the great majority of instances:

SOUTH.	SUTHERLAND.	
lorg	*larg*	foot-print.
bolg	*balg*	bag.
solus	*salas*	light.
dorus	*daras*	door.

But in a few cases we refuse to accept southern *a*, and change it into *o* —*falt, bainne, trasgadh,* become *folt, boinne, trosgadh.*

III. The most marked peculiarity of Sutherland Gaelic is, perhaps, its fondness for the *u* sound. We make all our participles (*adh, amh*) end in *u*; *bagradh, deanamh,* becomes *bagru, dean-u; dol, obair, domhail, drola, tobar,* are pronounced as *dul, ubair, dumhail, drula, tubar.*

IV. When we cease to compare ourselves with the south, we find three well-defined sub-dialects in Sutherland:

1. The dialect of Sutherland proper—*Cataobh*.
2. The Reay country dialect—*Duthaich-'ic-aoidh*.
3. The Assynt dialect.

These are the main sub-dialects; but a keen ear may easily distinguish differences in tone between natives of different parts of the same parish. The "twang" of a Portskerra man is quite different from that of Melvich, which is not half-a-mile distant.

Comparing these three sub-dialects then, it will be granted that the language of the people of *Machair-Chat*, as the low-lying east coast of Sutherland is called, is less pure than that of the Reay Country; and the dialect of the latter is less pure than that of Assynt. We may except one or two fishing communities from this comparison; for example, Embo, and Brora, whose natives can express themselves in fairly good idiomatic Gaelic. The language of Assynt or "*ma lamhan shuas*" as it is distinguished from the North and East, has preserved a good deal of its pristine purity. They are easily distinguished by a tendency to *eclipsis;* and resemble Lewis in this respect. *An duine*, the man, is pronounced *an nuine*, *n* of the article eclipsing *d*. As already mentioned, they conform to the Northern dialect in the case of the *ia* sound, and thus differ from the Reay Country: and on the whole, their command of the language is greater, both as regards vocabulary, idioms, and inflections.

The North coast or Reay Country man is easily distinguished by his preference for the broad *a*. To such an extent has he carried this tendency that in some districts *sin* is pronounced *san;* *teine*, *teana*. We shall by and bye account for this preference of *a* by a greater mixture of Norse blood in his veins—the element which evolved into broad Scotch in the English speaking counties of the north. Another peculiarity of this district is the number of words which have taken on permanently the prosthetic *f.* *Eagal, acain, rabhadh, easgain,* etc., become *feagal, fraghaidh, feasgainn.* Even *aithne,* command, is sometimes *faithne,* although there is danger of confounding it with *fainne,* a ring. The reason of so much confusion in our dialects regarding initial *f* is, that it disappears when aspirated; it is not sounded in oblique cases; thus *fear* is in gen. sing. *fhir,* where *fh* is silent. Consequently, as it disappears in oblique cases, it was also dropped in the nom. in many instances.

Inflections, or case endings, may be said to be disregarded. The old people, it is true, speak of *ceann na circe;* but the rising generation are quite satisfied with *ceann na cearc.* "*Tha e tional na caorich*" is oftener heard than the grammatically correct "*tha e tional nan caorach.*" A Reay Countryman has little regard for case-endings, with the exception of the dative plural *ibh,* which he has converted into *u.*

A very striking feature of the dialect of Sutherland is the extent to which it is permeated by foreign material. We have mentioned some of the causes that led to this, and ascribed a double share to the influence of the Norwegian stranger in our midst.

The influence of Norse on Scottish Gaelic is recognised on all hands. Both north and south have borrowed from it a good many terms connected with the sea. The Celts were not experts in navigation when the Vikings appeared upon the scene. It is not likely that they had advanced much beyond *the coracle* of St. Columba. Here, then, was quite a new vocabulary to them; and we find that they made good use of their opportunities ; they borrowed freely such terms as *bata*, boat, *barc*, bark, *seol*, sail, *sgiob*, crew, and the names for the different parts of a ship. Again, through the influence of Norse, the letter *t* has slipped in between *s r* in *strath*, *stron*, *strann*, *straid*. This much is admitted as Norse influence on the southern and northern dialects. But when we come to the far north, it will be found that the Scandinavian has left deeper footprints behind him. This is true not only of Sutherland, but also of Lewis. The writer recently saw a list of provincial words collected by a student, a native of Lewis, in the district of Ness and neighbourhood—words which do not appear in any Gaelic Dictionary, but most of which could be explained with the help of Cleasby's "Icelandic Dictionary," and are undoubtedly remnants of the Norse occupation. The same is true of north Sutherland. The effects of the Norwegian occupation may be classified as follows :

1. The preference for the broad *a* sound already referred to, so characteristic of the north coast. The English of Caithness is very broad, and is due to the same influence.

2. The habit of giving their Teutonic value to the letters *c, d, r*. The deep guttural *chd* sound of *c* in *mac*, is quite unknown in Sutherland. Again, *bàrd* is pronounced exactly as in English ; whereas in the south *d* has a broader sound, by flattening the tongue between the teeth and roof of the mouth.

3. A very large number of loan-words, which we are unjustly accused of borrowing from modern English, but which we have really borrowed from Norse ; examples are, *susdan*, thousand, N. *thusund ; preisteadh*, preaching, N. *priestr ; tùrn* for *cuis, deilig* (dealing), *bocaidh*, hobgoblin,

N. *bokki, barnaigeadh* (inviting to a feast), etc. These and a host like them have been in use in Sutherland long before modern English had any influence upon the language of the people.

4. What may be called the vituperative vocabulary is decidedly Norse. *Uilbh* is one of the most opprobrious terms in use, and comes from Norse *ulf*, a wolf. *Slaucar* is another, for an "awkward fellow," and *sgammal*, all of which may be found in Norse. This points to a period in our history when the Norse lorded it over the Celtic *bondi*, and applied to him such epithets in his wrath. They were carefully picked up, and being new, were preserved to the present day.

5. The nomenclature of peat-cutting is also Norse. One of the Earls of Caithness was called Torf-Einar, turf-cutter, being the first, no doubt, to point out the use of peats as a substitute for wood. Thus *bac* (N. *bakki*), bank, *storag, bassag, torra-sgian* (its first half) are all Norse.

(6) A few agricultural terms may also be mentioned, and words connected therewith. When a Sutherland herd calls a bull, he says "*tuadhi, tuadhi*." The Icelandic for a bull is *tuddi*, the usual changes being made on the loan-word, viz., diphthongisation and aspiration. The dairymaid's call is *huskus, huskus;* in Iceland it is *kuskus, kuskus* (root seen in Scotch qu-ey). The borrowing was not all on one side. The Norsemen who left Scotland on the fall of the Norwegian power at Largs, and went to Iceland, brought with them some Gaelic words, such as *calman*, a dove, and *tarf*, a bull. In driving away cattle by the dog a Reay Country herd makes use of a vocable which phonetically spells *trrrhi*. This is the word for driving off cattle in Iceland to the present day.

7. The last class we shall mention is the names for the different kinds of fish. A good many are Norse. *Lang*, ling, *cilig*, cod (N. *Keila*), *geddag*, grilse, etc. There is a Celtic word for cod, viz., *trosg*, in Assynt and the south; but the Reay Countryman uses *trosg* only as applied to an awkward fellow.

The following words are more or less peculiar to the county:

Lopan, a soft muddy place.

I, or *uidh*, a small stream with green patches on either side. It enters very largely into place-names, and is almost as common as

Rhidhe, or *rhidhean*, a sloping declivity with a burn at bottom. We have an innumerable number of place-names beginning with *Rhi*.

Riasgan, green patches on a hill-side: hence the place-name *Riasg*.

Rabhan, remains of a full tide on the sea shore or banks of a river.

Uar, a tempest, a waterspout, confluence of waters.

Baghan, churchyard.

Molldair, the miller's share; *bunndaist*, the weaver's share.

Bruthas, broth; *romag*, Athole brose; *a' bhuaicneach* is for small-pox; *na cnuimhean*, for toothache; *an t-siatag*, for rheumatism; *trom-altan*, a cold; *an cneatan*, and *trollaidh* in some parts.

Foit, an expression used when one is suddenly burnt. It is an old term, occurring on the margin of one of the Gospels in a Continental monastery as "*oit mo chrob;*" we have preserved it with prosthetic *f*. Probably this writer of the middle ages hailed from Ireland or Scotland, and had burnt his finger in snuffing the candle!

Troll, pronounced troull, awkward fellow. Norse, *troll*, hence *Traligill*. Norse, Troll's gill.

THE REGIMENTS.

By John Mackay (Ben Reay).

The military history of the Highlands, until a comparatively recent date, may be summed up as consisting of a series of clan feuds, attacks and reprisals. There were many warriors and fighting men, but bands of disciplined and trained soldiers, according to modern ideas, were unknown. Men were taught how to handle the sword, the battle-axe, and the bow, and in later times, the musket. The chief, or territorial magnate, who had many dependents, gave orders for the men on his estates to gather, and they obeyed: it may have been to engage in a foray against a hostile clan, and carry off spoil, or to make a raid on the territory of some leader against whom the chief had a grudge, or for the more deadly purposes of revenge. Our section of country was probably neither better nor worse in this respect than other districts. Tradition tells us of conflicts with the Danes and other invaders ; and later, that Highland chiefs with their followers fought under Bruce at Bannockburn, in the memorable battle which secured to Scotland her independence ; and also, that during the two succeeding centuries they frequently assisted the Scottish kings in their wars against England.

In treating of the Regiments of Sutherland and the Reay Country, I shall not attempt to give any account of the armed bands which rival chiefs brought into the field, when clan disputes had to be settled by the sword ; for although clan fights were often contests between large numbers of armed men, and showed a considerable display of military skill and strategy, the combatants could hardly be called soldiers. Clan feuds belong to the historical section of this volume.

The history of the regiments is of great interest, not only from the number of corps which were raised in the two districts, but also from the character of the men who composed them. It is also unique, inasmuch as the earliest printed military record in Great Britain is a narrative of the services of a regiment which was raised by the Chief of the Mackays, exactly two hundred and seventy years ago, and which served with great distinction in the terrible struggle known in history as "the thirty years' war." The exploits of the regiment were recorded by one of its officers in a volume which was published in London in 1637, under the title of "Monro: his Expedition with the Worthy Scots Regiment (called MacKeyes Regiment), levied in August, 1626, by Sir Donald MacKey," &c. &c.*

In 1631 the Marquis of Hamilton was authorised to raise a regiment of Scots soldiers for service in Germany, and

---

* But this was not the first regiment raised in the north of Scotland for service abroad. In the year 1612, Colonel George Sinclair, nephew of the Earl of Caithness, raised a body of men in his native county to assist the King of Sweden in his wars. His ships were driven ashore at Romsdal, in Norway, and he tried to make his way across the mountain to Sweden with his men. The people seem to have looked upon them as enemies, for they attacked the Scots when in a narrow gorge, by hurling large stones down upon them, killing the greater part, for only a few escaped. Colonel Sinclair was one of the first who fell. On a tablet erected at the place are words to this effect, "Here lies Colonel George Sinclair, who with 900 Scotsmen, were dashed to pieces like so many earthen pots by the peasants of Lessoe Vaage and Forsa. Berdon Sallatad of Ringeboe was their leader." The episode forms the subject of a Norwegian ballad, entitled *The Massacre of Kringelen*.

requested the Earl of Sutherland to assist him in recruiting. In response to this appeal, Adam Gordon, the Earl's brother, offered to go, and to take "with him a number of resolute soldiers to serve the King of Sweden." I have not been able, however, to find any record of the services of this company of men from Sutherland.

In 1642 the Earl of Sutherland and Lord Reay raised a small force—about 200 men—to assist in quelling a rebellion in Ireland. The division of the Royal Army to which they were attached was commanded by General Robert Munro, who had been Colonel of the Mackay regiment when it was in the service of the King of Sweden ; and it is highly probable that a portion of these men were tried soldiers, who, ten years previously, had fought in Germany under "The Lion of the North." I do not know of any special service in which they were engaged while in Ireland.

But unrest was thickening over the Kingdom, and troubles began between those who had subscribed the Covenant, and the adherents of the King. These troubles ultimately ended in the execution of King Charles the First, and the establishment of the Protectorate under Cromwell. All over the kingdom parties were divided, some remained true to the cause of royalty, while others declared for the Covenant and Cromwell. Among those who favoured the cause of the Covenant was the Earl of Sutherland, but Lord Reay remained loyal to the King. In 1645, the Earl called out 800 of his men to oppose Montrose, and sent them south to Inverness. This regiment was reported to have been raised at his own cost, but this does not appear to be correct, for in response to a petition which he presented to the Estates, a warrant was granted to him to receive 800 suits of clothes and 800 pairs of shoes for his men, and 1600 dollars for his own charges.

In 1649, shortly after the execution of the King, John Lord Reay joined the Earls of Ogilvie and Seaforth with "300 able men well provided with arms and necessaries" for the army which was being raised in support of Charles II., but the combined force, which amounted to not more than 900 men, was attacked at Balvainey by General Leslie's troops, and after an engagement in which they had 80 men killed and many wounded, the greater part of them were taken prisoners. The men were allowed to return to their homes, but the leaders were taken to Edinburgh as prisoners. Lord Reay was kept in prison about a year and a half. The romantic way in which his escape was effected by Lady Reay and a servant, is told in the Clan History p. 349-350.

In 1650 the Earl of Sutherland raised a regiment of about 1000 men, for the purpose of opposing Cromwell, and marched with them as far as Stirling. But the decisive victory gained by Cromwell at Dunbar put an end to the struggle, and peace was secured for a time. The Commonwealth was established, and Cromwell became ruler of the country.

For nearly forty years, that is, during the Commonwealth, the Restoration, and up to the abdication of James VII., neither the Earl of Sutherland nor Lord Reay took any active part in public affairs; but the troubles which had been gathering came to a head in 1688.

The advent of the Prince of Orange changed the aspect of affairs. The persecutions and cruelties which had been sanctioned by King James had completely alienated the affections of many of the best families who had formerly been devoted to his cause ; and in the north, the families of Sutherland, Mackay, and Munro, being staunch Protestants, were among the first in Scotland to attach themselves to the cause of the Prince of Orange. The events which quickly followed, viz: the abdication of the King, and the transference of the Crown to the Prince and Princess of Orange, as King William and Queen Mary, are too well known to be repeated.

When the Prince of Orange landed in England he had with him an army of about 14,000 men. The English and Scottish divisions were under the command of General Hugh Mackay of Scourie, who had for many years held a high command in the service of the Netherlands. He was appointed Commander in Chief in Scotland, but King William was so pressed for troops, that the only men he could spare for Scotland were detachments from the three regiments which formed the Scottish Brigade, and did not number more than 1,100 men. But the General immediately took steps to get what additional assistance he could from those noblemen and others who were favourable to the new dynasty. One of his earliest acts was to call upon the guardians of his kinsman, the youthful Lord Reay (the young Peer was only a boy) to "send without delay 200 chosen men, under two principal gentlemen of the clan," to assist him in his campaign against the forces of King James. These were at once sent; then he called for "other 200 well armed men," which he likewise speedily got. At the same time he sent instructions to Lord Strathnaver (the Earl of Sutherland's son) to levy, with all speed, the regiment

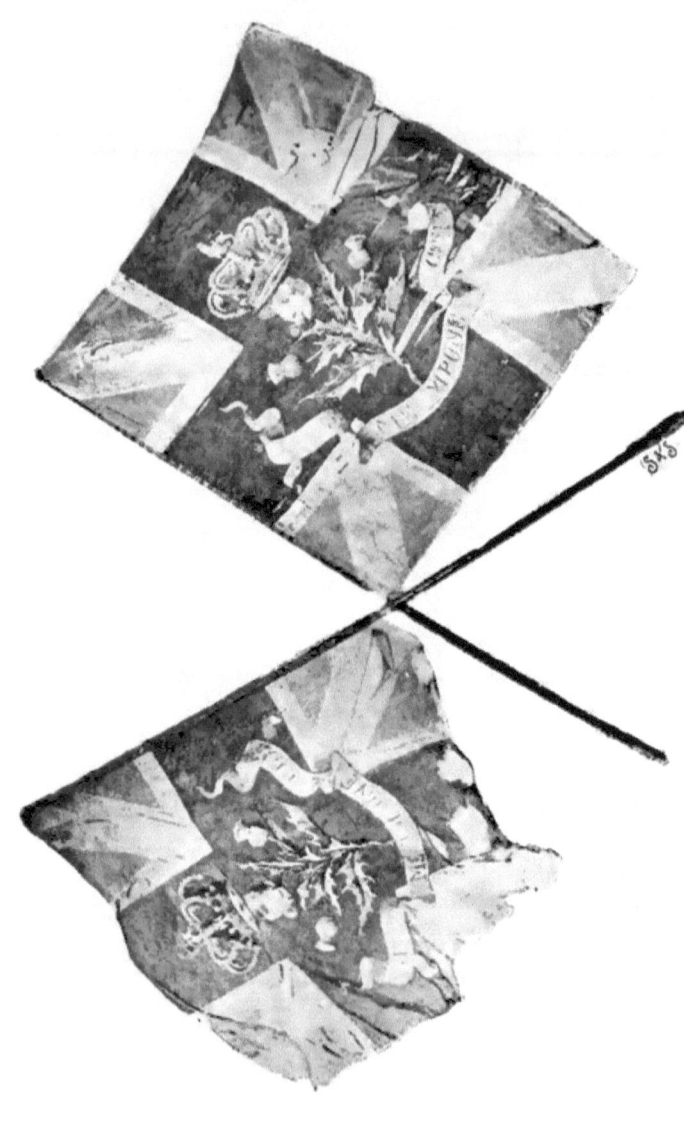

COLOURS OF MACKAY'S REGIMENT IN THE SERVICE OF HOLLAND.

for which he had received a commission, and "to arm as many of the men as he could with such arms as usually Highlanders make use of." Lord Strathnaver accompanied his men to Inverness, where "300 firelocks, with the necessary powder, match, and ball," were ordered to be delivered to him.

The two Reay Country contingents were commanded by Captain William Mackay of Kinloch, and Captain Hugh Mackay of Borley. Lord Strathnaver's men were quartered in Inverness and Elgin, the Mackays in Inverness and Perthshire. General Mackay wrote at this time "The Highlanders are absolutely the best untrained men in Scotland, and are equal to our new levies, though they are better armed than the Highlanders are."

The country was now plunged into civil war; and the issue to be decided was whether Scotland should remain under the yoke of the Stuarts, or obtain the freedom the people expected to enjoy under the government of the Prince of Orange.

King James's army, commanded by Dundee, and that of King William, commanded by Mackay, were soon to bring the question to a settlement, although the two commanders had not yet brought their forces face to face. Several minor engagements, however, between portions of the two armies had already taken place. For example, not far from Castle Grant, on the 1st May, a squadron of dragoons under the command of Colonel Livingstone, accompanied by about 200 Mackays, saw the enemy encamped on the other side of the Spey. Livingstone ordered his men to ford the stream. The Highlanders crossed first, followed by the dragoons, who put their horses to the spur, whereupon the Mackays outran the horse, and got first at the enemy. After a short engagement the latter were put to flight, and being pursued, had several of their number killed and wounded, and many were taken prisoners.

The battle of Killiecrankie was fought on the 27th July, 1689. The victory remained with King James's army, but Dundee having been mortally wounded, the advantage was not followed up. Some of King William's troops, as General Mackay stated in a letter to the Duke of Hamilton, when giving an account of the battle to that nobleman, "behaved like the vilest cowards." Mackay's own regiment,* commanded by his brother James (who was killed in the battle), was almost the only one in his army that showed any gallantry on this occasion, for most of the other regiments got into confusion and took to flight as soon as Dundee's Highlanders rushed at them, claymores in hand. But though the victory was with the army which Dundee had commanded, the advantage was with Mackay, for by the measures he took, the forces of the dethroned King, after a few months, were entirely broken up, and the new government was established. A period of peace at home now followed the recent troubles, and quietness prevailed in the Highlands.

Neither the Sutherland nor the Reay men appear to have been engaged in the battle of Killiecrankie; and shortly after that event most of them returned to their homes; but one company of the Reays, under Captain Hugh Mackay of Borley, was left as a garrison in Ruthven Castle, where they did duty for several months.

---

* Afterwards incorporated in the British Army as the 21st or Royal North British Fusiliers, now the Royal Scots Fusiliers.

But although the new dynasty seemed to be firmly established, many families in England and Scotland had a longing for the restoration of the exiled Stuarts, and the accession of the first of the Hanoverian family (George I.) to the Throne, in 1714, was made the excuse for a Jacobite rising. In Scotland this attempt to involve the country in civil war was headed by the Earl of Mar, and some other adherents of the late King James. They had his son proclaimed as King James VIII., and the chiefs of many of the western clans, with their followers flocked to the standard of rebellion.

The Earl of Sutherland, who was in the south when the rebellion broke out, hastened home as soon as it became known, having first arranged that a ship with arms and ammunition should be immediately despatched for the use of himself, Lord Reay, and others. But the rebels managed to seize the vessel, while she lay in Leith roads, and appropriated the stores. On reaching Dunrobin, the Earl, assisted by Lord Reay and Ross of Balnagowan, mustered a large number of men and marched towards Inverness. Lord Strathnaver, who held the rank of colonel, led the centre, and Lord Reay and the Earl of Sutherland, the right and left wings. A detachment of rebels, led by the Earl of Seaforth, had taken possession of the Highland capital, but leaving a strong party to guard the town, Seaforth hastened south to join the Earl of Mar. On the 13th November, 1715, the battle of Sheriffmuir was fought. It was a drawn battle; but it really ended the rebellion, for the Jacobite leaders could not again bring their men together.

After the battle, news reached the rebels that Inverness had been beset and taken by some of the loyal clans of the north. The force which had accomplished this consisted of about 300 men each of Mackays, Munros, Frasers, Forbeses, and Rosses.

The Sutherland and Reay men did not engage in active hostilities with any of the Jacobite forces, but were quartered in Inverness, and remained there for some time after the rebellion had been put down.

The government now took into consideration the desirability of arming a number of loyal Highlanders, and admitting them to the service of the Crown; but it was not till 1729 that they resolved to embody such a corps as part of the regular military force of the kingdom. Six Independent Companies of Highlanders were accordingly embodied—three of 100 men each, and three of 75 men each. The commanding officers of the larger companies were commissioned as captains, while those of the smaller companies got commissions as captain-lieutenants, and each company had in addition two lieutenants and one ensign. One of the small companies was commanded by George Munro, of Culcairn, and as the services of the companies were confined to the territories in which they had been raised, Munro's company did duty in Sutherland and Ross. The services of these companies during a period of nine years were so highly satisfactory to the Government, that in 1739 it was resolved to raise four additional companies, and incorporate the whole into a regiment of the line. In this way the famous corps, afterwards known as the 42nd Regiment, was established.

When the Independent Companies were raised, each company was dressed in the tartan of its commanding officer, and as these tartans were all dark coloured, the companies were known as *An Freiceadan Dubh*—the Black

Watch, to distinguish them from the regular troops, who, from the prevailing colour of their uniforms were known as *Saighdearan Dearg* —the Red Soldiers. But when the new regiment was formed, a special tartan was designed for it, and this pattern has ever since been known as the " Forty Second." The designation *Am Freiceadan Dubh* (at first given to the Independent Companies as a nick-name), was transferred to the 42nd ; and at the present day this regiment is officially known as "The Black Watch." But its history does not form a part of our volume, and I have merely mentioned the regiment because one of the Independent Companies was connected with our county.

In the Spring of 1745 the Earl of Loudon was authorised by the government to raise a regiment in the Highlands. He consulted with several of the chiefs and leading men of the north, and through their influence recruits came in so freely that in a short time about 1200 men were enrolled ; these were formed into a battalion of 12 companies, and designated Loudon's Highlanders. Sutherland and the Reay Country contributed their quota, and as representing these districts the Hon. Alexander Mackay, son of Lord Reay, and John Sutherland, of Forse, were appointed captains. When the rebellion broke out the regiment, before it had been drilled, was called to the field ; but this deficiency was of comparatively little importance, as the habits of the people made the change from ordinary to military life easy. At the battle of Prestonpans three of the companies—"every man and officer"—were taken prisoners by the rebels! The regiment was disbanded at Perth in 1748.

The Earl of Sutherland, desirous of assisting the Government at the time of the rebellion, raised and equipped a regiment of militia for the defence of the county. One of the captains of this regiment was George Mackay, younger of Melness. On the 25th March, 1746, an incident occurred in which he took the leading part, which is worth recording. A large sum of money had been shipped in France for Prince Charles, on board a sloop of war called the *Hazard*. This vessel was discovered by the government man of war *Sheerness*, and chased from the Moray Frith, along the coast to the Kyle of Tongue. The captain of the *Hazard*, finding that he could not escape from the man of war, ran his vessel aground on the sands below Melness, where the larger vessel could not follow. The money, which was in boxes, was safely landed, and the crew hoped to be able to march with their treasure to Inverness. They expected, also, that the country people would befriend them. But Captain Mackay, when he learned what had taken place, got together some other officers of the militia regiment and about 80 men, and attacked those who had landed from the *Hazard*. After a sharp engagement in which five of the *Hazard's* men were killed, and several wounded, Captain Mackay's company took the remainder—156 in number, mostly Frenchmen—prisoners, and secured also the money, amounting to upwards of £12,000. The treasure was taken possession of by Lord Reay, and sent south by him in the man of war *Sheerness*, as were also the prisoners. The *Hazard*, at the same time, was taken south as a prize. [See *Gentleman's Magazine* for May, 1746; and narrative by Colonel Ker, in *Lyon in Mourning*, vol. I., p. 358, published by "Scottish History Society," 1895].

I do not find that either Lord Reay or Captain Mackay received any acknowledgment—not even an expression of thanks from the government—for this valuable service. The account of this affair, given in Robert Mackay's Clan History, is entirely misleading.

The battle of Culloden which was fought about three weeks afterwards (on 16th April, 1746), put an end to any chance of the Stuarts being again placed on the throne.

I have given this short historical sketch because during the transition period, to some of the leading events of which I have made reference, many companies of fighting men were raised in the County of Sutherland. The Earls of Sutherland, the Lords Reay, and several others were true patriots, and when called upon by Government promptly equipped their followers in its support. I regret, however, that we have no reliable information as to the numbers, exact organization and special services of these companies. But during the second half of the last century several regiments for temporary service were raised in the county, and of these we have some trustworthy particulars—I refer to the militia or fencible regiments. There is also one regiment of the line, the 93rd (now known as the 2nd battalion Argyll and Sutherland Highlanders), identified with the county. The rank and file of this regiment when embodied consisted almost entirely of men belonging to Sutherlandshire, and showed a body of soldiers second to none in our military annals for bravery, good conduct, and morality.

A Sutherland local militia regiment was raised in 1808, but I have not been able to ascertain its strength, as there is no muster roll either at the War Office, or the Record Office, London. In the Record Office, however, there is a list of officers—24 in number—with the dates of their commissions; and if we take the same proportion of men to officers that we find in the fencibles, this militia regiment must have had a strength of about 600 men. Earl Gower was Colonel; Alexander Sutherland, Lieutenant-Colonel; Dugald Gilchrist, Major; and Kenneth Mackay, Senior Captain.

The regiment known from 1803 to 1860 as *The Ross, Sutherland and Caithness Militia*, and from 1860 to 1881 as *The Highland Rifle Militia*, had a company (the D company) composed of men from Sutherland, and officered by gentlemen connected with the county. On the introduction of the "territorial system" into the British army on the 1st July, 1881, the title of this regiment was changed to the *3rd battalion Seaforth Highlanders*, and there are now few Sutherlandshire men in its ranks—the number at present [1896] being only 25. Of these 10 are Mackays; while Macdonalds, Macleods, Morrisons, Munros, Gunns, and Rosses number 2 each; and Mackintosh, Campbell, and Docherty 1 each—all in D company. Private Docherty is of Irish descent.

I now take the regiments in the order in which they were embodied.

I.—MACKAY'S REGIMENT.

This regiment, as has been mentioned, was formed in 1626. The warrant for raising it was granted by King Charles I., who directed that a commission should be given to Sir Donald Mackay to allow him to levy and transport 2000 men, to assist Count Mansfelt in the war which he was then prosecuting by the King's direction. The Lords of the Council at Edinburgh accordingly granted the requisite authority on the 16th March, 1626. Subsequent warrants of a similar character were issued to Sir Donald, so that, between the years 1626 and 1631, he was empowered to raise and equip 8,000 men for service abroad. The war in which he was about to take an active part was that which was subsequently known in history as the '*Thirty Years' War*.' It was begun by the Elector Palatine (husband of the Princess Elizabeth Stuart), having accepted the crown of Bohemia, which had been offered to him by the Protestants of that country. This was not in accordance with the wishes of the Emperor of Austria, who at once interfered ; and in a short time the whole of Germany became involved in the struggle.

What may be called a pioneer portion of the regiment consisting of about 300 men, under the command of Lieut.- Colonel James Sinclair,* sailed from Aberdeen for Glückstadt on the Elbe, and arrived at its destination before the main body of the regiment embarked. Further detachments probably were sent off in the same way.

But the main body of the regiment (over 2000 men) embarked at Cromarty on the 10th October, 1626, and after a passage of five days arrived at Glückstadt. As Sir Donald Mackay, owing to sickness, was not able to accompany his men, the regiment was under the command of Lieut.-Colonel Arthur Forbes (a son of Lord Forbes). On landing, it was put into comfortable winter quarters, and remained in the "fat and fertile land of Holstein" for about six months.

---

* As there is no reference to this officer or his men in Munro's "Expedition," it is probable that on arriving in Holstein, Lieut.- Colonel Sinclair at once placed his small force at the disposal of Count Mansfelt.

In the meantime Count Mansfelt, under whose leadership the regiment was intended to serve, died, and it became necessary to make other arrangements for its employment. Sir Donald thereupon entered into an agreement with the King of Denmark to fight under his banner. This was a natural step, for the Danish King had embarked in the same cause; and besides, he was uncle to King Charles I. and the Princess Elizabeth, and service under him was quite in harmony with the feelings of the Scottish soldiers and their leaders.

Sir Donald on recovering from his sickness "tooke shipping from Scotland to Holland, and from thence overland" to Holstein, where he joined his regiment in the latter part of March, 1627. During the winter the regiment had been well exercised and put under good discipline, so that Munro when describing it, wrote, "mine eyes did never see a more complete regiment for bodies of men and valiant souldiers." When first embodied the greater part of the men would undoubtedly be from Sir Donald's own territory—the Mackay Country—but later, when detachment after detachment had to be sent out, the ranks were filled up by men from all quarters. It is a tradition that Sir Donald's own company was composed of gentlemen from Strathnaver.

Immediately after Sir Donald had joined his regiment, orders were given that it should proceed to Itzehoe, to be inspected by the King of Denmark, and take the oath of fidelity to that sovereign. The regiment was drawn up in three divisions "in good order of battaile, all officers being placed according to their stations orderly, colours fleeing, drummes beating, horses neying, his Majestie comes royally forward, salutes the regiment, and is saluted againe with all due respect and reverence used at such times ; his Majestie having viewed front flancks and reare, the regiment fronting alwayes towards his Majestie, who having made a stand, ordained the regiment to march by him in divisions, which orderly done, and with great respect and reverence, as became ; his Majestie being mightily well pleased did praise the regiment, *that ever thereafter was most praiseworthy.* The colonell and the principall officers having kissed his Majesties hand, retired to their former stations;" and the oath having been taken by officers and men, and the articles of war read and published, the regiment was marched off by companies to its quarters.

The next day Sir Donald received instructions to take seven of his companies across the Elbe, and for about ten weeks the regiment, in detachments, was marched from place to place till towards the middle of July, when all the companies met by arrangement at Boitzenburg, a pleasantly situated town at the junction of the Elbe and the Boitze. But to the disappointment of officers and men they were not destined to be long together. In a few days orders came that the regiment had again to be divided. Sir Donald, with Lieut.-Colonel Seton and seven companies, got orders to march to Ruppin, while four companies, under Major Dunbar, were to remain for the defence of Boitzenburg. It was known that a large force of Austrians under Tilly was approaching Denmark, and that one of the columns was marching directly upon the town which the Highlanders were left to defend. On the third day after the departure of Sir Donald with the main portion of the regiment, the approach of the enemy was announced. They halted within cannon-shot distance, and at once began the siege.

But Major Dunbar had not been idle. He was well versed in the theory and practice of war, and had left nothing undone that would enable him to defend his post like a man of honour. The small garrison of Highlanders numbered only about 800 men, while the attacking force was at least 10,000 strong. The first night a gallant and successful sortie was made under the personal leadership of Dunbar. The enemy, determined to be avenged for this, on the following day attacked the sconce at all points, but after a long and desperate struggle, were beaten off with a loss of over 500 men. Fresh troops were pressed forward, and the attack was renewed with increased fury, but the enemy were again baffled and had to fall back. A third and even more desperate attempt was made to carry the sconce. [The sconce defended the bridge, and if captured, the enemy's cavalry might have crossed the Elbe, and overrun Holstein, before the King could have been informed that Boitzenburg had fallen.] Storming parties came on in great force, and made a most vigorous assault, but the firing of the Highland musketeers told again and again with deadly effect. But in spite of heavy losses the Austrian soldiers continued to press on, and the gaps made in their ranks by the well directed fire of the Highlanders were constantly and steadily filled up. The loss was not, however, all on the side of the enemy, many of the defenders were killed, and a large number wounded. After a while the firing of the Highlanders suddenly ceased. Their supply of ammunition was exhausted! The Imperialists surprised at the unexpected silence, instinctively guessed the cause, and redoubling their efforts made a rush at the walls. The Highlanders, for a moment, were at their wits' end; but tearing the sand from the ramparts they threw it in the eyes of their assailants as they attempted to scale the walls, and furiously attacking them with the butt-ends of their muskets, drove them from the sconce. But it was a dreadful struggle. At last the storming party fell back, the fire of the artillery ceased and Boitzenburg was saved. The enemy had again over 500 men killed, and a very large number wounded. The Highlanders had two officers and forty men killed, while many were wounded, and "carried the true marks of their valour imprinted in their bodies, for their country's credit." Finding Boitzenburg so well defended, the Imperialists decided to cross the Elbe at another point. This they effected considerably higher up the river. In the meantime the King of Denmark had sent orders to Major Dunbar to retire from the sconce, bring off his cannon, if he could, and blow up the bridge. He was then to leave two companies of his men at Lauenburg, and retire with the rest to Glückstadt. These orders he carried out.

This was the first opportunity the Mackay regiment had of showing the quality of its men. They gallantly accomplished the hazardous task to which they had been detailed, and showed by their deeds that they were truly (as the King of Sweden afterwards characterised them) a band of Scottish Invincibles.

The two companies which were left at Lauenburg were speedily besieged, and Major Wilson, the officer in command, seeing he could not hold his position, asked for a truce to arrange terms of surrender. This was granted, and conditions were agreed upon. These were, that the garrison should march out with bag and baggage and drums beating, and that they should have a convoy to Glückstadt. But

Major Wilson had not been careful as to details. On leaving the castle his colours were taken from him, and on his complaining of what he considered a breach of faith, he was told to read the agreement. He was thus forced to march to Glückstadt without colours. For this oversight he was dismissed from the regiment with disgrace, and his command given to Captain Duncan Forbes.

Major Dunbar had no idle time, for the enemy having obtained a footing in Holstein, he was ordered, without delay, to take his four companies and defend the Castle of Bredenberg, which, he was instructed, was not to be surrendered on any condition. A large number of people had taken refuge in it when the Austrians first entered the land, and had carried with them a great amount of treasure. Dunbar had only about 400 men to maintain this important place, for Boitzenburg and Lauenburg had thinned the ranks of his four companies nearly one half. The castle was poorly fortified, and Dunbar had just got into it, but had scarcely time to get the drawbridge pulled up, when Tilly and his forces surrounded the place. A trumpeter was at once sent with a summons demanding an instant surrender. This, of course, Dunbar refused. The enemy immediately began a hot and vigorous siege, which lasted without intermission for six days. The defenders resisted bravely. At length the enemy's guns made two breaches in the walls, and the Imperialists approached the moat. Tilly then sent a drummer to the Major to see if he would now surrender; but the answer was that "as long as he had a drop of blood in his head, the place would never be given up." This answer so incensed Tilly that he swore that when he got "the upper hand they should all die without quarter." Shortly after Dunbar's answer had been given, the brave man was struck by a musket ball, and instantly killed. The other officers would not capitulate, and the siege was prosecuted with renewed fury. Officer after officer fell, and the enemy having passed the moat, got possession of the castle, and a wholesale massacre took place. The atrocities committed were brutal in the extreme. With the exception of Ensign Lumsden, who escaped almost miraculously, every officer and man of the Highland detachment was either killed while in the discharge of duty, or savagely butchered; while of the country people who had taken refuge in the castle, only a few were able to escape with their lives from the brutal soldiery.

The enemy had above 1000 men killed before they took the castle.

This terrible disaster left only the seven companies of the regiment with which Sir Donald Mackay had been ordered to march to Ruppin. They were then sent to Wismar, and remained there five weeks, waiting for arrangements to be made to transport the Danish army; and ships arriving from Copenhagen, about 8,000 men, including the Highlanders, embarked for Heiligenhaven, where the whole force was safely landed. Immediately after landing, orders were given to march to Oldenburg, where, it was hoped, the Danish forces there, if united with those just landed, might be able to defeat Count Tilly, who was known to be advancing with an immense army for the purpose of over-running Holstein. To the Highlanders was allotted the task of defending the Pass, which, by a strange overlook on the part of the Danish generals, had been left unfortified. As they drew near, the Holsteiners who were on service had all fled except their captain. The Pass was thus nearly lost; but Sir Donald hurried forward an officer with a platoon of musketeers, "mostly young gentlemen of his own company," to keep possession of the post. This they did; but being hard pressed, and suffering severely from the fire of the enemy, "many of them died in the defence of it." The first division of the regiment came steadily on, and a sharp engagement took place. The pikemen had a hard time of it; for they had to stand two hours exposed to cannon and musket shot, so that "their sufferings and hurts were greater both among officers and men, than the hurt done to the musketeers, for few of their officers escaped unhurt, and divers of them were killed." During the engagement a barrel of gunpowder exploded, by which Sir Donald was burnt in the face, several of his officers wounded, and many soldiers were killed. The enemy having seen the explosion, tried hard to force the Pass, but their efforts were in vain, and they were obliged to retire. The first division had been fighting for some hours, when the second division came up, and "falling on with man-like courage" the other "fell off to refresh themselves." The fighting continued for some time with unabated vigour; but after mid-day the regiment was enabled to keep the Pass "by companies, one company relieving another till night . . . and then darkness made the service to cease." This engagement lasted from 7 o'clock in the morning till about 4 o'clock in the afternoon. By the indomitable pluck of the Highlanders the Imperialists were kept in check, and the Danish army was saved that day. But it was a sad struggle for our brave countrymen; for in the unequal contest they had 3 officers and about 400 men killed, and 13 officers were wounded.

The Duke of Weimar, who was the general in command, came to Sir Donald, and after complimenting him and his regiment, requested that as they "had done bravely all day in being the instruments, under God, of his safety and of his army, he would once more request that the regiment might hold out the inch, as they had done the span, till it was dark, and then they should be relieved, as he was a Christian." The fact was, that apparently, out of his whole army, the Duke had no other regiment he could trust for the important duty of again guarding the Pass. A Council of War had decided that it would be hopeless to attempt to stand against Tilly's overwhelming forces. It had therefore been resolved that the army should retire with all speed to Heiligenhaven, get on board the ships there, and sail for Denmark. The Duke had insisted that as the Highlanders had behaved so heroically, they should have some special mark of favour, and as they "deserved best" that they "should be first brought off." Having arranged with Sir Donald that a company of Highlanders should keep guard at the Pass, the Duke rode off; and then Sir Donald left the camp for Heiligenhaven to engage ships for embarking his men. The agreement was that as soon as all was quiet on the part of the enemy at the Pass, Sir Donald's men were to retire, and marching quickly, reach the harbour and embark before any other portion of the Danish army. The Pass was guarded, and the Duke was as good as his word.

It was a moonlight night in October, and at 10 o'clock the regiment reached Heiligenhaven, and drew up on the shore. They had been instructed to wait there for Sir Donald, who had gone out to the roadstead to arrange for their conveyance. But he found the shipmasters panic-stricken, the incessant firing which they had heard during the day having so filled them with fright that they could not be induced to bring any of their vessels near the shore. So Sir Donald had to return disappointed.

What had been intended to be a quiet and orderly retreat had become a hurried and disorderly rout, for as soon as it was known that the Highlanders had left the Pass the rest of the army, horse and foot, made a rush from the camp to the seaboard ; and ere long the cavalry came galloping down to the water's edge in the greatest confusion. The officers had lost all control over their men, and discipline was at an end. The number of fugitives rapidly increased, and soon men and horses, pioneers, musketeers, and pikemen, baggage and ammunition, were crowded in an unwieldy and unmanageable mass on the pier and shore.

Sir Donald realised the gravity of the situation. The enemy was known to be in pursuit, and there was not a moment to be lost. The runaway cavalry, which consisted chiefly of German levies in the Danish service, had crowded the long pier, and were in the act of seizing the shipping for the conveyance of themselves and their horses. Sir Donald saw he had only one chance, and ordered his Highlanders to clear the pier of the horsemen. "Pikemen, to the front!" he cried; and formed in line, eight ranks deep, the whole length of the pier, the pikemen in front and musketeers in rear, the Highlanders advanced, and charging the horsemen forced them over the edges of the pier into the water. But the channel was shallow and they escaped drowning. The Highlanders then seized upon a ship, and after placing their colours and a number of men on board, had it moved a little from the shore to prevent its getting aground. This accomplished, the ship's boat was manned with an officer and some musketeers, who were sent to force other ships out in the roads into their service; and thus a sufficient number of vessels being secured, the regiment was safely embarked. It was hard work getting the men shipped. Some of the officers toiled all night ferrying the sick and wounded from the shore, and the last boatful was just leaving when the Imperialists entered Heiligenhaven. But the baggage and the horses of the mounted officers had all to be left behind. When day broke it was seen that Tilly's army had possession of the town; and the Highlanders from their ships had the mortification to witness the surrender of the Duke of Weimar's army to the Austrians. They gave themselves up without striking a blow. Of the whole of the Duke's army the Mackay regiment alone escaped. The German horsemen whom the Highlanders had driven from the pier, were mercenaries and nothing more, for they at once took service under Tilly. "We saw," said Munro, "the enemies army drawne up in battell, horse, foot, and cannon, and the routed Danish army opposite them. I did see six and thirty cornets of horse, being full troupes, without loosing of one pistoll, give themselves prisoners in the enemies mercy, whereof the most part took service. As also I did see five regiments of foote, being forty colours, follow their examples, rendering themselves and their colours without losing of one musket."

Sir Donald with his regiment sailed for Flensburg to report what had taken place to the King, and receive further orders from his Majesty. The King was much grieved on learning of the heavy loss his forces had sustained; but as he was not in a position to enter at once again on the offensive, he ordered Sir Donald to proceed to the island of Funnen, and there the Highlanders landed. It was only a year since they had left Scotland, and six months since they had entered on active service, but the struggles in which they had been engaged had been of so sanguinary a character, that the regiment mustered only about one third of the number of men who had embarked at Cromarty on the 10th October, 1626. It was after landing in Funnen that news reached them of the taking of Bredenburg by the Austrians, and the massacre of its brave defenders.

The heavy losses the regiment had sustained became matter for serious consideration. Sir Donald called his officers together for consultation, and the result of their deliberation was that he should at once proceed to Scotland and bring over 1000 men to recruit the regiment. A new agreement was also made with the King of Denmark to continue in his service. Sir Donald, accompanied by seven officers (one from each of the remaining companies) accordingly departed for Scotland; and Lieut.-Colonel Seton having gone to Holland on leave, the regiment was left in command of Robert Munro (author of the "Expedition"), who, when news had been received of the death of Major Dunbar, had been promoted to the rank of Major.

During the absence of Sir Donald Mackay the regiment took part in various minor battles, but the most important service in which it was engaged was the defence of Stralsund, one of the cities of the Hanseatic league. This city had hitherto remained neutral during the war; but its vicinity to the coasts of Sweden and Denmark, and its noble harbour, made its possession of great importance. Wallenstein, the Imperialist general, had declared that he would take it, whereupon the citizens sent a message to the King of Denmark begging for his assistance, for an Austrian army was already in the neighbourhood getting ready to lay siege to the town. The King at once promised help, for he knew if Stralsund fell into the hands of the Imperialists, the free navigation of the Baltic would be lost, and the Danish Islands be at the mercy of the conqueror. He selected the Mackay regiment for the hazardous duty, "having had sufficient proof of its former service . . . so that before others they were trusted on this occasion." Seven companies (or rather portions of seven companies) of the regiment had been left in Denmark. Orders were given that they should at once proceed to Stralsund, and on the 25th May, 1628, three companies under Lieut.-Colonel Seton arrived in the harbour, and were at once landed and put on duty. On the 29th, Major Munro arrived with the remaining four companies, and the worthy major records that no sooner were they drawn up in the market-place, than they were sent to the Franken Gate "to relieve the other division which had watched three days and three nights together uncome off, that being the weakest part of the whole towne, and the only poste pursued by the enemy, which our lieutenant-colonell made choice of being the most dangerous, for his countrie's credit." For six weeks their duty was hard and unremitting, neither officer nor soldier being "suffered to come off his watch, neither to dine nor suppe, for their meate was carried unto them, to their poste." Night and day they were kept at their posts without any respite. They made attempts to strengthen their position, but had, so to speak, to work with spade in one hand, and pike or musket in the other, for the enemy was always on the alert to attack them at any moment.

The loss of life was heavy on both sides. "Many rose in the morning," wrote Munro, "went not to bed at night: and many supped at night sought no breakfast in the morning. . . . Some had their heads separated from their bodies by the cannon, as happened to one lieutenant and thirteene souldiers, that had their fourteene heads shot from them by one cannon bullet at once." On the 26th June, Wallenstein, annoyed at the length of the siege, proceeded to the camp for the purpose of conducting operations himself. After examining the walls he swore he would "take the place in three nights though it were hanging with iron chains betwixt the earth and the heavens." "But," as the historian writes "forgetting to take God on his side, he was disappointed."

Between 10 and 11 o'clock that night the assault was made. The Highlanders, knowing that Wallenstein was in the camp, were prepared for a more than ordinary attack on their position, and when the storming party advanced, upwards of a thousand strong, were ready for them. After a struggle of an hour and a half, the enemy was driven back. But they had reliefs at hand, and a second party, equal in number to the first, renewed the attack. The Highlanders made short work of them, and these also were driven back. And so the night passed on, one storming party succeeding another, and meeting the same fate, until morning, when as day was breaking a last and desperate effort was made to force the Gate. They succeeded so far as to get within the outworks, but were beaten back with great slaughter, and forced to retire. The enemy had about a thousand men killed, and the Highlanders had "neare two hundred, besides those who were hurt." The moat was filled with the bodies of the slain; the works were ruined and could not be repaired, and this "caused the next nights watch to be more dangerous." That night there was again severe fighting with great loss of life on both sides. But as soon as the morning light shone, the Highlanders armed, some "with corslets, headpieces, with half-pikes, morgen-sternes, and swords," rushed out "pell mell amongst the enemies, and chased them quite out of the workes againe, and retiring with credit maintained still the triangle or raveline."*

Finding that he could not take the city so easily as he had imagined, Wallenstein sent a trumpeter to know if the defenders would treat with him upon terms. Lieut-Colonel Seton was glad of this offer, and an armistice of 14 days was agreed upon to draw up terms and ascertain the views of the King of Denmark on the subject. The treaty was just ready for signature, when orders came to Seton not to sign it, as troops were advancing with all haste for his relief. Shortly afterwards Lord Spynie with his regiment entered the town, and as he brought what the defenders were much in need of, a sufficient "provision of money and ammunition . . the treaty was rejected and made voide." At this time also an

---

* The sanguinary nature of the struggle, during the six weeks in which our regiment was employed in the defence of Stralsund, may be more easily imagined than described. Nearly "five hundred good men, besides officers, were killed, and of the remnant that escaped, both of officers and soldiers, not one hundred were free of wounds, received honourably in defence of the good cause." The siege lasted four months in all, and cost the Austrians upwards of 12,000 of their best soldiers. Notwithstanding this immense sacrifice they were compelled to retire, after spiking their cannon and setting fire to their baggage, so as to prevent any booty falling into the hands of the defenders.

agreement was entered into by the Kings of Denmark and Sweden by which the defence of Stralsund was undertaken by the latter. Sir Alexander Leslie was appointed Governor, and the forces employed by the King of Denmark were ordered to be withdrawn, and Swedish troops employed in their place.

The King of Denmark now made an attempt to secure for himself the province of Pomerania, and orders were given that Mackay's and Spynie's regiments should march from Stralsund to Wolgast, and join the Danish army there. The remnant of our regiment—it was only a remnant, for it was not 400 strong—was led by Captain Thomas Mackenzie, his superior officers being all disabled. The King decided to attack the Austrians, but his soldiers were no match for the Imperialists, and the greater part of his army was destroyed without ever coming to a regular engagement. Fearing that he might be taken prisoner, he resolved to embark for Denmark with the remainder of his troops; and as the enemy was pressing hard, he called upon Captain Mackenzie to take his regiment and keep the enemy in check, until the routed battalions were all shipped. Our regiment, we are told by Munro, "had got such a name for bravery that all the difficult and dangerous work" was allotted to it. Mackenzie did as his Majesty desired, and then got safely away himself with his soldiers, and sailed for Denmark in company with the King's ships.

On their way they met Lord Reay,* who had with him

---

* When home arranging for the recruits for his regiment, Sir Donald Mackay had visited London, and as a mark of appreciation of the services he had rendered in Denmark, the King [Charles I.] created him a Peer of Scotland, under the title of BARON REAY OF REAY, by patent dated 20th June, 1628.

over 1000 recruits for his regiment. Lord Reay's ships joined those of the King, and all sailed together for Copenhagen, where they arrived on the 9th of August. Lord Reay began at once to reorganise his regiment. Few of the band survived who had left Cromarty two years before, and the changes and promotions which were necessary in the various companies, made the task almost like forming a new regiment. When re-formed it consisted of 10 companies and numbered about 1500 men, besides officers and supernumeraries. This was a great reduction, in every way, when compared with the strength of the regiment when first embodied. Among the promotions I shall only mention that of Major Munro, who was appointed Lieut-Colonel, in place of Lieut-Colonel Seton.

The regiment being now thoroughly equipped received a month's pay, together with a settlement of all arrears, and as a security to Lord Reay for the payment of the money due to him, the King of Denmark gave him an "assignation on His Majestie of Great Britaine" for £4576 stg.* Leaving his regiment contented and in good quarters, Lord Reay returned to Scotland, taking with him Lieutenant Iye Mackay of his own company, and Captain John Munro.

But the services of the regiment under the King of

---

* It seems, however, that he had great difficulty in getting this money—indeed it is doubtful if he ever got the whole of it—and the payments on account were in small sums. After waiting three years he wrote (on 29th March, 1632), "his Majestie oweth me at present two thousand five hundred pounds," and begged that the Treasurer be authorised to pay him "the odd five hundred pounds to doe my present business . . . I am willing," he added, "not to presse the other two thousand pounds till God make an end of this triall."

Denmark came to an end sooner than had been expected. Preliminaries for a treaty of peace between that monarch and the Emperor of Austria had been agreed to in May, and in August, 1629, the treaty was signed. The terms were rather humiliating to the King; and one of the conditions was that the Scottish troops in his service were to quit Germany forthwith. Lieut.-Colonel Munro, on behalf of Lord Reay, settled for the companies which were under his command; the payment was on a liberal scale, and the King gave orders that shipping should be provided to convey the officers and men to Scotland, and also that until the ships were ready to sail the regiment should be furnished with free quarters at Elsinore. But the regiment did not return to Scotland. The war between Denmark and Austria certainly was ended, but the great struggle was only entering on its acute stage. While the Danes and the Austrians were arranging their treaty of peace, Lieut.-Colonel Munro, acting under instructions from Lord Reay, entered into negotiations with the King of Sweden for the services of the regiment; and the Swedish monarch, who had formed a high opinion of the Scots, was glad to secure the assistance of a corps which had made itself so famous. Conditions, satisfactory to all concerned, were agreed upon; and the regiment, immediately after it had been graciously dismissed by his "Majesty of Denmark and honestly rewarded," instead of returning to Scotland, entered on a new service in which it gained, if that were possible, even greater honours than it had achieved when serving the King of Denmark.*

---

* *The Administrative Staff* of the regiment when it entered the service of Sweden (and probably it was the same in that of Denmark), was composed of 21 members, viz: The Colonel,

The strength of the regiment when it entered the Swedish service, according to the official Military Lists, was two battalions of 1200 men each. As soon as the arrangements were completed, six companies, then at Elsinore, were in obedience to orders from Gustavus Adolphus despatched at once by Munro to Braunsburg in Prussia, where they remained for more than a year without being engaged in active service. Lord Reay arrived in Denmark in November, and gave instructions that six companies, which had been waiting in Holland for orders, should proceed from that country to Sweden. He remained in Denmark (where Lieut.-Colonel Munro joined him) till February, 1630, when both proceeded to Sweden to wait upon the King. His Majesty received them very graciously, and immediately after their arrival reviewed the six companies, expressing himself as so highly satisfied with the condition and discipline of the Highlanders, that he "did wish in open presence of the army that all his foot were as well disciplined." Lord Reay remained in Sweden with this division of his regiment, but Munro was directed to proceed to Braunsburg to take command of the six companies which were there.

Lieut.-Colonel, Major, Quarter-Master, 2 Chaplains, 4 Surgeons, a Regimental Judge, an Executioner, and 9 inferior officers (clerks, orderlies, &c.).

The Companies, of which there were 12, contained each 190 men of all ranks, including 1 Captain, 1 Lieutenant, 1 Ensign, 1 Armourer, 1 Muster Clerk, and 6 Drummers and Pipers.

The Pay of all ranks was very high when compared with the military allowances of the present day. For example (converting the Swedish money of 1630 into the British equivalent of 1890), the Colonel had £360, the Lieut.-Colonel £160, Major and Captains each £108, Lieutenants and Ensigns each £59 10s., Sergeants about £22, and Privates £8 6s. 3d., all *per month*.

It would occupy too much space to give even the briefest outline of the various engagements in which the regiment took a part while it served under the Swedish flag; but a few of them may be mentioned. The first service was with Gustavus Adolphus when he began his great campaign of 1630-1632. The Swedish army, led by the King in person, and numbering in all about 13,000 men, landed at Penemünde on the 24th June, 1630. Lord Reay, with the portion of his regiment which had remained in Sweden all winter, formed a part of this army. About a month after landing Stettin was taken. This was effected without bloodshed by Lord Reay and his men, on the 26th July. While the drawbridge was down Lord Reay secured the gate, whereupon "the Towne garrison retyred from thence within the port, and the Scots entering *pell mell* with them, the port was also taken. By this did the King presently enter the Towne, with his whole army." The Duke of Pomerania having thus lost his principal city, dismissed his garrison, "who thereupon took Oath and Pay for the King's service"; and Gustavus, on getting into Stettin, appointed a solemn thanksgiving for the easy victory which had been gained. The next work was the taking of Damm. But there was no resistance, and after the town had been taken possession of in the name of the King of Sweden, Lord Reay and his soldiers returned to Stettin. The siege of Colberg, where "Lord Reay led the valiant Scottish men of his owne nation," was the next service in which they were engaged. The siege lasted about four months, and ended by the garrison (who were without provisions) capitulating. When the Austrians quitted the post they had defended so well, the Highlanders were under arms to receive and salute them when they marched away.

The battalion which had been sent to Braunsburg, and was now under the command of Lieut.-Colonel Munro, got orders on the 12th of August to march to Pillau, and there embark for Wolgast. Two ships were chartered and started on their voyage, Munro with three companions being on board one of them—the "Lilly Nichol," while the other vessel—the "Hound" took Major Sennot and the remaining companies. During a gale the vessels got separated; the "Hound" reached her destination in safety, and the soldiers on board were sent to Stettin; but the "Lilly Nichol," after various mishaps, was wrecked near Rugenwalde, a town on the coast halfway between Stettin and Danzig. All on board got safely to land, excepting a sailor and one of the soldiers, who attempting to swim ashore were drowned. The only articles saved from the wreck were "swords, and pikes, and some wet muskets." The town was held by the Austrians, but Munro, by a bold stroke, secured both it and the castle for the Swedish King. The following is a German version of how this was accomplished:

"The bold and successful attack of the Scottish Colonel Munro has a tinge of romance about it. The ship on which several companies of Mackay's regiment were being conveyed from Prussia, was stranded in the neighbourhood of Rugenwalde. The soldiers lost their ammunition and baggage, and had only about 500 muskets and a few swords and pikes for their armament. But the courageous and determined Scot did not hesitate on that account to attempt to carry out the commission he had undertaken, when he was appointed to the command of these men. The governor of the castle was secretly a friend of Sweden, and Munro being informed of this, requested him to open a back gate for the

Scots to enter on the following night, when he doubted not that he would be able to drive out the Imperialists. Everything succeeded as was desired, and the town and castle were taken. . . . When the King of Sweden was informed of the great feat which Munro had accomplished, he said that he did not in the least doubt that the favour of God was clearly shown by the wonderful way in which this had been brought about."

Munro kept possession of Rugenwalde for nine weeks, and then, being relieved by Sir John Hepburn, was instructed to take possession of and defend the castle of Schiefelbein. This was an important position, and according to the *Swedish Intelligencer* Munro was selected for this work because his "men were knowne to be fortunate by their former taking of Rugenwaldt, and valiant too by their bravery in other services." But I need not lengthen out the story. After the taking of Colberg, Lord Reay returned with his men to Stettin, and shortly afterwards Munro was ordered to join the head-quarters with his three companies. When united, the regiment, although it consisted of 12 companies, had only about 1,200 men, or half its strength. On his way to Stettin, Munro met Lord Reay by appointment at Greifenburg. His Lordship was proceeding to Great Britain under a new commission from the King, not only to raise men to complete the ranks of his own regiment, but to raise several new ones for the Swedish service. He did not again take any personal part in the campaign, but remained in Great Britain, doing good service, however, for the King of Sweden by executing the commissions with which he had been entrusted. He sent over the recruits for his own regiment, bringing it up to its full strength; and raised another regiment of Scots, to which he appointed field officers from his own regiment. Other regiments in England and in Scotland were likewise raised under the authority he held from the King of Sweden ; and in addition he secured the services of a regiment which was to act as a Body-Guard to his Majesty.*

During the latter part of 1630, the plague raged in Stettin. According to the Swedish Lists 285 men of our regiment were ill of this disease at the end of the year, and "divers brave souldiers died."

In January, 1631, Gustavus Adolphus, "the Lion of the North," as he was designated, made preparations for the campaign which virtually decided the fate of Germany, and the Protestant religion. Lord Reay's regiment had its share in the honours of this war, but it got also more than an average share of the hard knocks which were given in the struggle. Having at this time been reinforced by the recruits which his Lordship had sent out from Scotland, it consisted of 16 companies (2 battalions), and numbered 2,400 men. [In 1631 the King of Sweden had eight Scottish regiments in his service, with a total strength of 12,600 men.] Before starting on the campaign the King formed what was known as THE SCOTS BRIGADE. It consisted of four regiments, and from the tartan of the Highlanders, and the colour of the doublets and standards of the other regiments, it was commonly called *The Green Brigade*.

---

* "Mackay, our countryman, is in great honour," wrote James Baird, the Commissary, to his brother, from Edinburgh, 17th March, 1631, "and is General over three regiments, and Captain of the King of Sweden's Guards, quhilk consist of an hundred horse and an hundred foot, *and sall be all Scottismen*. '[AN ACCOUNT OF THE SURNAME OF BAIRD, p. 63, Edinburgh, 1857.]

A movement of the Swedish troops was made towards the Oder; but the Austrians in great force, under General Tilly, were also on the move, and laid seige to New Brandenburg, in which about 1000 of Lord Reay's men, under Lieut.-Col. Lindsay, and an equal number of Swedes, under General Kniphausen, had been left as a garrison. The town was in a wretched condition for defence, the walls being in ruins; and there were only two small guns as the whole artillery of the defenders. Tilly had with him about 22,000 men and 26 guns, and beset the town on all sides. He summoned the garrison to surrender. They refused, and for nine days made a desperate and heroic resistance. Worn out, and seeing no chance of succour, they at last asked for terms, but Tilly now refused to give them any quarter. Then followed the last assault, and after a dreadful struggle the town was taken. A merciless slaughter was the result. The fury of the Austrians was directed chiefly against our countymen; and on that memorable day (26th March, 1631) over 600 of Lord Reay's Highlanders were cut to pieces. Five officers and a few soldiers were taken prisoners; two officers escaped by leaping from the walls, and making their way across country were fortunately able to join Munro; but all the other officers, including Lieut.-Colonel Lindsay, were killed.*

The news of this terrible disaster reached the Scots Brigade while the Swedish army was on its way to lay seige to Frankfort on the Oder, and filled the whole camp with

---

* "Half Lord Reay's Regiment was here massacred almost to a man. Lieut.-Colonel Lindsay, who commanded this corps in his colonel's absence, was killed in the breach, as were also Moncrieff, Keith, and Haydon—all Scots." [Harte's Life of Gustavus, Vol. I., p. 275 [

horror, but especially the six companies of the Reays, which were under the command of Lieut.-Colonel Munro. This Frankfort was a rich and strongly fortified town, and had a garrison of about 10,000 men. Lord Reay's and Hepburn's regiments took the leading part in the assault* which led to the capture of the town. This was on Sunday, the 3rd April, 1631. There was a desperate resistance, and inch by inch, every foot of the way was contested. "Quarter!" cried the slowly retreating Austrians. "New Brandenburg! New Brandenburg!" shouted the Scottish soldiers. Shoulder to shoulder, Highlander and Lowlander advanced like moving castles, the long pikes levelled in front, while the rear ranks of musketeers fired in volleys from behind. It was a dreadful retribution,—40 officers and about 3000 soldiers of the Austrian army were left dead in the streets; 50 colours were taken, and an immense quantity of treasure. The Swedish loss was about 800 men, and of this number 300 belonged to the Scots Brigade. No wilful injury was done to the town, and as soon as order was restored, the King appointed a day of thanksgiving to be observed for the victory.

Many towns and strongholds fell before the victorious Swedish army. In May it rendezvoused in the the neighbourhood of Berlin, and remained in that quarter till the end of July. About the middle of August a large number of recruits, sent out by Lord Reay, arrived at Stettin, and under the command of Lieut.-Colonel John Munro, joined the regiment

---

* Before the attack began, the King, addressing the Scottish leaders said, "Now, my valiant Scots, remember your countrymen who were slain at New Brandenburg." [Harte's Life of Gustavus, Vol. I., p. 279.]

at Wittenburg. But I shall pass over the services of the regiment (although it took part in many important engagements) until the 7th of September, when the great battle of Leipzig —"the most remarkable battle recorded in history"—was fought. The result of the battle was a severe defeat to the Austrians, and their retreat from the battlefield was described as being like a race for life. Tilly was wounded; but he escaped, leaving many of his best officers dead on the field, and "full 15,000 of his men were slaine upon the place of battle or in the chase." Gustavus had a little over 4,000 Scottish soldiers in his army on this occasion, and they did the bulk of the fighting. Of the Mackay regiment about 1,300 were present. They formed the leading column, and had "the honour of first breaking the Austrian ranks. The Imperialists regarded them with terror, calling them *the invincible old regiment*, and the "right hand of Gustavus Adolphus." I do not know what loss our regiment sustained, but it must have been heavy, for two weeks after the battle the strength of the first battalion is returned as 600 strong "and 600 wanting."

The victorious army marched towards the Rhine, and before the end of the month all the towns between Leipzig and Würzburg had surrendered to the King; then Frankfort on the Maine, Oppenheim and Mayence were taken. The last-named, the most strongly fortified city in Germany, surrendered after a three days' siege, and redeemed itself from pillage by paying a large ransom—300,000 dollars—but our countrymen did not get any share of the money, and Munro made some strong observations thereanent, to the effect that the Scots had on many occasions to endure all the hard knocks, while to the Swedes and Germans were given all the plums. The next important engagement was the battle of the Lech, where on the 5th April the famous Austrian general, Tilly, was wounded, and died three days afterwards. Then the progress of the Swedish army was an uninterrupted series of successes, and in a short time the whole of Bavaria, as far as the capital, lay open to Gustavus. On the 6th May the victorious troops halted before Munich. Lord Reay's Highlanders were the first to enter, and their appearance spread terror among the citizens; but the leading men had faith in the magnanimity of the conqueror, and received Gustavus and his army with all due respect. Only the Scottish regiments were permitted to have their quarters within the walls; and to the Mackays was entrusted the honourable duty of being body-guard to the King during the three weeks they were in the Bavarian capital. But Wallenstein, who had succeeded Tilly as Commander-in-chief of the Austrian army, was marching towards Nürnberg, and Gustavus Adolphus, in order to checkmate him, left Munich and proceeded in the same direction. Both armies encamped in the neighbourhood of the city. Wallenstein had a force of about 60,000 men, and Gustavus, though at first he had only about 18,000 men, before the end of July had probably nearly as many as Wallenstein. From the end of June till the middle of August, the two armies lay in sight of each other without coming to a regular engagement. It seemed to be a game of masterly inactivity on both sides, and the question was—which could hold out the longest. Provisions were exhausted, and it was impossible to obtain supplies. It was necessary that decisive steps should be taken, and on the 22nd of August, the long expected battle may be said to have begun. The fighting, which continued for three days, was of the most desperate character, and ended in a drawn battle. No less than 10,000 citizens and 20,000 soldiers were left dead in and around the devoted city. Both armies remained in their respective positions till the 14th September, when Gustavus, leaving 5,000 men in Nürnberg, retired with the remainder of his forces towards the south, and Wallenstein, as soon as he discovered that Gustavus had marched away, also took his departure, marching however towards the north, and burning all the villages that were near.

The heavy losses sustained by the Scots Brigade had so reduced its numbers that the King, at the end of September, gave orders that it should go into quarters to rest and wait for recruits. On the 11th of October he took leave of what was left of the gallant Scottish regiments, in view of the whole army, and thanked them for their services. They never saw their great leader again, for in less than a month (on the 6th November, 1632) he was found dead on the battlefield of Lützen.* It is remarkable that the battle of Lützen was the only one in which he had engaged the enemy without the mass of his Scottish troops. Several

---

* The death of Gustavus Adolphus was a mystery. His body was found on the battlefield, and it was reported that no one saw him killed. But in the Archives at Marburg I found a document giving a circumstantial account of his murder. The witness of the deed had one of his legs shot off shortly before the foul act was committed, and was unable to move or render assistance. The murderer is believed to have been the Duke of Lauenburg, who had a grudge against the King, and had sworn to be revenged. [See article on this subject by the present writer, in *The Scottish Review*, Vol. XIX., p. 400.]

Scottish officers, however, were with him, and among those who were killed was Colonel William Mackay (son of Donald of Scourie) who had been a captain in Lord Reay's regiment. But although the King was slain, victory remained with the Swedish army, for Wallenstein was totally defeated, and forced to retreat to the mountains of Bohemia.

There is little more to say regarding the services of the Mackay regiment. After the death of Gustavus, Lord Reay ceased to take any active interest in it, and in the month of December, 1632, his name disappears from the Swedish army list. Lieut.-Colonel Munro was promoted to the rank of Colonel, and the regiment then became known under the name of its commander, as *Munro's regiment*. Munro, desirous of having the regiment made up to its full strength, left for Scotland in July, 1633, to procure recruits. At this date it numbered only about 240 men; but recruits arriving from time to time, the ranks got well filled up, and within a year it numbered 12 companies with a total strength of about 1,800 men. On the 26th August, 1634, the terrible battle of Nordlingen was fought. The loss of life was dreadful; and of our regiment, out of its 1,800 men, scarcely sufficient were left to form one company. Of the whole Scots Brigade not more than 200 men came out of the sanguinary conflict.

After the battle of Nordlingen, the regiment as a separate corps, ceased to exist; and the one company to which it had been reduced was placed, with the remnants of the other Scottish regiments, under the command of Duke Bernard of Saxe Weimar. In the following year an arrangement was come to between Sweden and France, by which the Scottish troops were taken into the pay of the latter country. Sir

John Hepburn, when he resigned his commission in the Swedish service,* entered that of France, and it was under him (to many of them their old leader) that these troops were to serve. A new regiment was organised and named after its commander, *le Regiment d' Hebron*—Hepburn's Regiment. It represented in its ranks many corps; the remnant of Hepburn's own old regiment, the one remaining company of Mackay's Highlanders, all the other Scottish regiments of Gustavus, and the Scottish Archer Guards of the French Kings. Probably it was the latter circumstance that led the King of France to order that it should take precedence of all other regiments in his service. Hepburn was killed at the battle of Saverne in 1636, and the regiment then became known as *le Regiment de Douglas*, from the name of its new colonel. It bore this designation till 1678, when it was incorporated in the British army as *Dumbarton's Regiment*, after its next colonel. In 1684 it was designated the *Royal Regiment*, and is now known as the ROYAL SCOTS. It is probably the oldest regiment in Europe, and takes precedence of all other regiments of the line in the British army. As the "one remaining company" of Mackay's regiment formed a part of *le Regiment d' Hebron*, when it was made up in 1635, I claim that our regiment is now represented by the Royal Scots.†

From first to last Lord Reay sent over to "the German wars" upwards of 10,000 men, and as Munro expressed it,

---

* He had quarrelled with the King on some religious question.

† This regiment has had the following titles:—

Le Regiment d' Hebron,	1633—1636.
Le Regiment de Douglas,	1636—1678.
Dumbarton's Regiment, ...	1678—1684.

"our noble colonell did engage his estates and adventure his person," not with a sordid view of gain, but "for the good cause." To meet the debts he had thus contracted he was obliged to sell his lands in Ross-shire and Caithness, then his hereditary sheriffship of Strathnaver (this to the Crown for £1000), and last and saddest of all, what was the pride of the Mackay country—the beautiful and fertile district of Strathnaver.

II.—FENCIBLE REGIMENTS.

FOUR of these regiments were raised in the county, and finer bodies of men were never brought together in any part of the United Kingdom. Three bore the title "Sutherland" Fencibles, and the other was designated the "Reay" Fencibles. The services of all the Fencible regiments were restricted to military duty in Great Britain and Ireland.

THE SUTHERLAND FENCIBLES.

1. THE 1ST SUTHERLAND FENCIBLE REGIMENT was raised in 1759. William, Earl of Sutherland, was Colonel, and the Hon. Hugh Mackay, son of Lord Reay, Lieutenant-

The Royal Regiment, ...	1684–1751.
1st or The Royal Regiment, ...	1751–1812.
1st or The Royal Scots, ...	1812–1821.
1st or The Royal Regiment, ...	1821–1871.
1st or The Royal Scots, ...	1871–1881.
The Lothian Regiment—The Royal Scots, ...	1881 -

Colonel. The Royal Warrant authorised the enrolling of 1000 men, but about 1500 assembled at the call of the Earl within nine days after his Lordship had arrived in the north with his letters of service. Of course only 1000 could be taken, and the disappointment of many was great when they found they were not wanted. Numbers returned to their homes, but the more hardy and determined followed on to Perth (where the regiment was to muster), and insisted on being with their chief. The military authorities in Edinburgh were consulted, and the result was that permission was given to add another company of 100 men to the regiment. It thus became 1100 strong. "The martial appearance of these men when they marched into Perth in May, 1760, with the Earl at their head, was never forgotten by those who saw them," for over 200 of them were about 6 feet in height, and formed two grenadier flank companies. Their service was entirely confined to barrack duty in Scotland, and during the four years in which they were together, no one was punished in the regiment. It was disbanded in 1763.

Rob Donn, the celebrated Mackay bard, joined the regiment when it was formed, and remained with it during the four years it was embodied. He was rather a privileged character, and was not asked to do duty excepting in a way that left him very much master of his own time. He was, in fact, bard of the regiment, and while his companions were at drill, he was at liberty.

2.—THE 2ND SUTHERLAND FENCIBLE REGIMENT was raised in 1779. The Earl of Sutherland having died shortly before, and his only child being an infant girl, William Wemyss of Wemyss, nephew of the Earl, was appointed

Colonel, and Nicholas Sutherland, Lieut.-Colonel. The regiment was 1000 strong. Two companies came from Caithness, but all the others were raised in Sutherlandshire. The services of this regiment, like that of the 1st Sutherland Fencibles, was simply doing barrack duty in Scotland. It was disbanded in 1783.

3.—THE 3RD SUTHERLAND FENCIBLE REGIMENT. This corps was commanded by Colonel Wemyss of Wemyss, who had been Colonel of the last mentioned regiment; and the Hon. James Stewart, son of the Earl of Moray, was Lieut.-Colonel. It was raised in 1793, and when embodied was over 1000 strong. There was one Ross-shire company, of which Macleod of Cadboll was Captain. After being stationed in Edinburgh for some time, it was sent to Ireland, but, with the exception of some rapid marches, and one skirmish with the rebels, the men had no opportunity of showing their prowess in the field. When the troubles were over the regiment returned to Scotland, and was disbanded at Fort-George in 1798.

Samuel MacDonald, commonly called "Big Sam," was a Sergeant in this regiment. He was 6 feet 10 inches in height, strongly built, muscular, and well proportioned. His strength was enormous, but he was never known to abuse it. He joined the 93rd when it was raised, and died at Guernsey while the regiment was stationed there, in May, 1802. A full length figure of "big Sam" is given in Kay's "Edinburgh Portraits." From his great size, the Countess of Sutherland thought that he required a larger amount of food, &c., than men of ordinary stature, and gave him an allowance in addition to his regimental pay.

General Stewart in his "Sketches" gave currency to an error when he stated there were "104 *William* Mackays in this regiment . . . and 17 in one company." The Muster-Roll shows that there were in all 211 Mackays, including 7 officers, in the regiment; and out of this number 16 only had the Christian name *William*. With a strength of 1084 men of all ranks, the leading names were as follows: Mackay, 211; Sutherland, 128; Murray, 42; Ross, 34; Macleod, 29; Macdonald, 29; Munro, 28. The clan names in the 1st and 2nd Regiments were in almost identical proportions.

THE REAY FENCIBLES.

The Royal Warrant for raising this regiment was dated 24th October, 1794. Colonel Mackay Hugh Baillie, a military officer of note and experience, and a near kinsman of Hugh, Lord Reay, the then chief of the Mackays, was selected to command the regiment, and George Mackay of Handa (afterwards designated of Bighouse) was appointed Lieutenant-Colonel. The strength of the regiment was fixed at 800 men, and a few weeks sufficed to obtain the required number. When placed on the Establishment (18th June, 1795) it consisted of 46 officers and 754 non-commissioned officers and men, and of these 11 officers and 209 rank and file were Mackays, while 381 had the honourable Gaelic prefix "Mac" to their names. The uniform of the regiment was similar to that of the 42nd. Scarlet coat with dark blue facings and silver lace, and kilt of Mackay tartan.

The regiment was inspected at Fort George in March 1795, and after being drilled, uniformed, and armed, was ordered to Ireland, where the steady conduct and soldierly bearing of the men soon attracted the notice of Generals Lake and Nugent, commanding in that country. The service of the regiment, which had been stationed in Belfast and neighbourhood, was of an uneventful and routine character until 1798, when the rebellion broke out and assumed formidable proportions. The object of the rising was to bring about the separation of Ireland from Britain, and for this purpose the conspirators had been promised substantial aid from France. A day had been fixed when Ireland was to rise in arms, but the scheme had been made known to the Government, and many of the leaders were arrested. Those who escaped determined that a general insurrection should take place, and the 23rd of May was fixed upon for that event. It was under these circumstances that the Reays were moved from Belfast to Cavan, and then to Dublin. The battle of Tara-hill was fought on the 26th of May, 1798. In this engagement the rebels had a force of about 4000 men, while the Government had only the Reays, less than 800 strong, and two troops of yeomanry. The rebels were well posted on the top of the hill, protected by old walls and other shelter, which gave them a great advantage, but the Reays marched boldly on and gradually fought their way up, when, reaching the top, notwithstanding the great odds against them, they furiously charged the rebels with the bayonet, tumbling them over at every stroke, and eventually dispersed and chased them off the hill. The yeomanry then charged the retreating masses, who fled panic stricken and in disorder. The loss of the Reays was 30 killed and a considerable number wounded. The rebels had about 500 killed, besides many wounded. It was a complete victory, and the battle broke the back of the rebellion. After this engagement the Reays marched to Dublin, where they met with a hearty reception from the citizens.

But the troubles were not quite ended. On the 22nd August a French force of about 1,300 men landed at Killala. General Lake, hearing of this, hastened with two regiments of Irish Militia, the Fraser Fencibles, and some dragoons, to resist the advance. The Reays at the same time were ordered to Tuam, to keep in check the rebels in the west. General Lake encountered the Frenchmen near Castlebar. The French began the attack and soon threw the Militia into disorder, and they, in retiring, threw the Frasers into disorder, so that the whole gave way, and the French soldiers, still advancing, Lake was forced to retire. Overwhelmed with grief at the unsteady and cowardly conduct of the militia (many of whom went over to the enemy), he was frequently heard to exclaim, "If I had my brave and honest Reays with me, this would not have happened." The Irish insurgents and their French auxiliaries had everything in their own hands for a few days, and they began an indiscriminate slaughter of the Protestants and Loyalists of Castlebar. But Lake, who had fallen back on Tuam, had re-formed his army, and this done, he determined to attack the Frenchmen. On this occasion he took his "honest Reays" with him. After four days march his advance troops got up to and skirmished with the French, bringing them to a halt. General Lake soon afterwards appeared with the troops under his immediate command, and then all resistance on the part of the Frenchmen ceased ;

COLOURS OF THE REAY FENCIBLES.
(Now preserved in St. Giles' Church, Edinburgh.)

they laid down their arms and surrendered unconditionally; and the Reays had the honour of conducting them as prisoners of war to Dublin. Few Irish were taken, for when they saw the Frenchmen laying down their arms, they threw their own away and fled to the hills. This practically ended the rebellion, and comparative tranquility was restored to Ireland. The Reays were afterwards quartered in various towns for about four years; and in 1802 the regiment was ordered home to Scotland. It embarked at Belfast on the 10th September, and landing at Stranraer marched to Stirling, where, on the 26th of that month, General Baillie gave his parting address to the officers and men, paying high compliments to both, for their loyalty, good discipline, and distinguished gallantry. The regiment was disbanded on the 13th October, 1802.

One of the sergeants of the Reays became famous among "The Men" of Sutherland. This was Joseph Mackay. He served with the regiment until it was disbanded, and afterwards entered the 1st Foot or Royal Scots, and got a commission as Ensign. He was wounded at Waterloo, and returning to his native parish, devoted the remainder of his life—about 40 years—to evangelistic work in the Highlands. Many stories are told of his piety and benevolence; and the few old people left in the Reay country still speak with the greatest reverence of Ensign Joseph.

I cannot do better, in bringing this short story of the Reay Fencibles to an end, than quote what Mr. Mackay, Hereford, says in the closing part of his account of the services of the regiment: "They were an honour to their race and to their country, descendants of men who always bravely held their own, and defended their territory against

GENERAL SIR JOHN A. EWART, K.C.B,
93rd Sutherland Highlanders.

great odds . . and who remained ever loyal to their Sovereigns, and repeatedly performed great services to the State. . . . They produced heroes and warriors . . . whose fame will remain in the story of their country, and on the Continent of Europe. In Ireland, as has been shown, they exhibited many proofs of the valour of their race, and eminently manifested that they were the genuine sons of the valiant Mackays of the North."

III.—THE 93RD OR SUTHERLAND HIGHLANDERS.*

THE 93rd or Sutherland Highlanders, now known as the Second Battalion Princess Louise's Argyll and Sutherland Highlanders, was, at one time, considered the most Highland of the Highland regiments. It was raised on a "Letter of Service" granted in May, 1800, to General William Wemyss of Wemyss, (the same who had commanded the 2nd and 3rd regiments of Sutherland Fencibles) and was at first known as "General Wemyss' Regiment of Infantry," because no number had been assigned to it. The strength was fixed at 600 men, but was augmented to 1000, with

---

* I am largely indebted to General Sir John Ewart's interesting volumes "The Story of a Soldier's Life" for several of the incidents mentioned in this sketch. The various histories of the 93rd have also been consulted, and I have made free use of Colonel Percy Grove's volume, which is the most recently published account of the regiment.

officers in proportion. In 1811 it numbered 1049 officers and men, of whom 1014 were Scots, 18 English, and 17 Irish.

A striking peculiarity in the raising of this regiment, was, that the original levy was made by a species of conscription, and not by the ordinary mode of recruiting. It was in this

PLACE AT SYRE WHERE THE STRATHNAVER MEN WERE ENLISTED IN THE 93RD.

way: A census having been taken of the population on the estates of the Countess of Sutherland, her agents requested that a certain proportion of the able bodied sons of the tenants should join the ranks, as a test of their duty to the chief and to the Sovereign. The appeal was well responded to, and in a few months the regiment was completed.

Naturally some of the parents grumbled at the taking away of their sons, but the young men themselves never seem to have questioned the right thus assumed by their chief over their military services. The levy was made up to a considerable extent of men who had served in the 3rd Sutherland Fencibles, which had been disbanded about two years previously, and many of the men, as well as the non-commissioned officers, were the sons of highly respectable farmers. The officers were mostly well known gentlemen connected with Sutherland and the adjacent counties. The whole body of 600 men, without a single absentee, assembled in Inverness in the Month of August, and during their stay in the Highland capital they were so orderly and well behaved that no place of confinement was required in connection with the regiment. In September it received its number, and was entered in the Army List as the 93rd. In this month it also embarked at Fort George for Guernsey, where it was for the first time armed and fully equipped. It remained in Guernsey till September 1802, and was then ordered to Scotland to be reduced; but in consequence of the renewal of war with France, the order for reduction was countermanded, and instead of being disbanded, the regiment was sent to Aberdeen. In February 1803 it was removed to Ireland, and in August 1805, it embarked at Cork, for the Cape of Good Hope. It formed with the 71st and 72nd regiments, the Highland Brigade which was under the command of Brigadier General Ferguson.

In landing at Table Bay the 93rd lost 35 men by the upsetting of a boat in the surf. Its first engagement was in the battle of Blue Mountains. This was a decisive victory, for the enemy were completely routed with a loss of upwards

of 600 in killed and wounded. The British loss was 16 killed
and 191 wounded: of this number the 93rd had 2 men killed
and 5 officers and 53 men wounded. The regiment remained
8 years at the Cape, when to the general regret of the colony,
it embarked in 1814 for England, and arrived at Plymouth on
the 15th August. Of the 1018 non-commissioned officers
and men who disembarked, 977 were Scots. During all the
time the regiment was at the Cape, "the men conducted
themselves in so sedate and orderly a fashion that . . .
severe punishment was unnecessary, and so rare was the
commission of crime that 12 and even 15 months have been
known to elapse without a single court-martial being assembled
for the trial of any soldier of the 93rd."

It had not been many weeks at home until it was again
ordered on foreign service, and on the 16th September it
sailed for North America, the United States, at that time,
being unfortunately at war with Great Britain. The expedition, of which they formed a part, had for its object the
reduction of New Orleans. This was a disastrous and grossly
mismanaged undertaking; and "the gallant 93rd lost a larger
number of officers and men in it, in a few hours, than it did
throughout the whole of the Indian Mutiny campaign," in
which it had probably hotter work to do than ever fell to the
lot of any single regiment. The siege of New Orleans, as it
was called, was a miserable failure, not on the part of the
troops, but through the incapacity or want of understanding
of the general officers; and it is sad to think that neither gain
nor glory resulted from the dreadful carnage. One illustration will suffice. "The 93rd, led by Lieut.-Colonel Dale (he
was killed in the engagement), were advancing in close
column towards the centre of the enemy's line, exposed to a

tremendous fire of grape and musketry, when within 100 yards of the breastwork they were ordered to a halt. In this miserable position they had to stand, being neither allowed to advance nor retire . . while they were being mowed down by the murderous artillery and rifle balls." General Lambert at last ordered the regiment to retire, but only a fragment of the 93rd was left, for 6 officers and 120 men had been killed (including those who died of their wounds the following day); and 12 officers and 363 men wounded.

After this disastrous action it was decided to abandon any further attempts on New Orleans. Colonel Groves, in his History of the Regiment, says, "the splendid courage and steadiness of the 93rd Highlanders on the 8th January, 1815, elicited the admiration, not only of their fellow soldiers, but of the enemy: indeed, had all the regiments exhibited similar devotion and discipline, New Orleans might never have been numbered among British defeats."*

Peace being established between Great Britain and the United States, the troops were shortly afterwards ordered to embark and sail for England. The fragment which was left of the 93rd arrived at Spithead on the 15th May, 1815, but

---

* This great disaster was occasioned by the culpable neglect of the Lieut-Colonel of the 44th regiment, to carry out instructions which he had received on the previous night, to take his men forward with scaling ladders, for an assault which was intended to be made on the enemy's works. The 93rd had been selected for this perilous task. When advancing at daybreak, and near the breast work, it was discovered that there were no ladders, the regiment was called to a halt. This made their presence known to the enemy, who poured merciless showers of grape and rifle balls upon the almost defenceless Highlanders, and literally mowed them down, as stated above.

being in too weak a state to take part in the stirring events on the Continent, it was ordered to Ireland.

A second battalion had been added in 1813. In 1814 it embarked for Newfoundland, under command of Wm. Wemyss, a son of General Wemyss. After a little over a year's service, the battalion returned home, and on the 24th December, 1815, was disbanded at Sunderland, when 30 sergeants, 23 corporals, 11 drummers, and 303 privates were drafted to the first battalion.

The 93rd did not take part in any event of importance for many years. From Ireland it was sent to the West Indies in 1823, and after ten years returned to England. In 1838 it was sent to Canada, and remained in that colony about ten years. Between 1844 and 1848 it was stationed in Montreal and Quebec, and I have heard old people, in both towns, speak most highly of the regiment, the exemplary conduct of the men being warmly praised. On the 27th July, 1848, it embarked at Quebec for Leith, where it landed on the 31st of August, and was at once sent to Stirling. From Stirling it was removed to Edinburgh, where it was stationed one year, then in Glasgow one year, and in 1852 it was sent to England.

In 1854, being then stationed in Plymouth, the regiment received notice, in consequence of the threatening aspect of affairs in the East, to hold itself in readiness to embark on active service It was then on the peace establishment, and in order to bring it up to its proper strength, volunteers were called for, when 170 fine seasoned soldiers from the 42nd and 79th responded to the call. The regiment sailed for Malta on the 22nd February, and landed on the 8th of March. The total strength which embarked was 27 officers and 911 non-commissioned officers and men. The news of the declaration of war with Russia reached Malta on the 4th of April, and on the 6th the 93rd sailed for Turkey.

The services of the 93rd during the Crimean war* and Indian mutiny are of such recent occurrence, that I shall not attempt to give an account of these struggles, but merely narrate a few incidents in which the regiment took a prominent part.

On the 14th September, 1854, the 93rd landed in the Crimea. The 42nd, 79th, and 93rd regiments had been formed into the Highland Brigade, the command of which was given to Sir Colin Campbell (afterwards Lord Clyde). Six days after landing, the battle of the Alma was fought. The Highland Brigade struck terror into the hearts of the Russians. To their superstitious eyes "the strange uniforms

---

* The Crimean war began in this way. A Russian army having entered Turkey and attacked some of the Provinces, Great Britain and France entered into an alliance to defend the territory of the Sultan, and declared war against Russia. The allies were afterwards joined by Sardinia. War was declared on the 28th March, 1854; the struggle lasted about two years; and peace was proclaimed on 29th April, 1856. The vastness of the undertaking was not at first realised, and Great Britain began by calling out an army of 10,000 men for the struggle; but this number was soon found to be far short of what would be needed, and it had to be augmented from time to time, until about 100,000 men were embodied, of which number 70,000 were sent to the Crimea. The British losses during the campaign were 3,532 killed or died of their wounds, and 15,782 who succumbed to disease, making a total loss of life of 19,134.

France sent 309,268 men, and lost 82,133; while the Russian loss was stated to be about 500,000, of whom 90,000 lay buried on the ensanguined heights of Sebastopol.

of those bare-kneed troops seemed . . terrible; their white waving sporrans were taken for the heads of low horses, and they cried to each other that the angel of death had departed, and that the demon of death had come." In this engagement the 93rd had 1 officer and 7 rank and file killed, and 44 rank and file wounded.

The conduct of the 93rd at Balaclava has received universal praise. This was just a month after the battle of the Alma. The regiment was formed in line—that is, front and rear rank. "I would not even form them four deep," said Sir Colin Campbell, when remonstrated with for not placing them so as to be able to throw themselves into a square, when the Russian cavalry was galloping towards them. There they stood, "that thin red line, tipped with steel," awaiting the onslaught of the Russian dragoons, the ground trembling beneath their horses' feet, and gathering strength at every stride. The Highlanders stood cool as if on parade, until their foes were within 600 yards, then down on their knees dropped the front rank, and delivered a steady volley. But the distance was too great, and though a few saddles were emptied, the Russians pressed forward unchecked. On they rode till scarcely 200 yards separated them from the intrepid Highlanders; then the rear-rank men brought their rifles to the present, and over the heads of their comrades poured a withering fire into the enemy's masses. Shaken to their very centre, the Russian dragoons fell back; but they made one more bid for victory, and encouraged by their leaders, endeavoured to turn the Highlanders' right flank. But they were checkmated by the Grenadier company, which received them with such a volley that they wheeled about and rushed off to seek the shelter of their guns. The 93rd is the only Infantry

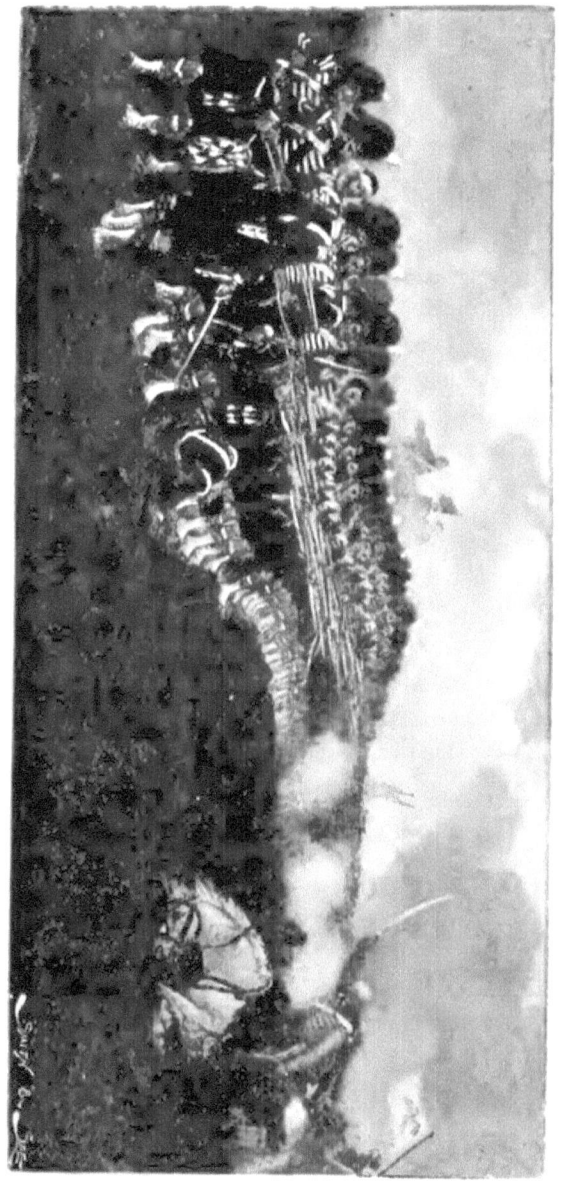

THE "THIN RED LINE" AT BALACLAVA.

regiment in the British army which has the word "Balaclava" on its colours.

During the siege of Sebastopol the 93rd had its full share of dangerous and harassing duties. On the 8th September, 1855, the second grand assault was made, but the stronghold was not taken. The Highland Brigade was then moved forward to occupy the advanced trenches, so as to be ready if the enemy should make a sortie. About midnight, when everything was quiet, Lieutenant MacBean left the trenches, and approaching the Redan was struck with the idea from the stillness which prevailed, that the Russians had deserted it. He returned to the trenches, saw Sir Colin Campbell, and obtained permission to enter, if he could get 2 officers and 20 men to volunteer to accompany him. He got the officers and men, and with them entered the Redan, but finding the work apparently unoccupied, hastened back to Sir Colin with the news. General Ewart, in his "Story of a Soldier's Life," gives the following account (he was then a Major in the 93rd). He did not know what prompted him, but he determined to follow the little party to the Redan : "Just as I arrived they were re-crossing the ditch. . . I at once stopped two of the 93rd named Peter Mackay* and John White, and asked if they would mind again entering the

---

* At the close of the Crimean war, the Emperor of France presented a few military medals to each British regiment which had taken part in the campaign. These medals were exclusively for non-commissioned officers or privates, the only exception being some general officer who had held some special command. [The Duke of Cambridge is the only British officer to whom it was granted by the Emperor.] To the 93rd nine medals were given, and it was a great honour to be selected to be one of the recipients.

Redan. They said "No," so they descended the ditch, and scrambled up the other side. All was perfectly quiet, but I could not help thinking that possibly some trap was being laid, so proceeded cautiously to search whether any Russians were lying in ambush . . but the Redan appeared to be untenanted." On returning to the advanced trench Major Ewart at once went to Sir Colin Campbell, who was glad to receive a confirmation of the report which had been made to him by MacBean. While they were talking, an Engineer officer came up and requested that, as the Redan had been found deserted, it might be immediately occupied by the Highlanders. But this the old general declined; "and the wisdom of his refusing was shortly afterwards made manifest by a tremendous explosion taking place in the work." A trap had been laid by the Russians. Had the place been occupied probably all within would have been killed The evacuation of the Redan by the Russians rendered any further assault unnecessary. Sebastopol was in possession of the allies, and the war was practically at an end.

While waiting at Varna and Aladja, in July and August, for orders, cholera, fever, and dysentry raged in the camp, and large numbers of soldiers died,—416 men of the 93rd having been in the regimental hospital, and in the Crimea,

---

Private Peter Mackay, above-mentioned, was awarded one—" for bravery, and for being the first man to enter the Redan on the night of the 8th September, 1855." The other soldiers of the regiment, who, for special acts of bravery, were selected for the honour, were: Colour-Sergeant Alexander Knox, Sergeant Archibald Crabtree, Sergeant James Kiddie, Lance-Corporal William Mackenzie; and Privates John Leslie, John Forbes, James Davidson, and James Cobb.

during the first winter, the regiment suffered severely. "Only those who lived through those dreary days," wrote Dr. Munro, "know what it was to be without proper shelter and clothing, and without sufficient food and fuel, while cold keen winds blew, and rain and snow beat down upon the earth, converting it into a sea of mud, through which we had to wade with half shod feet. . . . The tents afforded poor protection against the piercing cold, the boisterous wind, and the rain : and our clothes, of which at one time we had not even a change, became so worn and filthy" that it was almost impossible to wear them. Until the 30th November many officers and men had only the clothes they had on when they landed on the 14th September. The daily dole of salt beef and pork was left untasted, because the men would not, or could not eat, or because they had no fuel, or did not know how to cook so as to make the food palatable. . . The consequence was that numbers of them became ill and many died of dysentry. It was not till February, 1855, that anything was done to remedy this miserable state of affairs. The men were then hutted, and the health of the regiment materially improved. The second winter the health of the men was good, excepting for a short time in December, when cholera re-appeared. But in March, 1856, peace was proclaimed, and on the 16th June the 93rd embarked for England. The regiment landed at Portsmouth on the 15th July, and proceeded to Aldershot, where, on the following day it was reviewed by Her Majesty. It was then moved to Dover, and was joined there by the depôts from Malta and Dundee.

The red doublets of the pipers were at this time exchanged for green.

On the 31st January, 1857, the regiment was ordered to prepare for immediate embarkation for India, and as its strength had just been reduced to a peace footing, volunteers were called for from the 42nd, 72nd, 79th, and 92nd regiments:—201 men promptly responded. Shortly before embarkation it was notified that the destination of the regiment had been changed to China, but when the transports arrived at the Cape of Good Hope, they were directed to sail for Calcutta, in consequence of a mutiny in the Bengal army. The ships reached Calcutta on the 20th and 26th September, and no time was lost in sending on the regiment in detachments to Cawnpore. The detachment which was under the command of Major Ewart was the first division of the regiment to reach Cawnpore. Here is what he wrote after visiting the scene of the massacre and seeing some of the proofs of the atrocities which the rebels had committed, " As I looked around I could almost have cried with rage, and when I left the house where this frightful crime of unsurpassed brutality had been committed, I felt that I had become a changed man. All feelings of mercy or consideration for the mutineers had left me. I was no longer a Christian, and all I wanted was revenge. In the Crimea I had never wished to kill a Russian, or even tried to, but now my one idea was to kill every rebel I should come across."

On the 10th November, all the detachments of the regiment had arrived in the neighbourhood of Lucknow. Sir Colin Campbell had assumed the command on the previous day, and on the 11th he inspected the entire force (about 4,000 men), which had been drawn up on the plains near the Alum-bagh. Addressing the 93rd he said, " Ninety-third!

We are about to advance to relieve our countrymen and countrywomen besieged in the Residency of Lucknow by the rebel army. It will be a duty of danger and difficulty, but I rely upon you!" To this laconic speech the Highlanders replied with a loud cheer, which was taken up by the other regiments, as the brave old general rode along the line. Every man was actuated by the same feeling, namely—a determination to avenge Cawnpore, and rescue the women and children in Lucknow. On the 14th the army began its approach. The 93rd was the leading regiment in the main column. A force of rebels had taken up a position near a village to the south of Lucknow, but these having been driven off, the 93rd passed into an open space directly opposite the Secunder-bagh—a palace, with a high-walled loop-holed enclosure, about 150 yards square. A breach having been made in the walls, the assault was begun by the 93rd, supported by the 4th Punjab Rifles, and detachments of other regiments. "Never," said Sir Colin in his despatch, "was there a bolder feat of arms." The greater part of the 93rd dashed straight at the breach. It was an exciting attack. On rushed side by side in generous rivalry, the Sikh and the Highlander, the latter straining every nerve in the race, led gallantly by their officers. The opening of the breach was so small that only one man could enter at a time, but a few having gained entrance, they kept the enemy at bay until a considerable number of Highlanders and Sikhs had pushed in, and then commenced what was probably the sternest and bloodiest struggle of the whole campaign. The Sepoys made a stubborn resistance, and fought with the courage of despair, for they knew that no mercy would be shown to them. The carnage was dreadful, over 2000 Sepoys having been slain. The 93rd had in this eventful struggle 2 officers and 23 men killed, and 7 officers and 61 men wounded. Many of the latter died of their wounds, and most of the others were permanently disabled. That evening an effort was made to capture the Shah Nujjiff. Brigadier Hope, with about 50 men, guided by Sergeant Paton crept cautiously through some brushwood to a part of the wall which the Sergeant had discovered, so injured, that he thought an entrance could be effected. One man was pushed through the hole, and seeing none of the enemy near, several of the others scrambled up and stood on the wall. Brigadier Hope and his small party reached the main gate almost unopposed, then threw it open, and in rushed the 93rd just in time to see the rebels in their white dresses gliding away in the darkness of the night. Thus ended the desperate struggle of the day, and the relief of the Residency was ensured. A deep silence now reigned over the entire position, and the little army, weary and exhausted by its mighty efforts, lay upon the hard won battle-ground to rest, and if possible to sleep.

Many a heroic deed was done that day. Ewart, Burroughs, Stewart, MacBean and other officers were ever foremost in the fray, setting an example of dauntless courage to their men, although no example was needed. Lieutenant-Colonel Ewart slew eight rebels with his own hand, and captured a colour, after receiving two sword-cuts on the right arm and hand. The colour belonged to the 2nd Loodiana regiment, the only Sikh corps which had mutinied. Private David Mackay, of the Grenadier Company, captured the other colour of this corps, and received the Victoria Cross for his gallantry. Eight days afterwards (at Cawnpore), Lieutenant-

Colonel Ewart was struck by a cannon shot on the left elbow. "I was aware," he wrote, "that I had been struck violently on the left side, but did not know what had actually taken place until I looked down and saw the bleeding stump. . . . The blow did not knock me down, nor did I feel any inclination to fall, but a soldier of the 93rd, named Peter Mackay, (the same man who had been with me in the Redan, on the night of the 8th September, 1855), ran up at once and tied his handkerchief tightly round the stump."

Although Lucknow was relieved there was still much to be done. The troops under Sir Colin Campbell and those in the Residency, had, as it were, shaken hands, but the difficult task remained of getting the women and children out, without risking the lives of any of those that still remained. The Residency was evacuated during the night of the 22nd (November), the women and children were rescued, and the regiment moved to the Alum-bagh, and encamped in its old position. Sir Colin decided to convey the women and children and the wounded to Cawnpore, and selected the 93rd to be the escort. They started from the Alum-bagh on the 27th. A few hours after setting out news reached Sir Colin that the mutineers of the Gwalior contingent, in great force, were attacking General Windham at Cawnpore. Sir Colin immediately decided (though encumbered with the women and children and the sick) to push on with all possible speed, and by a forced march of about 40 miles, reached the Bridge of Boats, opposite Cawnpore, the following evening. Early the next morning, by the artillery distracting the attention of the enemy, the 93rd were enabled to get across the bridge, and the other troops followed. The rebels numbered fully 20,000 men, and had about 40 guns ; they kept up a continued fire, but did not venture on an attack. On the 3rd December the women and children, and a great number of the wounded, were sent off under a strong escort to Allahabad, and Sir Colin, no longer hampered by these defenceless ones determined to attack the enemy. On the 6th, what is known as the battle of Cawnpore was fought. The rebels were completely defeated, and retreated during the night, but they were quickly pursued and entirely dispersed, leaving a large number of killed and wounded, besides losing all their guns, ammunition, and baggage. In this engagement the 93rd greatly distinguished itself.

The British army was now employed in clearing the district around Lucknow of the rebels. By the end of February, 1858, the troops destined for the second siege of Lucknow were collected. On the 2nd of March a movement was made, and on the 9th the Martiniere was carried by the 42nd and 93rd. On the 11th the 93rd was selected to storm the Kaiser-bagh. The assault was successful, but the regiment had two officers and 13 men killed, and two officers and 45 men wounded. Lieut. MacBean and Pipe-Major MacLeod particularly distinguished themselves during the assault. MacBean killed 11 rebels with his own hand, while the Pipe-Major was, one of the first to get through the breach, and when through struck up the regimental gathering, and continued playing during the fighting, in places where he was perfectly exposed. The British had now gained possession of Lucknow, and there was no further fighting there after the 27th. During the operations against the city no regiment was more frequently employed, or suffered more severely than the Sutherland Highlanders.

On the 6th April the 93rd was brigaded with the 42nd and 79th under Adrian Hope. At the unsuccessful attack on Fort Rooyah on the 16th, Hope was killed, to the great sorrow, not of the 93rd only, but of the whole Highland Brigade. The regiment was subsequently present at the battle of Bareilly, and other minor affairs, and fully maintained the glorious reputation it had earned at Lucknow. In February, 1859, the mutiny having been suppressed, the 93rd was sent to a station in the Himalayas. During the campaign, between September 30, 1857, and December, 31, 1859, the regiment lost in killed and died of wounds, 5 officers and 78 men, and by disease 97 men, and there were invalided and sent to England 1 officer and 83 men. I have not been able to ascertain the actual number wounded.

The regiment made an unusually long stay in India, for it did not return to its native shores until March 25, 1870, when it arrived at Leith. After eight years home service it sailed for Gibraltar, where it was quartered until April, 1881. On the introduction of the "territorial system" into the British army, when numerical titles were abolished, the 93rd was linked with the 91st, and became the second battalion of the Argyll and Sutherland Highlanders. In 1892 the battalion again proceeded on foreign service, and is now stationed at Dalhousie in Bengal.

Although the "93rd" at present can only be said to have a *nominal* connection with the county after which it is named (for since the time of the Crimean war and the Indian mutiny, few Sutherlandshire men have been in the regiment), it is to be hoped that some efforts may be made by the military authorities to get young men from the county to join its ranks, so that it may be, what its name implies, the

Sutherland Highlanders; for, strange as it may appear, *the regiment*, under the territorial system, *is not allowed to recruit in Sutherlandshire!*

" During the 90 odd years of their existence the Sutherland Highlanders have been remarkable for their gallantry in the field and excellent discipline in quarters, the kindliest feeling has ever existed between officers and men, and though the regiment no longer bears its original designation, it is still animated by the same spirit which was so conspicuous in the 'auld 93rd.'"

. . . .

While the 93rd was stationed in Edinburgh in 1850, the regiment was reviewed in presence of Jung Bahadour, the Prime Minister of Nepaul, who was then on a mission to Great Britain. He was delighted with the regiment, especially with the pipers, and begged to be allowed to purchase the latter to take with him to India. He was disappointed that his request could not be entertained, but the reason being explained to him he was satisfied. About a dozen years later (after the Indian Mutiny), he, however, got a piper who had obtained his discharge from one of the Highland regiments. I am not certain, however, whether from the 93rd or 78th, but from what I was told by the Residency surgeon, who was then at Nepaul, I am pretty sure he was a 93rd man.

But Henry Mackay, who was a Pipe-Major of the 93rd, and served in the Crimea and the Indian mutiny, on obtaining his discharge from the regiment, was taken into the service of one of the Indian princes (the Maharajah of Puttiala), and held quite a lucrative appointment. He was treated with great liberality, and the Maharajah bestowed a rank upon him equal to that of Colonel of a regiment. Mackay trained 14 pipers and a corresponding number of drummers. The Maharajah wished to have the pipers dressed in the kilt, but Mackay (who could not brook the idea of Indians wearing the Highland dress) insisted on trews, and carried his point. They were dressed in green cloth tunics and 93rd tartan trews.

At a conference held at Umballa in 1869, the Maharajah attended with a strong force. The official report of the conference referred to this force as follows : " In equipment and drill it is very fair indeed. It is drilled by a man named Mackay, formerly a piper in the 93rd Highlanders. His work does him credit. The pipers played uncommonly well."

After being about six years in the Maharajah's service, Mackay's health broke down, and he was compelled, greatly to his own regret, and of the Maharajah also, to leave India. He returned to Scotland, and died in Aberdeen on 22nd March, 1893.

. . . . .

Seven Victoria Crosses were won by the 93rd during the Indian Mutiny Campaign, and the regiment received the Royal Authority to add " Lucknow " to the battle honours already emblazoned on its colours. The recipients of the Victoria Cross were :

    Captain WILLIAM GEORGE DRUMMOND STEWART, for distinguished gallantry at Lucknow, 16th November, 1857.

    Lieutenant and Adjutant MACBEAN, for distinguished personal bravery in killing with his own hand 11 rebels in the main breach of the Begum-bagh, 11th March, 1858.

Colour-Sergeant JAMES MUNRO, for devoted gallantry in the Secunder-bagh, in having promptly rushed to the rescue of Captain E. Welsh, when wounded and in danger of his life, whom he carried to a place of comparative safety, to which place the Sergeant was brought in shortly afterwards dangerously wounded, 16th November, 1857.

Sergeant J. PATON, for distinguished personal gallantry at Lucknow, 16th November, 1857.

Lance-Corporal JOHN DUNLEY, for being the first man of the regiment, who, on 16th November, 1857, entered one of the breaches in the Secunder-bagh with Captain Burroughs, whom he most gallantly supported against superior numbers.

Private DAVID MACKAY, for great personal gallantry in capturing an enemy's colour after a most obstinate resistance, at the Secunder-bagh on 16th November, 1857. Mackay was afterwards severely wounded at the capture of the Shah-Nujjiff.

Private PETER GRANT, for great personal gallantry at the Secunder-bagh, 16th November, 1857.

The following officers were promoted from the ranks of the 93rd. There may have been others, but I have not been able to trace them.

General WILLIAM MACBEAN, V.C. Enlisted in 1835 ; promoted to rank of Ensign, 11th August, 1854. Within 20 years thereafter he became Lieut.-Colonel commanding the regiment, and commanded it 4 years. Retired as Honorary Major-General, 16th February, 1878, and died about four months afterwards.

Lieut.-Colonel JOHN JOYNER. Promoted as Quarter Master, 6th July, 1855, and appointed Paymaster, 29th May, 1863. Retired with rank of Lieut.-Colonel.

Major WILLIAM MACDONALD. Enlisted in 1812 ; promoted to rank of Ensign, and appointed Adjutant 23rd August, 1827 ; was Adjutant 21 years; promoted as Captain, 3rd December, 1847, and retired with rank of Major, 11th June, 1852.

Major HARRY MACLEOD. Enlisted in 1848 : promoted as Quarter Master, 13th June, 1863. Retired with rank of Major, 26th December, 1887. Major Macleod is a recipient of the *Reward for Distinguished and Meritorious Service*.

Captain DONALD SINCLAIR. Promoted as Quarter Master, 22nd March, 1844, and retired with Honorary rank of Captain, 6th July, 1855.

Captain WILLIAM MORRISON. Enlisted in 1860; promoted as Lieutenant in Army Hospital Corps, 17th September, 1879; Captain, 17th December, 1889, and retired 5th May, 1896.

Captain SINCLAIR FORBES. Enlisted in 1864; appointed Quarter Master, 27th August, 1884; and retired with rank of Captain, . . , 1895.

Captain WILLIAM MACKAY. Enlisted in 1864; promoted as Lieutenant in Army Hospital Corps, 1st April, 1876; Captain, 1st April, 1886; and retired 21st March, 1896.

Captain JOHN BREEBER. Enlisted in 1860; appointed Quarter Master, 24th September, 1873; Captain, 24th September, 1883; and died in Glasgow, 20th October, 1886.

Lieutenant ROBERTSON MACKAY. Enlisted in 1823. While a Sergeant was promoted and transferred as Lieutenant to 5th Fusiliers, on 4th September, 1840, and appointed Adjutant, 8th June, 1843. He was shot dead by a private of the latter regiment two months afterwards (on the 11th August). Mackay was a native of Reay. His brother, Quarter Master Sergeant Adam Mackay, also in the 93rd, served through the Crimean War, and was offered a Commission, but declined. The following extract is from the regimental records of the 5th Fusiliers:

"On the afternoon parade of the 11th August, 1843 (at Birr), a private . . . . . a sanguinary monster in human shape, fell out of the ranks, asking the permission of

> Lieutenant and Adjutant Robertson Mackay, who was at the moment engaged in drilling the battalion . . . . and retiring to an adjoining hollow, loaded his firelock, and then returning and coming up *behind* the Adjutant . . . suddenly presented his firelock, and before he could be prevented by the horror-struck lookers-on, shot the unfortunate officer through the body. Thus was cruelly and deliberately murdered, in the prime of life, and in the active discharge of his duty, Robertson Mackay, an excellent man, an estimable Adjutant, an attentive, zealous, and talented officer, and most worthy member of society."

Lieutenant JAMES IRELAND. Promoted to the rank of Ensign, and appointed Adjutant, 25th April, 1813; Lieutenant, 17th March, 1815; died in 1827.

Lieutenant JAMES MACPHERSON. Enlisted in 1848; Quarter Master, 1859. Transferred to 70th Foot, and was Lieutenant and Adjutant.

Lieutenant JOHN GORDON. Promoted to the rank of Ensign, 5th November, 1854; Lieutenant, 17th April, 1855; and died in India during the Mutiny Campaign in 1858.

Lieutenant WILLIAM FORBES. Promoted to the rank of Ensign, 10th December, 1858; Lieutenant, 30th October, 1862; and retired in 1865.

Lieutenant ALEXANDER MACRAE. Enlisted 1871; Quarter Master, with rank of Lieutenant, 1st April, 1887.

Ensign ROBERT MACKAY. Promoted as Quarter Master, 3rd June, 1813; Ensign, 10th March, 1814; and retired in 1816.

Quarter Master A. DALLAS. Promoted as Quarter Master, 31st August, 1820.

Quarter Master ALEXANDER CROZIER. Promoted as Quarter Master, 24th October, 1831, and transferred to 55th Regiment in 1835.

Quarter Master GEORGE MACDONALD. Enlisted in 1824 ; Quarter Master, 13th December, 1839 ; Half Pay, 22nd March, 1844 ; was afterwards Staff Officer of Pensioners at Wick. (Brother of Major William Macdonald).

Quarter Master JAMES KINNAIRD. Promoted as Quarter Master, 6th May, 1882.

Quarter Master ALEXANDER BEATTIE. Enlisted 1874 ; Appointed Quarter Master, 27th February, 1895.

ARGYLL AND SUTHERLAND HIGHLANDERS—

Lieutenant GILBERT GUNN. Enlisted in 1883 ; promoted to the rank of 2nd Lieutenant, and transferred to *Royal Scots*, 12th April, 1893 ; Lieutenant, 14th August, 1895.

VOLUNTEERS.

By Quarter-Master James Morrison, Golspie.

The County of Sutherland did not lag behind the rest of the country when, in 1859, the movement for establishing volunteer companies for defence against foreign invasion was so heartily entered upon, for, so early as the 6th June of that year, a meeting was held within Golspie Inn, "for the purpose of organising a corps of volunteers for the defence of the country."

The chair on this occasion was occupied by Mr. Charles Hood, Inverbrora, and a motion that companies be raised in the east coast parishes of Dornoch, Golspie, Clyne, and Kildonan, was unanimously adopted, as was also one that Lord Stafford (afterwards third Duke of Sutherland) be respectfully asked to join the volunteers as commandant. Before the meeting separated the following gentlemen enrolled themselves, and to them must belong the honour of being the originators of the volunteer movement in Sutherland, viz: Charles Hood, Inverbrora, Brora; Sidney Hadwen, West Garty, Loth; Sutherland Murray, Kirkton, Golspie; William Houstoun, Kintradwell, Brora; M. C. MacHardy, Accountant, Golspie; John Mackenzie, Golspie Mills, Golspie; John B. Dudgeon, Crakaig, Loth; James Lindsay, Ironmonger, Golspie; Major Charles S. Weston, Golspie; Robert B. Sangster, Banker, Golspie; Marcus

OFFICER, SERGEANT, PIPER, AND PRIVATES OF THE SUTHERLAND COMPANIES,
IN FULL MARCHING ORDER, 1743.

Gunn, Culgower, Loth ; Donald Gray, Solicitor and Banker, Golspie ; Dr. R. K. Soutar, Golspie ; George Dudgeon, Crakaig, Loth ; John Grant, Writer, Golspie ; Hugh Ferguson, Accountant, Golspie.

Several other general and committee meetings were held during the summer and autumn of 1859, at which matters of detail were discussed and progress reported, until at a meeting of committee on 17th October, it was intimated that the Lord Lieutenant of the county (His Grace the Duke of Sutherland) had "accepted the services of the enrolled company of the Sutherland Rifle Volunteers, called the "Golspie Company," that he had appointed Major Charles Samuel Weston (late of the Indian army) Captain of said company, and that the company numbered 107 men, but would be restricted to 100 "effectives."

Mr. W. S. Fraser, Dornoch, reported to this meeting that he had enrolled the Dornoch Company to the number of 126, that he had numerous further applicants, but that a selection of 100 "effectives" would be made. The meeting resolved to ask the Lord Lieutenant to offer the services of the Dornoch Company to Her Majesty, and to nominate a suitable gentleman for Captain of the same.

At their meeting of 1st November the Committee added to their number Messrs. Charles Hood, Inverbrora, and George Lawson, Clynelish, who conveyed the pleasing intelligence that a third company was in process of formation at Brora, and that 60 men had been already enrolled, with every prospect of increasing the number to 100.

The selection of a suitable uniform appears to have given very considerable trouble, but ultimately, one consisting of dark grey tunic and trousers, shako of same colour, with

OFFICER, 'CAITHNESS COMPANIES.

black horse hair plume in front, and brown leather belts, was adopted. The clothing and accoutrements for the three companies which had now been raised cost about £1,000, and of this sum £800 was subscribed by the Duke of Sutherland, while the remaining £200 was made up by the volunteers themselves and others in the county friendly to the movement.

While the choice of a uniform had been exercising the minds of the committee, drill had not been neglected. The first drill instructor of the corps was Colour-Sergeant David Ross, from the staff of the Ross-shire Militia at Dingwall, who, in October, began to drill the Golspie and Dornoch Companies on each alternate week. In the following year two sergeant-instructors were told off by Colonel Ross of the militia for drilling the three companies.

It has already been stated that Major Weston was appointed, by the Lord-Lieutenant of the county, Captain of the Golspie Company, while Messrs. Sutherland Murray and Joseph Peacock were elected by the volunteers Lieutenant and Ensign respectively. Mr. W. S. Fraser, Procurator-Fiscal, was appointed first Captain of the Dornoch Company, with Sheriff-substitute Thomas Mackenzie as Lieutenant, and Mr. Donald Taylor, Sheriff-Clerk, as Ensign. Brora Company had, as its first officers, Charles Hood, Inverbrora, Captain ; George Lawson, Clynelish, Lientenant ; and John B. Dudgeon, Crakaig, Ensign. In 1861 Major Weston was appointed Adjutant of the Corps, and was succeeded in the command of the Golspie Company by Lieutenant Murray, Ensign Peacock becoming Lieutenant, and Mr. James Lindsay, Ensign.

The volunteers had not long to wait until an opportunity

SERGEANT AND PRIVATES OF THE CAITHNESS COMPANIES
IN FULL MARCHING ORDER, 1795.

presented itself for parading before their Sovereign. The Queen had reviewed some 18,000 English volunteers in Hyde Park, on 23rd June, 1860, and no sooner was this great event over than a strong desire was expressed that she should also inspect her Scottish volunteers at Edinburgh. This she most graciously consented to do, and the 7th August was fixed as the date. Thanks to the generous aid of the Duke of Sutherland and Lord Stafford, the three Sutherland Companies were enabled to take part in this great national event. The companies mustered at Little Ferry at 11 a.m, on Monday, 6th August, and, after refreshments had been served, they embarked, 169 strong, on board the steamer "Heather Bell" for Inverness, thence they were conveyed to Edinburgh by rail *via* Aberdeen, and at the Review they formed part of the second battalion, third Brigade of the first Division of Rifles. A hearty cheer was accorded them by the spectators as they marched past the saluting point.

The next event of importance in connection with the movement was the formation of a fourth company at Rogart. The desire to raise a Corps there took practical shape at a meeting held in Rogart School, on 13th October, 1860, when it was unanimously resolved to form a company. Special attention was to be exercised that the men enrolled should be temperate, and of good moral character. Messrs. John Hall, Sciberscross; Robert B. Sangster, Banker, Golspie; and George Barclay, Davochbeg; were elected Captain, Lieutenant, and Ensign respectively. The Rogart Company had, from its commencement, the distinction of adopting practically, the uniform of the 93rd Sutherland Highlanders, viz: scarlet doublet, Sutherland tartan kilt and plaid, glengarry bonnet, and white belts, with a plate on the front of

GROUP OF OFFICERS OF BATTALION.
INVERGORDON CAMP, 1895.

the shoulder belt bearing the inscription "Duchess (Harriet's) Company, Rogart," and it is the boast of the Rogart men that their dress, a few years later, became the uniform of the whole battalion.

The War Office, in December, 1863, issued an order converting the Sutherland Rifle Volunteer Corps into an Administrative Battalion, composed of the four Sutherland Companies, and the 1st Orkney at Lerwick; and, later on, the 1st Caithness (Thurso), 2nd ditto (Wick), and 3rd ditto (Halkirk), were added to the battalion.

The Duke of Sutherland who, as Marquis of Stafford, had been appointed commanding officer in 1859, with the rank of Major, was in 1864, promoted to the rank of Lieut.-Colonel.

1863 saw a complete change in the uniform of the three grey clad companies, the new dress consisting of scarlet Highland doublet, Sutherland tartan trews, diced glengarry bonnet, and white belts. This uniform, however, does not appear to have given satisfaction to either officers or men, for, in 1867, it was put to the vote of the men whether the Corps should adopt the full Highland dress or remain in trews, and it is almost needless to say that "the kilt" was carried with acclamation. The officers, from the Colonel downwards, had previously resolved "for the kilt," if the men agreed.

H.R.H. The Prince of Wales paid his first visit to Dunrobin Castle in September, 1866, when he received a tremendous ovation, a leading part in which was taken by the volunteers. The Dornoch Company formed a guard of honour at Clashmore, while Golspie, Clyne, and Rogart Companies received him at Dunrobin. His Royal Highness was so impressed with the appearance of the volunteers that, at the request of the Duke of Sutherland, he consented to

GROUP OF PIPERS OF BATTALION
INVERGORDON CAMP, 1893

become Honorary Colonel of the battalion, a rank which he still retains.

A fifth company was added to the strength of the county rifles in 1867, at Bonar Bridge. The work of enrolling was taken up with enthusiasm, and in a very short time a strong company was raised. At the date of writing (1896), E or Bonar Company is the strongest in the battalion. Mr. Dugald Gilchrist, of Ospisdale, was appointed Captain; Mr. A. S. Black, Banker, Bonar, Lieutenant; and Mr. John Mackenzie, Creich, Ensign.

The sergeants of the battalion had an honourable and pleasant duty to perform in August, 1871. On the 4th of the month Her Grace the Duchess of Sutherland presented a new set of colours to the 93rd Sutherland Highlanders, then lying in Edinburgh Castle, to replace those which that gallant corps had carried through the Indian mutiny. The officers of the 93rd resolved, in return for the kindness of the Duchess, to hand over their old colours to the custody of the Duke, to be kept in Dunrobin Castle, and His Grace issued orders that the Sergeants of the Sutherland volunteers should proceed to Edinburgh to receive the colours and bring them north. When the Duke himself went to Edinburgh to be present at the ceremony, he took with him, as a bodyguard, 20 privates of the Rogart Company, not a man of whom stood less than six feet high.

On the occasion of Her Majesty's visit to Dunrobin Castle in September, 1872, the volunteers formed a guard of honour, and the following reference to them appears in the Queen's book—*More Leaves from the Journal of a Life in the Highlands:*

BATTALION AT INVERGORDON CAMP 1895

"At six we were at Golspie station, where the Duchess of Sutherland received us, and where a detachment of the Sutherland volunteers, who looked very handsome in red jackets and Sutherland tartan kilts, were drawn up."

The next eight years of volunteer existence appear to have been comparatively uneventful, but steady progress was being made year by year in drill, shooting, and general efficiency.

By a War Office order, dated 1st June, 1880, the several companies composing the Administrative Battalion ceased to exist as separate corps, and became *lettered* companies of a new consolidated battalion entitled the 1st Sutherland (the Sutherland Highland) Rifle Volunteer Corps. The establishment was fixed at 10 companies and 1 sub-division (since increased to 11 companies), with a maximum strength of 1059 of all ranks.

In 1881 the greatest event in the history of the Scottish volunteers took place. On the 25th August, Her Majesty the Queen reviewed over 40,000 Scottish and North of England volunteers at Edinburgh. Thanks again to the munificence of the Duke of Sutherland, the Sutherland men were able to attend this great review with but trifling cost to their company funds. The Duke himself took command on this occasion, Major Weston, the Adjutant, being the only other mounted officer with the corps.

The total strength of the battalion at the review was 18 officers and 457 non-commissioned officers and men (including a detachment of the Thurso Company), divided into six companies, and anyone who had the privilege of seeing the battalion marching past, will not readily forget the grand physique of the leading company under the command of the

BATTALION MARCHING PAST, JUBILEE REVIEW, INVERNESS.

Marquis of Stafford. To give an idea of the size of the men composing this company, it is only necessary to say that the height of the centre man was 5 feet 10 inches, while the flank men stood each 6 feet 3 inches.

The position of the battalion was third, in the third brigade of the first division, the Brigadier being Colonel Duncan Macpherson of Cluny, commanding the "Black Watch." The *Scotsman*, in describing the march past, said of the Sutherland men:

> "But the cheers that were raised were for the 'Queen's ain men' . . . and for the Sutherlandshire regiment—a regiment that was under the command of the Duke of Sutherland, and which, in their showy scarlet jackets and tartan kilts, fairly caught the eye, and almost effaced by their impressiveness recollections of what had gone before. In this regiment there were, it is true, the same weaknesses (distances between companies) as have already been noticed. The promise held out by the leading company by their all but faultless dressing, was not altogether borne out by those that followed; but, on the other hand, taken as a body, they were as strong and heavy men as ever stepped in kilts."

The *Times* said:

> "Splendid men the Duke's corps are, reminding some of the spectators of the 93rd in its Crimean days. They marched also as well as they looked."

Major Weston, who had served as Adjutant since 1861, retired in 1882, and was succeeded, under the new regulations, limiting the tenure of the office to five years, by Major Webber Smith, from the first battalion South Staffordshire regiment. Major Webber Smith did not complete his term with the corps for, on his regiment being ordered for service in the Soudan Expedition of 1884, he volunteered for active service and was accepted. He was succeeded as Adjutant by Captain Francis Maude Reid, 71st H.L.I. Major Reid was, in his turn, succeeded by Major H. G. Lang, 1st Seaforths, and he, on retiring from the army in 1894, was followed by Captain Granville C. Feilden, 2nd Seaforths, the present energetic Adjutant.

The company of rifles at Lerwick formed, as has already been mentioned, one of the companies of the Sutherland battalion; but, on account of its isolated position, the War Office, in 1884, resolved to convert it into a company of artillery, and transfer its equipment to Lairg, where a company was to be raised. The latter part of this scheme was carried through most successfully, and a splendid company was enrolled at Lairg, with Messrs. D. Munro, Banker, Lairg, and J. R. Campbell, Shinness, as officers.

The regiment was present at the review of Highland volunteers held at Inverness in honour of the Queen's Jubilee, on 27th June,- 1887, and the following are the remarks of the *Inverness Courier* on its appearance there :

> "The Sutherlandshire volunteers were a magnificent body of men, all of good size and of splendid physique, and as they stepped along (790 strong) to the music of between 30 and 40 pipers, they elicited the hearty admiration of all. In point of physique the Sutherland battalion carried off the palm."

The Duke of Sutherland handed over the command of the regiment in 1882 to Captain the Marquis of Stafford, who held it until 1891, when he was succeeded by Major Clarence G. Sinclair, Younger of Ulbster. Colonel Sinclair retiring in 1893, a petition, signed by every officer and man in the regiment, was presented to their former colonel, now 4th Duke of Sutherland, requesting him to resume the command, but as His Grace had, in the interval, become colonel of the Staffordshire Yeomanry, and the regulations prevented him holding two commissions, he found himself unable to comply, much to the regret of all ranks. Major Duncan Menzies, Blarich, the present popular and enthusiastic commanding officer, was then gazetted Lieutenant-Colonel.

In 1885 the regiment had its first taste of camp life. A battalion camp was formed at Dunrobin on 27th July in this year, and lasted for six days. Everything passed off so satisfactorily that a second was held on the same ground in the beginning of August, 1887. These were the only battalion camps held, for after the formation of the volunteer force into brigades, the Sutherland battalion joined its brigade—the Highland—on the three occasions when it went into camp, viz : 1891, at Fort George, and 1893 and 1895, at Invergordon. On the day of the inspection and review at Invergordon, in 1895, the regiment numbered on parade 923 of all ranks, and on all these occasions it has compared most favourably, in every respect, with the other corps composing the brigade.

No notice of the Sutherland volunteers would be complete without a reference to the two great events of the volunteer year in the county, viz : the prize meetings of the Sutherland Rifle Association, and the reviews at Dunrobin Castle.

The Sutherland Rifle Association was founded in 1861, and has held its meetings continuously at Dunrobin in the autumn of each year ever since. Thanks mainly to the Dukes of Sutherland, and other friends of the volunteers in the county, it has offered a most attractive prize list every year, and its influence on the shooting of the corps has been most beneficial.

The volunteer review at Dunrobin Castle has always been one of the great events of the eastern portion of the county. Started in 1860 by the second Duke of Sutherland, reviews were held annually in the autumn, down to 1880. In 1881 the great Edinburgh review took place, and it was deemed sufficient demonstration for that year. They were resumed, however, in 1882, and have been held since then in 1883, '84, '91, and '94. At the review of 1876 the Caithness companies first appeared, and created a most favourable impression.

The *Enfield* muzzle-loading rifle, with which the volunteers were first armed, was exchanged in 1871 for the *Snider* breach-loader, which again gave place in 1885 to the *Martini-Henry*, with which the force is now armed; but there is every prospect that 1896 will witness the issue of the new *Lee-Metford* rifle.

Considering the great distance which the Sutherland men have to travel to the meetings of the National Rifle Association their successes at Wimbledon and Bisley must be regarded as highly creditable to their prowess with the rifle. It was not till 1873 that a representative of the corps appeared at an N.R.A. meeting, and up till 1880, only trifling prizes were won. Since then members of the Sutherland companies have won: The *Daily Telegraph* Cup; first prize Grand Aggregate (twice); first prize Volunteer Aggregate; Wimbledon Cup; Olympic; and ten "Queen's" badges; besides a considerable number of substantial, though less important, prizes, while representatives have shot five times in the Scottish Twenty team for the International Trophy. It was in 1883, however, that the crowning glory of the shooting world came to the county, when Sergeant Robert Mackay of the Dornoch Company carried off the Queen's Prize. That

COLOUR-SERGEANT ROBERT MACKAY, QUEEN'S PRIZEMAN, WIMBLEDON, 1883.

was a great year in the annals of the Dornoch Company, for, at the Highland Rifle Association meeting at Inverness, their team won the Bannockburn Shield, a trophy open for competition to teams of eight men from any volunteer company in Scotland.

Golspie, Dornoch, and Clyne companies organised first flute, and then brass bands, shortly after they were raised, and these continued until 1883, when it was resolved that brass bands should be entirely abolished in the battalion, and a pipe band formed instead. Rogart and Bonar Companies, it should be mentioned, had pipers from their formation. The change has proved eminently successful, the pipers of the battalion, consisting usually of 28 or 30 performers (besides drummers), forming probably the largest military pipe band in the world. The battalion now possesses an ambulance corps at Golspie and Wick, and a cyclist section in Caithness. The strength of the whole battalion, as at 31st October, 1895, was 1082 of all ranks, 598 being in Sutherland and the remainder in Caithness. This is the greatest strength the corps has yet attained to. The maximum authorised establishment is 1111.

LIST OF NOBLEMEN AND GENTLEMEN WHO HAVE HELD COMMISSIONS IN THE SUTHERLAND RIFLE VOLUNTEERS.

HON.-COLONEL.—H.R.H. The Prince of Wales.

LIEUT.-COLONELS COMMANDING.—The Duke of Sutherland, Marquis of Stafford, Clarence G. Sinclair, Duncan Menzies.

MAJORS.—W. S. Fraser, E. H. Horne, J. H. Buik, Earl of Cromartie, Clarence G. Sinclair, D. Menzies, R. Robertson, D. Sutherland, J. MacKintosh, John Morrison.

ADJUTANTS.—Major C. S. Weston, Major J. Webber-Smith, Major F. M. Reid, Major H. G. Lang, Captain G. C. Feilden.

CHAPLAINS.—Revds. W. MacBeath, D. Grant.

SURGEONS.—J. Craven, J. B. Simpson, A. Alexander, S. Elliot.

QUARTERMASTERS.—John Blake, James Morrison.

SUTHERLAND COMPANY OFFICERS.—A. (Golspie) Company—C. S. Weston, S. Murray, J. Peacock, J Lindsay, A. J. T. Box, R. Wright, W. Murray, John Morrison, H. Grant, A. N. MacAulay, T. P. Eykyn.

B. (Dornoch) Company.—W. S. Fraser, T. MacKenzie, D. Taylor, T. Barclay, A. Leslie, R. Macdonald, J. Barclay, J. MacKintosh, L. Hoyes.

C. (Clyne) Company.—C. Hood, G. Lawson, J. B. Dudgeon, R. Wright, G. R. Lawson, A. J. T. Box, G. Sutherland, W. J. Dudgeon, R. C. Ross.

D. (Rogart) Company.—J. Hall, R. B. Sangster, G. Barclay, D. Gray, Marquis of Stafford, Master of Blantyre, D. Menzies, G. G. Tait, P. B. Sangster, John Mackay, A. J. T. Box, J. Milligan, R. B. Sangster.

E. (Bonar) Company.—D. Gilchrist, A. S. Black, J. MacKenzie, A. Harper.

F. (Lairg) Company.—D. Munro, J. R. Campbell, J. A. Butters.

ARTILLERY COMPANIES.

It will be remembered that at the first meeting in connection with the volunteer movement, held at Golspie on 6th June, 1859, the gentlemen there assembled resolved to raise a company in the parish of Kildonan. This company was formed as the 1st Sutherland Artillery in March, and was formally sworn in in April, 1860,—Messrs. George Loch, Uppat; William Houstoun, Kintradwell; Robert Rutherford, and Dr. Rutherford, Helmsdale ; being appointed Captain, 1st Lieutenant, 2nd Lieutenant, and Surgeon respectively.

The company did not take part in the Royal review of 7th August, 1860, but was present at the greater one of 25th August, 1881. It has always taken a most prominent part in the local reviews at Dunrobin, the smart handling of the two field guns belonging to the company forming one of the chief attractions on these occasions.

The Helmsdale Company has for years possessed a goodly number of first-rate carbine shots, and probably, in this respect, it is second to no company in the north. It has also taken a good position in gun practice and repository drill, and is at present one of the most efficient companies in the Caithness Artillery Brigade, of which it forms part.

In 1867 the late Duke of Sutherland resolved to raise a company of artillery volunteers at Golspie, having in view the utilization of the splendid physical material existing in the young fishermen of that village. A very strong company was soon enrolled, and it is worthy of remark that, at its first parades, the two flank men stood each fully 6 feet 6 inches in height. The Duke's youngest brother, Lord Ronald

Leveson Gower, was appointed Captain, and Ensign Donald Gray, of the Rogart Rifle Company, 1st Lieutenant.

The company has taken its share, along with its companion of the same arm in Helmsdale, in all the local volunteer events, and it has been highly successful in its great gun shooting, both locally and at Inverness, where, for some years previous to the disruption of the Inverness Artillery Association, it carried off some of the principal prizes.

Both the Helmsdale and Golspie companies have been in camp with their Brigade, and they have sent contingents frequently to the Scottish Artillery camp at Barry.

The following are those gentlemen who have held commissions in the Sutherland Artillery Companies:—

Helmsdale Company.—George Loch, W. Houstoun, R. Rutherford, Dr. T. H. Rutherford, J. Campbell, J. Paterson, David Sutherland, R. R. Hill, Donald Sutherland.

Golspie Company.—Lord Ronald L. Gower, D. Gray, C. MacLean, J. MacLeod, O. Ross, W. Traquair, D. Peters. A. Barclay, W. Ross, George M. Ross, H. A. Rye, W. Barnes, J. W. Cameron, C. J. Wahab.

POETRY AND MUSIC.

By Henry Whyte and Malcolm MacFarlane.

Not being natives of the county, we cannot pretend to have that knowledge of the poetry and music of Sutherland which would enable us to submit an exhaustive treatise on the subject.

Rob Donn Mackay is the bard of the county, and others are mere rush-lights compared with him—indeed, with the exception of the brothers Gordon, he is the only bard in the county whose works have been published in a collected form. It may be interesting, however, to mention that the late Charles Mackay, LL.D., author of "Cheer, Boys, Cheer," "There's a good time coming," etc., and perhaps the most popular and voluminous song writer of his generation, was the son of a Durness man, born on Loch Hope side (Rob Donn's native parish): and the mother of George Macdonald, the distinguished poet and novelist, was a sister of the Rev. Dr. Mackintosh Mackay, the editor and collector of the first edition of Rob Donn's poems, published in 1829. Doubtless, these eminent poets derived their poetic tastes from their parents, who could hardly fail being influenced by the poetry and music of Rob Donn, the bard of their native district. In the year 1802 William Gordon, a native of Creich, born in 1770, published a collection of Gaelic Hymns.*
He was in the Reay Fencibles until their being disbanded in

---

* See Reid's *Bibleotheca Scota-Celtica* pp. 164-165.

1798. It was during the time that the regiment was in Ireland that his little volume was published. When the regiment was disbanded, he returned to his native parish, and was employed as a teacher of one of the Gaelic schools. He died in 1820. A few of the best of Gordon's hymns were afterwards reprinted in a Collection of Hymns by John Munro, Glasgow, in 1819. He also composed an elegy on his brother, Peter Gordon, which has been much admired for its simplicity of diction and deep pathetic feeling. This elegy was published in a volume of original poems by his brother, George Ross Gordon, in 1804. The work contains, besides the elegy, a love song by William Gordon, and two small pieces of considerable merit by Alexander Gordon, another brother, who was a master mason in Tain. After leaving the army George Ross Gordon was successfully employed as teacher of a Gaelic School at Morness. The elegy on Peter Gordon will be found in the *Teachdaire Gaelach*, Vol. I. (1829) page 171. We might also refer to the sacred poems of the pious Donald Matheson, who was born in 1719, in the heights of the parish of Kildonan, where he spent his lifetime. He died in 1782. His hymns were first published about 1816, and a second edition in Tain, 1825. A number of his best poems and a brief English memoir will be found in "Metrical Reliques of the Men in the Highlands.†"

During the present century a number of minor poets have tuned their Gaelic harps, but we are not aware that any of

---

† *Metrical Reliques of the Men in the Highlands, or Sacred Poetry of the North*, with Introduction and Brief Memoirs in English, collected and edited by John Rose, Inverness, 1851.

them have published a collection of their poems. These have been successfully dealt with by the Rev. Adam Gunn, in his "Unpublished Literary Remains of the Reay Country" —a paper read before the Gaelic Society of Inverness in 1889, and published in Vol. XVI. of that Society's Transactions.

Instead of attempting to traverse so wide a county alone, we have sought the guidance of those who are familiar with its every lake and river, hill and ben, and so led we proceed upon our musical excursion through this great county. The following paper is from the facile pen of Mr. John Mackay, Hereford, and he has kindly given us permission to interpolate such songs and airs as shall best illustrate the great bard of the Reay country. We may here state that for many of the airs we are indebted to a MS. collection left by the late John Munro, a native of the county, who resided for many years in Glasgow. We do not deem it necessary to give the Gaelic words of the songs, as these can easily be found in any of the editions of the works of Rob Donn.

ROB DONN.

By John Mackay, C.E., J.P., Hereford.

In the olden times the bards were sufficiently provided for from within, they had need of little from without. The gift of imparting lofty ideas, emotions, and glorious images to men, in words and melodies that charmed the ear, and fixed themselves inseparably on whatever they might touch, of old enraptured the bard, and served the gifted as a rich inheritance. At the courts of kings, at the tables of the great, under the windows of the fair, the sound of their lays was heard, while the ear and the soul were closed to all beside.

> " High placed in hall, welcome guests
> They poured, to lords and ladies gay,
> The unpremeditated lay."

Robert Mackay, the celebrated Gaelic bard, whose proper name has yielded to the more familiar one of Rob Donn (brown Robert), from the colour of his hair and swarthy complexion, was born in the winter season of 1714, as he tells us in his exquisite elegy on William, eighthteenth Earl of Sutherland, who died at Bath, 16th June, 1766—

> Rugadh mise anns a' Gheamhradh
> Measg na beanntaidhean gruaimeach,
> 'S mo cheud sealladh do 'n t-saoghal
> Sneachd is gaoth mu mo chluaisibh.

> 'Twas in winter I was born,
> 'Midst the wild frowning mountains,
> And what first met my gaze
> Was the snow, and frost-bound fountains.

The birth-place of Rob Donn, *Allt-na-Caillich* (nun's burn), at the head of the valley of Strathmore, is the centre of the most wildly grand and picturesque scenery in the Highlands. This Alpine valley lies embosomed in lofty hills. Its upper extremity terminates in an assemblage of mountains piled together, as if nature in a fanciful mood meant to exhibit the rude yet majestic grandeur of its handiwork, in assembled mountain and rock, river and cataract, glen and corrie. At its lower extremity, and along its eastern side, rises Ben Hope, in abrupt and towering magnificence, rearing, as it were, its imperial head in the midst of numerous

kindred mountains around, which seem to show their
diminished height, as if to do it homage. Beyond this awe-
inspiring mountain opens at once upon the view the fine
expanse of Loch Hope, washing the northern base of the
mountain. The observer is now left to contrast this overpowering sublimity with the adjacent wilderness of fell and
morass, the banks of Loch Hope—decked on each side with
tufts and groves of the healthy sweet-scented native birchwood—divided by spots of emerald green, images as it were
of delicate protected innocence, stretching from the shores
of the lake up to the base of the mountain, as if anxious to
seek its august and magnificent protection.

Such is a brief description of the scenery which surrounded
Rob Donn in his youthful days. If such sublimity of local
environment can inspire poetic imaginations, or conduce to
the formation and training of poetic genius, truly the nursery
of our bard might well lay claim to that merit, " The emblem
of deeds that were done in its clime." It forms part of the
parish of Durness, in the centre of that extensive district of
the county of Sutherland, which, having been inhabited from
a period almost beyond the reach of history by the Mackays,
has always been designated in the native language, *Dùthaich
Mhic-Aoidh* (the territory of the Mackays), and sometimes
"Lord Reay's Country," the chief of the Clan Mackay, and
will probably be so called for ages to come, although the
whole of it has passed for the last sixty-six years into the
hands of the house of Stafford and Sutherland.

Although Rob Donn's talents, even in very early childhood, excited much attention, he never received a particle of
what is too exclusively called education : he never knew the
alphabet, but the habit he inherited and learned from his

Highland mother of oral recitation, enabled him before attaining manhood to lay up an amazing amount of poetic and other lore, as has from time immemorial constituted the intellectual wealth of his countrymen and women, such as the Ossianic poetry, and numberless other minstrelsy of his native country. His mother was remarkable for her recital of these. She died at a very advanced age. An anecdote is related of her, evincing a singular instance of heroic fortitude at the age of eighty-two. Being out on the hills, some distance from home, she had the misfortune to break her leg. No way daunted, she bound it up as well as she could, and contrived to get home unassisted ; and while enduring the operation of setting the fracture, she soothed away the pain by softly humming or "crooning" one of her favourite Gaelic airs. Robert's mastery of Highland traditions, ballads, and *orain* of all sorts had become extraordinary, and his knowledge of Holy Writ was equally remarkable, and, be it remembered, at the time he lived no Gaelic Bible had reached the county.

At a very early age the boy poet attracted the attention of John Mackay, better known in his own county as *Iain MacEachain* (John, the son of Hector), tacksman of Musal, an extensive grazing farm in Strathmore, less than two miles from Rob's home. Mr. Mackay persuaded his parents to let him, young as he was, come into his family. He was put to tend calves. His master was not only a grazier but also a cattle dealer, a business then followed in the North Highlands by comparatively few gentlemen, but those few were gentlemen of good birth and breeding, of the highest probity, superior attainments and intelligence. Mr. Mackay was one of these, liberal minded, upright, gentlemanly, and of a disposition the most amiable and benevolent to all around, especially to his poorer neighbours—in short, a man universally respected. In this gentleman's family the boy poet remained to the period of his marriage. When he advanced in years and strength, it became part of his duties to assist in guiding droves of Highland cattle to the southern markets and into England. Meantime, his witty sayings, his satires, his elegies, and above all, his comic and love songs, had begun to make him famous, not only in his native glens, but wherever the herdsmen and drovers of a thousand hills could carry an anecdote or a stanza, after their annual peregrinations to and from such scenes as the Falkirk Trysts or Kendal Fairs.

During this period many anecdotes have been preserved of the boy-herd's and the young man's precocity. His quickness of mind, his amazing power of repartee, were sources of frequent amusement and astonishment to his master, and unceasingly to younger members of the family, with whom he became a great favourite. In this estimable household the youthful poet experienced the most liberal treatment and encouraging kindness, of which he ever afterwards retained a lively and grateful recollection. On the death of Mr. Mackay our poet composed an elegy to his memory, one of his best, which combines an impressive, effective description of character with as pure poetic power as can be found in any elegiac poetry. We are tempted to give a translation of two stanzas of this excellent production.

> "Though there be some who laugh to scorn
> The man of liberal heart and hand,
> This prayer to heaven should be borne
> From all the quarters of the land,

> That that blest day we soon may see
>   When man shall love his brother men,
> Nor barter all eternity
>   For selfish three score years and ten.

This stanza reminds us of Burns and his immortal ode, "A man's a man for a' that." The next depicts the general sadness caused by the demise of his former master and friend, Iain MacEachann.

> "Who needs advice must want it now,
>   And see the prosperous times depart;
> All clouded is the poet's brow
>   With none to reverence his art.
> None seek to make the sad rejoice—
>   And when I ask why joys are fled
> They answer me, with tearful voice,
>   'Alas! is not MacEachainn dead?'"

In the latter years of Rob Donn's service with the estimable Mr. Mackay, he was entrusted by his master with the chief care of his droves to the southern markets. In these annual expeditions we cannot doubt that in this capacity the young man, with that native sagacity and quick discernment belonging to the Highlanders and his own genius, acquired no small share of that knowledge and insight of character and manners which are so apparent in his poetical compositions. To nature he was greatly indebted; so was he also to the form and structure of that society to which he had access at home, yet not a little to the sphere of observation that his frequent journeying disclosed to a mind singularly acute and circumspect.

The following translation is from the pen of the gifted Thomas Pattison, author of "The Gaelic Bards.*"

THE SHEILING SONG.

(*'S trom leam an óividh.*)

* THE GAELIC BARDS, and Original Poems, by Thomas Pattison. Glasgow: Arch. Sinclair, 1890 (second edition).

Oh! sad is the sheiling and gone are its joys!
All harsh and unfeeling to me now its noise,
Since Anna—who warbled as sweet as the merle—
Forsook me, my honey-mouth'd, merry-lipped girl!
 Heich! how I sigh; while the hour
 Lazily, lonelily, sadly, goes by!

Last week, as I wander'd up past the old trees,
I mourn'd, while I ponder'd, what changes one sees!
Just then the fair stranger walk'd by with my dear—
Dreaming, unthinking, I had wander'd too near,
 Till, "Heich!" then I cried, when I saw
 The girl, with her lover, draw close to my side—

"Anna, the yellow-hair'd, dost thou not see
How thy love unimpair'd wearieth me?
'Twas as strong in my absence, when banish'd from thee—
As heart-stirring, powerful, deep as you see.
 Heich! it is now at this time,
 When up like a leafy bow, high doth it climb."

Then haughtily speaking, she airily said,
"'Tis in vain for you seeking to hold up your head:
There were six wooers sought me while you were away,
And the absentee surely deserved less than they.
 Ha! ha! ha! are you ill?
 But if love seeks to kill you—bah! small is his skill!"

Ach! ach! Now I'm trying my loss to forget—
With sorrow and sighing, with anger and fret.
But still that sweet image steals over my heart,
And still I deem fondly hope need not depart.
 Heich! and I say that our love,
 Firm as a tower gray, nought can remove.

So fancy beguiles me, and fills me with glee,
But the carpenter wiles thee, false speaker! from me.
Yet from love's first affection I never get free;
But the dear known direction my thoughts ever flee.
    Heich! when we strayed far away,
      Where soft shone the summer day through the green shade.

A young man of such a poetic temperament could not be expected to remain long a stranger to the more tender susceptibilities of his nature. He early wooed his "yellow-haired Annie" Morrison, but being detained at Crieff in charge of his master's drove for several months longer than usual, the fair Annie plighted her troth to a rival and disappointed her poet-lover. Robert, on his return, finding how matters stood, keenly felt the slight, and made it the subject of two of his finest love songs, *'S trom leam an airidh*, being one of them. In these exquisite songs, to original airs his passion for the faithless "Anna" breathes with an innocent simple faithfulness, with an ardour and truth of poetical recital that no lays of the kind can perhaps surpass.

Robert recovered from his disappointment, and within a few years married Janet Mackay, daughter of a respectable farmer in his native parish, a young woman of ready wit, much good sense, and of a most amiable disposition, a fit help-meet for the poet in every way, and he, unlike many of the erratic ill-starred sons of genius, ever proved the best, the most faithful of husbands, and an equally good, indulgent, and dutiful parent to a numerous and respectable family.

About this time Donald, fourth Lord Reay, a true-hearted chief, claimed for himself the care of the rising bard of the clan. This nobleman was one of nature's nobility, "a stay-at-home" amongst his clan; genial and kind to all, liberal minded and generous, one of the best of chiefs and landlords. He personally knew all his tenantry and their condition. His constant aim was to elevate the minds, as well as assist in increasing the means of his humbler clansmen. He never permitted any arrears of rent to be recorded in the estate books. He himself attended the annual rent collections, and to such of his tenants as were able to pay, but not fully prepared, he lent the deficiency, and to such as were unable from unforeseen circumstances, he discharged the debt, giving them full receipts. This generous conduct was never taken advantage of, his people, though comparatively poor, were educated by him to a degree of highmindedness and morality seldom met with elsewhere. This generosity and careful attention produced the highest sense of gratitude and manliness in the minds of his brave and unsophisticated clansmen, evinced in the grand orderly conduct of the first, second, and third regiments of Sutherland Fencibles, the Reay Fencibles, and the 93rd regiment of the line. This estimable nobleman, and his co-temporary, Earl William of Sutherland, were intimate friends, men of like dispositions. They were the last of the grand Highland chiefs of their respective clans, adored, idolised by clansmen for their conduct, benevolence, and generosity, equally esteemed by either clan, and on their demise lamented by both.

For his own chief, who died in 1761, Rob Donn composed a most pathetic elegy, setting forth the virtues of his heart and mind, and comparing him with his predecessors in the following terms, much weakened by translation into English :

There have been lofty men among thy sires,
  In mind and wisdom, courage and renown,
Who in the proud pursuits of their desires
  Have acted like the wearers of a crown !
Yet far less praise than thee they must receive,
  For Christian grace, and faith, and charity,
It is less hard to hope than to believe
  That better men will e'er come after thee !

For Earl William, who died in 1766, Rob, who knew him well, composed a most touching elegy, regretting that no bard in his own country had a word to say in memory of the " High Chief of Dunrobin," but that his own feelings would not permit him to be silent on an event so melancholy and disastrous to the whole county. The poet in this excellent lament depicts, "in words that burn," the sorrow and sadness of the people, descants upon the moral and mental virtues of the deceased, his lovely and devoted young spouse, Mary Maxwell, and his immediate predecessors ; expatiates upon their personal gifts, their genial kindness to all, their hospitality, their greatness without pride, their love of order, their great desire to improve the condition of the tenantry, who had no cause of complaint, for "not a penny was exacted but they were able to pay," and concludes by invoking the blessings of Heaven upon their young orphan daughter, left to their people as a remembrance of them, and hopes he will see or hear of her marriage with a *hero* (brave man) who will follow in the footsteps and habitudes of her ancestors.

After his marriage Rob Donn resided on a small out farm, belonging to his late employer. He was one of the most expert deer stalkers in the country. Being so well known for this attainment Lord Reay soon provided him with a habitation, house and lands, on the eastern side of Loch Erribol, and made him his gamekeeper. His functions were not very well defined, but he was to shoot as many deer from time to time as his Lordship's family and friends might require. This employment was eminently suited to the poet's predilections, and everything went on very satisfactorily for some years. When the preservation of a separate deer forest became necessary, its charge devolved upon another. Our bard sometime afterwards was reported of being somewhat unscrupulous as to the number of deer he shot. The accusation was not denied. At this period nothing could possibly be imagined more difficult to be understood by Highlanders than that there could be any moral evil in killing any animal of the chase. In itself it was a pastime and sport to which all were more or less trained from boyhood. It begets enthusiasm for itself which largely partakes of practical poetry in its character, and so wholly suited to all their native predilections that its interdiction was considered as an assumption of power entirely unwarrantable on the part of their superiors. The saying "'S ionraic a' mhèirle na fèidh" (righteous is the theft of deer), became a proverb, and has still outlived its literal application over all the Highlands of Scotland. Our bard upon this subject exposed himself to the visitations of the law, but he always escaped, though threatened, for there was scarcely any of the gentlemen of the county who would not have gone any length to protect him. On one occasion, when rather alarmed, he called upon Mr. Mackay of Bighouse to befriend him. Mr. Mackay seemed deaf to all Rob's protestations. "Would you accept of security for future good behaviour?" he asked. "No."

"Will you not accept of your son, Hugh, as security?" added Rob. "No." He then got up to leave, and before turning round to go, exclaimed, "Thanks be to Him who refuses not His Son as security for the chief of sinners." Robert heard no more of the affair.

When William, Earl of Sutherland, "the beloved," was commissioned by the crown in 1759 to raise a regiment of Fencibles, 1000 strong, so popular was he in Sutherland and the Reay country that in nine days 1500 Sutherlands, Mackays, and other countrymen, assembled on Dunrobin Green to be enrolled under the Earl's banner, as Colonel. Urged by several of the gentlemen holding commissions in the corps to accompany them, Rob, no way loath, joined as a private.

The admiration of his talents and genius, joined to his own becoming and respectable demeanour, had long previous to this time procured him admittance to the society and the family circles of all the better and higher classes in the county, even to Dunrobin Castle, the apartments of which with their paintings and pictures he describes in his Elegy for the Earl William, now his colonel.

In this regiment he was not required, by the consent of the officers, to do duty as a soldier, except in a way that left him master of his own movements. In one of his rambles he was accosted by Major Ross, who had only joined the regiment, and asked to what company he belonged. "To every company," retorted the bard. The major next demanded his name. The bard's fitting reply was in a stanza of four lines, "I am a Sutherland among the Sutherlands, a Gordon among the Gordons, a Gunn among the Gunns, but at my own home, a Mackay." He then walked off! The major was very angry at this gross breach of military etiquette and discipline. This officer shortly after meeting Earl William, the colonel, reported the circumstance. The Earl, knowing it could be no other than Rob Donn, explained to the irate major that the poet was privileged, and that when he made his acquaintance he would be still more inclined to forgive him. The bard did not forget the incident; he composed several songs in which he sarcastically rallied the major upon his strictness of discipline. In 1763, on peace being made with France, the regiment was disbanded, and the poet, with every soldier enlisted, returned to their homes.

Upon his return home, George, fifth Lord Reay, a nobleman like his father whom he succeeded in 1761, exemplary, pious, of excellent parts and acquirements, exceeded by none of his predecessors in the affections of the people,—invested his clan bard with an office that more than satisfied his ambition, and carried with it abundant respect in the eyes of his fellow-mountaineers. He became Bo-man, or superintendent of his Lordship's dairy and other cattle on the home farm of Balnakill in Durness. His business was to account for the safety and increase of the cattle entrusted to his care, while his wife superintended the dairy. He was bound by agreement to make certain annual returns of dairy produce.

In this situation he remained for several years, giving the greatest satisfaction, till Mackay of Skibo became manager of the estate. It was part of the Bo-man's duty to thresh, or assist to thresh out corn for supplying the cattle with fodder during the winter months. The bard was not used to the exercise of the flail; he employed servants to do this laborious work, which he had not previously been asked to do. He was informed he must wield the flail or quit. The bard chose the latter alternative. It has been rightly supposed that this was not the real cause. Rob had sometime previously severely animadverted upon the conduct of Lady Reay, in a satire, because she had tried to screen a favourite waiting-maid from the censure of the Church, using all her influence with the clergyman for that purpose, and on his refusal, threatened him with legal proceedings to compel him. The minister was firm. Rob heard of it all and severely satirized her Ladyship. This being reported to her, she conceived a great dislike to the bard, and prevailed upon Mackay of Skibo, on his being appointed estate manager, to find some plausible excuse to get rid of the satirist.

Rob retired to Achmore on the confines of Cape Wrath. When Balnakill became the residence of Colonel Hugh Mackay, son of his early employer and friend, he was solicited to enter his service. The bard assented. The fond associations of boyhood and youthful days were not forgotten by either, notwithstanding the difference of age, now more separated by that of rank. Rob's attachment to the colonel was sincere, in fact he was very partial to him and composed several songs in his favour; but even this did not prevent the bard, when he considered it due, to make some severe strictures upon the colonel and upon his wife's penuriousness. These animadversions were borne by the colonel with becoming temper, and at the bard's interment no one felt the loss more sincerely than Colonel Mackay.

The following translation of a song in praise of Hugh Mackay, Bighouse, is by Mr. L. MacBean, and appears with music in " Songs and Hymns of the Scottish Highlands."

Lament for Hugh Mackay.

(Cumha do h-Uisdean Mac Aoidh.)

Oh, sad this voice of woe we hear,
    And gone our cheer and pleasantry;
One common grief without relief,
    Has seized on chief and peasantry;
In hut or hall or merchant's stall,
    There's none at all speaks cheerfully;
Since that sad day he went away,
    Naught can we say but tearfully.

It is not private loss or woe
    That makes the blow so rigorous,
But his sad fate whom none could hate
    With mind so great and vigorous.

For none could find in heart or mind
    A fault in kind or quality,
Now he is not, though we forgot,
    Our common lot, mortality.

Oh, many a man was filled with gloom
    That round thy tomb stood silently ;
Hearts that were buoyed with hope—now void—
    By death destroyed so violently.
By clansmen prized and idolized,
    His worth disguised humanity.
But this fell blow, alas ! will show
    There's naught below but vanity.

He was excelled by none on earth,
    Wit, wisdom, worth, adorning him ;
But none can fill his place but ill
    Of those who will be mourning him.
The hearts are wrung of old and young,
    The mourner's tongue is failing him.
Oh, never more shall we deplore
    One man so sore bewailing him !

    Rob continued in the colonel's employ till his wife, now feeling the infirmities of age, was no longer able to undergo the fatigue of her laborious office. They retired to the neighbouring small farm of Nuybeg. They had not long been there when his excellent wife, whom he tenderly loved, died, and whom he did not survive many months. He deeply grieved for her loss. His greatest earthly treasure was gone. He continued, however, to attend to his usual avocations till within a fortnight of his death, which took place on the 5th August, 1778, at the age of sixty-four. His death caused a universal feeling of sadness over the whole county. He was honoured with a funeral like that of a chief, the highest and lowest of his clan standing side by side with tears in their eyes when his body was laid in its last home. In 1829 a monument was erected over his remains at the expense of a number of his devoted clansmen, with appropriate inscriptions in Gaelic, English, Greek, and Latin.

His stories of wit and humour were inexhaustible, and next to superior intelligence and mental acuteness, formed possibly in his every-day character the most conspicuous feature. He had ever a correct and delicate feeling of his own place in society; but if any, high or low, superior or equal, drew forth the force of his sarcasm upon themselves by assuming any undue liberty on their part, it was an experiment they seldom desired to repeat. His readiness and quickness of repartee frequently discovered him where he had previously been unknown

Rob Donn's moral character was uniformly respectable. To those acquainted with the moral and religious statistics of the bard's native country at that time, it will furnish no inconsiderable test, not only of his morals, but of his strictly religious demeanour, that he was chosen a ruling elder of the Kirk session of his native parish. In that country such an election was never known to be made where the finger of scorn could be pointed at a blemish of character. It hardly needs be mentioned that his company was courted not only by his equals, but still more by his superiors in rank.

In the bosom of his family, humble yet respectable, he was a pattern in happiness and temper. His discipline of his children was kindly, more by ridicule than by harshness, and thus a family of thirteen were spared to rise around their estimable parents, trained to habits of thrift, industry, and virtue. The ordinary pastime of their long winter evenings was, "the tale and the song," and the parent priest absent or present, the whole family exemplified the most sacred lineament of the immortal picture in "The Cottar's Saturday Night." One of the sons enlisted in the 73rd, Lord MacLeod's Highlanders, now the 71st. At the battle of Porto Novo, in Southern India, 1st July, 1781, this gallant regiment charged the enormous army of Hyder Ali seven times during the day. In one of these charges John Donn Mackay came out with his bayonet twisted like a corkscrew; and Sir Hector Munro, in his narrative of the battle of Arnee, fought on 2nd June 1782, states, "I take the opportunity of commemorating the fall of John Donn Mackay, corporal in MacLeod's Highlanders, son of Rob Donn, the bard whose singular talent for the beautiful and extemporaneous composition of Gaelic poetry was held in such high esteem. This son of the bard has frequently revived the spirits of his countrymen when drooping in a long march, by singing the humorous and lively productions of his father. He was killed by a cannon shot, and buried with military honours by his comrades the same evening."

From his birth to his death, Rob Donn was the celebrated bard of the Reay Country. Though there were in that magnificent country other bards of less note during his time, yet he is the only one of whom we have any record. It is therefore no wonder that his countrymen should esteem and honour him. There were heroes before the Fingalians but Highland poetry has not kept their deeds nor their names in remembrance. Bards there may have been in the Reay country before Rob Donn, but nothing is known of their songs or names. As a bard, Rob Donn stands alone in his own country. The Mackay clan were, and still are, famous for many excellent qualities. They were, and still are, very clannish. It is a lasting credit to the gentry of that country that they considered the bard worthy of an honourable position among them. It is also a lasting credit to the bard that he never did anything unworthy of his functions as a poet to gain or keep that position. Like his contemporary, Duncan Bàn, and many other Gaelic bards, he had no school education; but we must not suppose that the man who could not read in those days was so ignorant as the man who cannot read nowadays. It may be doubted if there can be found in our day a herd or gamekeeper, however well schooled, so intelligent or so well educated as were Rob Donn and Duncan Bàn. Both these men had extraordinary natural talents. They had knowledge which in our day can only be acquired from books. They had secured a culture which books cannot provide. There is no school in the Highlands in which Rob Donn could obtain the education he received in Ian MacEachainn's house and amongst the gentry of the Mackay country. Not only did those ladies and gentlemen know the poetry, the history, the traditions, and the customs of the Highlands, but they also possessed accurate information regarding the government and politics of their own day.

It may be that more praise and distinction have been lavished on Rob Donn in his own district than have been bestowed upon poets of greater parts. Out of his own country, but more particularly among other Highlanders, he has not been appreciated as he deserves. There is none of our Highland bards--Ossian perhaps excepted—who left so many pieces of poetry behind him, and none at all who composed so many songs ; aud in comparison with our Highland bards in general, Rob Donn is notable for the brevity and number of his songs. Probably we have not amongst them all one who composed so many airs as he did. We have none at all who composed songs upon such a variety of subjects. There is not a chord of the Highland harp which he has not touched. His mind may not have been filled with the charm, the beauty, and the grandeur of the scenery of his country, as were the minds of the three bards who were his contemporaries, MacDonald, Buchanan, and Duncan Bàn ; but we find on more than one occasion that the glory and grandeur of the creation were not hid from his eye or from his heart.

There are two things that helped to diminish Rob Donn's fame out of his own district, these are his language and versification. Many of his words are unintelligible to the Highlanders of the south and west. Rightly or wrongly, little of the Reay country Gaelic, except Rob Donn's compositions, has been published to familiarise the knowledge of that dialect to the ears of other Highlanders, in whose vocabulary many words he uses are not found, though essentially good Gaelic, met with in dictionaries, and easily understood by his own countrymen. This fact, combined with the terseness of many of his expressions, may have militated adversely against his productions being so well accepted in the south as in the north. See his elegy to *Ian Mhic Raibeart Mhic Nèill* (Mackay of Mudal), page 150 Edition 1871.

> "Corpa calma, bha fearail,
> Inntinn earbsach, làn onoir,
> Làmh a dhearbhadh na chanadh am beul."

It is of great value to get the productions of a penetrating intellect warm from the heart. Rob Donn could not write, MacDonald and Buchanan were school teachers. They wrote and published their works. The Rev. Mr. Stewart of Killin wrote his songs for Duncan Ban Macintyre. It is a great loss for Rob Donn's permanent fame that he had not taken the same opportunity; nevertheless, so long as a tale will be told, or a song sung in Gaelic, "The Song of Death," "Fillan," and the "Geigan," "Smart John," and the "Grey Buck," "MacRory's Breeks," and the "Rispond Family," will be a source of instruction and delight to thousands of his countrymen in every quarter of the globe.

The Rispond Family consisted of two brothers who lived together in single blessedness. They were mean, sordid misers. They had a stock of sheep and cattle on the hills. They amassed gold, and, like the man in the parable, hid it in the earth, in a spot it is said where from their house windows they could see its hiding-place. They had a housekeeper. In the dead of winter, and late on a Saturday night, a poor woman came to their door for shelter, but they closed it in her face—an act which at that time, and for at least one hundred years subsequent, was in those parts looked upon as a heinous crime. Before that night week the three were dead—the housekeeper first, and the two brothers within a day and a night of each other. The two were borne to their last resting-place by the same company of men, and laid together in mother earth. The following translation is by the late Miss M. M. Scobie, Keoldale, Sutherland.

THE RISPOND FAMILY ELEGY.
(Marbhrann Chloinn Ruspainn.)

Quite hale and strong and hearty
    At the opening of the year
Were the three whom we have buried,
    And now lie so lowly here ;
Ten days have only passed as yet
    Since the New Year began,—
Who knows when this dread messenger
    May call for any man?

Within the circle of a year
    Were both of these men born ;
Closest of comrades ever were
    Since days of life's gay morn ;
Ev'n Death, who heeds not closest bonds,
    No separation made,
For in the space of one brief day
    He both in silence laid.

No wrong had they to any done,
    Judging by human ken ;
But neither had they helped in aught
    Their needy fellow-men ;
And all that can be said of them
    Is—they were born—survived
Some years upon this earth—and then
    The hour of death arrived.

But after all that I have said,
    The whole of which is true
(For in this song most faithfully
    I've told but what I knew),
I fear you will not heed my words,
    Nor help the needy more
Than those poor fellows who last week
    Were buried at our door.

"The Song of Death" is an elegy or *Marbhrann* upon Rev. John Munro, Eddrachilis, and Mr. Donald Mackay, Schoolmaster, Farr. The translation is by Mr. L. MacBean.

The Song of Death.
(Marbhrann.)

O Death! thou art still a herald of ill,
  Thy grasp, hard and chill, ne'er faileth;
Where warriors fight, thou showest thy might,
  To shun thee no flight availeth.

O Messenger drear, no pity or fear
   Saves peasant or peer before thee ;
For gold or for gain thou has but disdain,
   And victims in vain deplore thee.

The babe at its birth, ere sorrow or mirth
   It knows upon earth, thou takest ;
For the maid to be wed, ere to church she is led,
   An eeriesome bed thou makest.
If old or if young, if feeble or strong
   In wisdom, or wrong and error ;
If small or if great, whatever our state,
   We have the same fate of terror.

O Power, from whom our sorrowful doom
   Of death and the tomb descendeth,
How happy is he whose confident plea
   On Thy promises free dependeth !
Our Father, Thou art the widow's sure part,
   Ne'er shall Thy support forsake her ;
All good is bestowed, all favour is shewed
   By our bountiful God and Maker.

Rob Donn's mind was, as a poet's mind ever must be, clear, keen, susceptible. It was especially lively and quick : but a bard, be his endowments ever so high, never attained the highest fame without subjecting his mind to patient study. The son of man, with head or hand, never did, or never shall do, any deed that shall endure without labour or exertion.

In personal appearance, Rob Donn was of medium stature, strong and well formed, brown-haired, brown-eyed, good looking : the glance of his eye keen and penetrating, and the expression of his countenance indicated much animation of mind and energy of will.

Rob Donn's poetic compositions may be classed into four kinds—humourous, satirical, solemn, and descriptive. All these severally, with few exceptions, partook of the lyrical. To him the artificial part of poetry was unknown. He seemed proud of his own power of satire, which was not vindictive or rancorous, more calculated to annoy than to wound. As a writer of elegies he is more distinguished for sober truth than poetical embellishment. He detested flattery, and in concluding a lament on the demise of a friend he vouches for the truth of the virtues he recorded. His most celebrated composition of this description is "Ewen's Elegy." The circumstances under which it was composed were these: Rob was benighted on a deer stalking expedition, at the head of Loch Erribol, and took shelter for the night in a hut in which dwelt an old man named Ewen, whom he found stretched on a pallet, apparently at the point of death. Rob had heard that morning of the death of Mr. Pelham, Prime Minister of England, 1754. The idea of his death called away from the summit of his ambition and worldly greatness, contrasted with poor Ewen's condition, invoked the bard's muse. Ewen, though unable to converse with the poet, had still a quick sense of hearing, and also of pride. When the bard went on repeating aloud his composition, and came to the last stanza, the dying man felt so incensed that he crept from his pallet of heather, seized a stick and aimed a blow at the poet's head, which was dexterously avoided. He soon afterwards pacified the frail old man, and passed the night peacefully in the hut. The following is a specimen of this elegy in an English garb:

All men, O Death, thy face shall see,
   And all be forced with thee to go!
Watchful and ready should we be
   'Twixt Pelham high and Ewen low:
Thou makest grief in court and hall,
   When at thy touch earth's glories fade:
The ragged poor man thou dost call
   For whom no mourning will be made!

. .

Friends of my heart! and shall not this
   Make all our thoughts to Heaven tend?
Society a candle is
   That flames away at either end!
In Scotland, where's a humbler man,
   O Ewen than thy father's son?
And in all Britain, greater than
   This Pelham—save the King, was none!

His elegies are mostly of the solemn. His descriptive poems are spirited and true to nature. The Song of Winter is one of his best. We subjoin two stanzas:

How mournful in winter
   The lowing of kine;
How lean backed they shiver,
How draggled their cover,
How their nostrels run over
   With drippings of brine,
So craggy and crining
   In the cold frost they pine.

'Tis Hallowmas time, and
To mildness farewell!
Its bristles are low'ring
With darkness o'erpowering,
And its waters aye show'ring
With onset so fell;
Seem the kid and the yearling
As rung their death knell.

To sum up, it may be said that in the properties of true poetic fertility, of wit and humour, when he is playful, elevation of sentiment when he is solemn, soundness of moral principle and moral feeling when he is serious, we may place him as a bard beside the most popular of the minstrels of his country, and if we dare not say that he stands the first of Gaelic bards, we may say with Mackay of Melness, himself a bard,

With every judge of poet's fame
Rob Donn's will live a deathless name.

SONGS AND MELODIES CONNECTED WITH THE COUNTY.

IN addition to the airs interpolated into the biography of Rob Donn, we submit the following specimens of melodies which he composed to his own songs and laments.

The county has produced not a few musicians, who have given us many pretty melodies and stirring airs. To this county we are indebted for the first collection of Gaelic vocal music that we possess; we refer to the Collection of the Rev. Patrick MacDonald of Kilmore, Argyll, a son of Rev. Murdoch MacDonald, of Durness, whose death Rob Donn laments so sorely. This musician was born in Durness in 1729, and died in 1824. In 1781 he issued "A Collection of Highland Vocal Airs, never hitherto published, to which are added a few of the most lively Country Dances or Reels of the North Highlands and Western Isles, and some Specimens of Bagpipe Music." The work contains two hundred and twenty specimens of Gaelic music.

SONG AND MELODY BY ROB DONN.

(Ach ma ni thu baragan.)

His brother, Joseph MacDonald, was born in Strathnaver in 1739, and died in the East Indies about 1762. He assisted his brother Patrick in compiling his Collection, and left in MS. a Collection of Pipe Music, which was published long after his death (1803), by his brother.

The well-known Queen's piper, Angus Mackay, was

connected with the county by birth or parentage. In 1838
he published a Collection of sixty Pibrochs, which are highly

valued—and the work, being now out of print, commands a
high price. Mackay was accidentally drowned in the river

Nith in 1859. A nephew of Angus, Donald Mackay, was piper to the Prince of Wales, and was allowed to be the best piper of his day. He died only a few years ago. Among the present exponents of bagpipe music, natives of the county occupy a leading place, so long as we have among

Duke of Sutherland's March.

us Pipe-Major Robt. Sutherland, Hamilton, and Pipe-Major John Mackay, Paisley, 93rd Argyle and Sutherland Highlanders. Among modern poets and composers, we find Mr. Eric Mackay, son of the late Dr. Charles Mackay, nd Mr. J. Lindsay Mackay of Glasgow.

MACKAY'S SLOW MARCH.

318 SUTHERLAND AND THE REAY COUNTRY.

There is not a collection of Highland music but contains several tunes claiming connection with Sutherlandshire. We subjoin a list of tunes which are to be found in a work published by Messrs. Logan & Co., Inverness, and known as Fraser of Knockie's Collection.

DORNOCH LINKS.
(March.)

FRASER OF KNOCKIE'S COLLECTION.

Briogais Mhic Ruaraidh—MacRory's breeks.
Caisteal Dhùnrobainn—Dunrobin Castle.
Mac Aoidh—Lord Reay.
Mor, nighean a' Ghiobarlain—Marion, the Knab's Daughter.
Nighean donn a' buain nan dearcag—Maid of Sutherland.
Rob Donn—Rob Donn Mackay, the Poet.
Rìbhinn àluinn éibhinn òg—Beauty charming young and fair.

We cull the following from a collection of pipe music published by Wm. Gunn, Glasgow, in 1876.

WM. GUNN'S COLLECTION OF PIPE MUSIC.

Am Boc glas—The gray Buck.
Baintighearna Bhigeis—Lady Bighouse's Reel.
Baindiùc Chataobh—Duchess of Sutherland's Reel.
Brigis 'Ic Ruaraidh—MacRory's Breeks.
Bruachan Mheilinis—Braes of Melness.
Caileagan Ghaillspidh—Golspie Lasses.
Caileagan Bhaile-dhuthaich—Tain Lasses.
Caisteal Dhunròbainn—Dunrobin Castle.
Chuireadh mnathan Dhuthaich 'Ic Aoidh—The Reay Country Wives.
Lingis Dhornaich—Dornoch Links.
Mac Aoidh 'n oidhche 'rugadh Seònaid—Birth of Lord Reay's Daughter.
Maraichean Ghaillspidh—Golspie fishermen.
Morair Mac Aoidh—Lord Reay's Jig.
Nighean a bhodaich a bha 'n Eadrachaoilis—The Maid of Eaddrachilis.
Port Bhunailidh—Helmsdale, a jig.
Port-siubhal Diuc-Chataobh—Duke of Sutherland's March.

Port-siubhal Iain 'Ic Eachainn—John Mackay of Skerry's favourite quickstep.

Port-mor Iain 'Ic Eachainn—John Mackay of Skerry's favourite reel.

Soiridh 'Ic Coinnich le Cataobh—MacKenzie's farewell to Sutherland.

MacKenzie's Farewell to Sutherland.

RELIGIOUS HISTORY.

By Rev. ADAM GUNN, M.A., Durness.

I.—DRUIDISM.

DRUIDISM was the earliest system of religion in the British Isles. Cæsar mentions Britain as *the seat* of the Druids, from which it would appear that it attained to its fullest development on British soil. The Druids were priests and legislators, judges and teachers ; they also practised medicine and soothsaying. As to their tenets, it is now generally admitted that they taught the doctrines of the immortality of the soul, and of future rewards and punishments. They also practised human sacrifice occasionally, and they held the oak (Gr. *drus*) in great reverence.

The remains of this system are among us to the present day.

(1.) Druidic circles are found at the following places in the county: at Badnabay in Eddrachillis ; at Corrie in Rogart ; at Clachtoll in Assynt ; and between the Mound and Morvich in Golspie. A good specimen of a vitrified fort is on the hill of Creich, and according to some antiquarians, these forts mark the sites of Druidic sacrificial rites.

(2.) Certain words and practices among the natives of Sutherland, as elsewhere throughout the Highlands, can be explained only by reference to this Sun-worship. The moral significance of the Gaelic terms for north and south may be cited. *Tuath*, north, gives an adjective *tuathail*, which means wrong, morally and physically; while *deas*, south, yields *deiseal*, which is right or opportune in every sense. *Bealltainn* and *samhuinn*, the first of summer and winter respectively, and the customs associated with these in certain quarters, point in the same direction. The use of *Clachan* as the native-name for the village where the parish church stands (compare Clachan in Farr) is probably to be attributed to a time when people actually worshipped at *the stones*. Certain superstitions also may be traced to this era. A boat going to sea should turn sunwise if the fishing is to be successful; and in burying the dead, care must be taken to approach the grave sunwise. These are doubtless relics of a Pagan age, when the sun was an object of worship. This system prevailed in the far north until the sixth century of the Christian era.

II.—THE CULDEES.

It is probable that Christianity entered the south of Scotland in the train of the Roman legions. But the influence of Rome did not extend to the northern Picts. These were found in a state of heathenism when Columba came over from Ireland in 563 A.D. After establishing his college in Iona, he paid a visit to Brude MacMeilchon, King of the Picts, whose residence was on the river Ness. Adamnan, the saint's biographer, relates the difficulties which St. Columba encountered from the *Magi*, meaning, no doubt, the Druids. But, in the end, he prevailed, found access to the King, and converted him to the Christian faith. The way was thus opened up for the spread of the Gospel among the Northern Picts, and the Culdees, as Columba's followers were called, eagerly undertook the work. Their *modus operandi* seems to have been as follows:—They first selected a suitable site—an island by preference—for building their bee-hive cells. They next turned attention to agriculture, for the establishment must be self-supporting. In this way they civilized, as well as Christianized, the rude barbarians. Some time would thus be spent in settling themselves in their new quarters, and in gaining a knowledge of the dialect. In the southern counties, where the Dalriadic colony from Ireland had previously settled, they would not require an interpreter. In the north it was different; the Celtic speech of Pictland was more nearly allied to the Brythonic than to the Goidelic branch, and Columba required an interpreter both in his negotiations with King Brude, and in the conversion of the Skye Chieftain Art-brannan.

As was natural, the chief opposition came from the Druid, for his influence waned in exact proportion to their success. The chief soon discovered that he had little to fear from the presence of the *Cele-dei*, but a good deal to gain. Columba took care to secure the favour of the native chieftains at the outset; and so when Cormac and his followers went to the Orkney Islands, they brought with them a recommendation from the Pictish King to the Orkney *reguli* for the protection of their lives. This accounts for the quiet manner in which Culdee settlements were effected in the far north. There is no record of any martyrdom, save that of St. Donan, who was killed either in Kildonan, Sutherlandshire, or more probably in the island of Eigg; and he fell a victim rather to the avarice of a native chieftainess, than to the intolerance of the old faith.

There is hardly a parish in the county which has not some relics of Culdeeism. The most popular saint, judging from the topographical record, was St. Columba, whose name is enshrined on the north coast in Coomb Isle, and in Kilcolmkil in central Sutherland. St. Donan, a contemporary of Columba, may have laboured in Kildonan, where some Irish authorities say he lost his life. Culmaillie, in Golspie, and Kilmacholmaig, and other *Kills* in the county, such as Bailenakill, Durness, all point to Culdee worship. Saint Bar, the patron saint of Cork, may have preached for a time in Dornoch; for the festival of St. Bar was held as a fair or term day down to the sixteenth century. His church existed probably in ruins in Robert Gordon's day (circa 1630). Kintradwell, from St. Triduana, who also figures in Orkney dedications, is another saint name of later times; and the inference may safely be made that a Culdee establishment existed once upon a time in every parish in the county. Towards the close of the ninth century, the people were completely civilised. Hamlets sprung up in the vicinity of the monasteries, and civilization made rapid progress. It was now that that scourge of early Celtic Christianity—the Norse invaders—broke loose upon Scottish shores, and for more than two centuries enveloped the land in heathen darkness. The counties of Caithness and Sutherland came early under their sway, owing to the proximity of Orkney. The Culdee establishments were plundered, and the ecclesiastics slain; and when, in 1150 A.D., the church was again established in the county, it was no longer a Culdee church, but a well-organised Romish hierarchy supplanted the primitive Columban order and continued until the Reformation.

III.—ROMAN CATHOLICISM.

The story of the gradual decay of the Columban church is outside the limits of this paper. As a matter of fact, its disappearance in Sutherland was due more to the successive Norse invasions, than to the aggressions of the Papal See. When the North became more settled, and the Norse Earls came under the sway of the Scottish Kings, Romanism had made sufficient progress at court to become the recognised religion of the land. There is abundant reason, however, to conclude that it was regarded by the native Celts of Sutherland as a foreign importation. No Celtic name appears among the early Bishops of Caithness; and so hostile were the Celts to the new system, that it was found expedient to remove the Bishop's residence from Dornoch, the Cathedral seat, to Halkirk in the vicinity of Thurso. The Norse Earls promised a certain amount of protection to the Saxon ecclesiastics. and being now Christianized themselves since 1000 A.D., they made good their promise to the Scottish Kings when it suited themselves.

The first Bishop in authentic records is Andrew, 1150 A.D. King David I.—that "sore saint to the Crown"—gave him a grant of land, called *Hoctor Comon*. His diocese was co-extensive with the old Earldom, including Sutherland and Caithness. He seems to have been a good deal about the Court of David, and his name appears in the charters of the period. In 1165 he witnesses a charter of Gregory, Bishop of Dunkeld. In 1181 he signs Earl Harold Maddadson's grant of one penny to the See of Rome from every inhabited house in Caithness.

The next Bishop was John. He refused to collect " Peter's Pence," and got into trouble in consequence. On 27th May, 1198, Pope Innocent III. enjoins Bjarni of Orkney and Reginald Gudadson, King of the Hebrides, to compel him on pain of censure. About this time Caithness was taken from Earl Harold by William the Lion, and given to Reginald; but in 1202 Harold regained possession, and took vengeance on the Bishop by cutting out his tongue and eyes. He lived until 1213. The King heard of these things, and came north with a great army to " Eysteindal, where Sudrland and Caithness meet." Peace was made on condition of getting every fourth penny found on all the land of Caithness. The place where they met is not located with certainty; the probable locality is modern Dalharald, not far from Loch Naver, which would at that time be the boundary line between Katanes and Sudrland. The "King's Stone," or Clach-an-righ, erected there points to this spot as the meeting-place.

The third Bishop, Adam, a man of low birth, was consecrated by Malvoisin, bishop of St. Andrews, in 1213. He made a pilgrimage to Rome in 1218. He exacted the Church revenues too harshly. "By an old custom a spann of butter for every twenty cows was paid to the bishop by the husbandmen. He reduced the number of cows first to 15, then to 12 and finally to 10, exacting in every case the spann of butter." In 1222 the Katanes men complained to Earl John, who in vain attempted to induce the Bishop to be more moderate. The irate husbandmen assembled at Hakirk in Thorsdale (the Bishop's seat at that time), threatened violence, and notwithstanding the intercession of Rafn, King William's *logmadr*, burned the Bishop in his own kitchen. King Alexander II. took fearful vengeance on the leading perpetrators by cutting off the heads of eighteen of the murderers.

The fourth bishop, Gilbert de Moravia, appointed in 1223, was by far the ablest and most enlightened representative of the Papal See in Sutherland. It was he that built the Cathedral church at Dornoch. There was a monastery there before 1158, for we find King David stipulating with Rognvald for the protection of the Monks of "*Durnach* in Katanes" during the disturbances of Harold Maddadson, the Earl of Caithness. Very soon after the appointment of Bishop Gilbert,, he set about the task of extending the worship of God in his diocese. At his own expense he built a cathedral, and dedicated it to the Virgin Mary. He saw this structure completed, the glass of which is said to have been made at Sytherhaw (Sygurd's Hoch), west from Dornoch. Gilbert's Charter of Constitution is still preserved, and published in Sir William Fraser's "Sutherland Book." The Chapter, modelled on Elgin and Lincoln, had ten members, of whom the Bishop was chief. The Sutherland churches were Clyne, Dornoch, Creich, Rogart, Lairg, Farr, Kildonan, Durness, Golspie, and Loth. The church of Dyrnes (Durness) was bestowed upon the Cathedral to find light and incense. From this it is evident that he was a splendid organizer. Several things conspired to make his rule a successful one for church development. First, he was a native Celt, from the ancient kingdom of Moray—whose Celtic Maormors were powerful enough to set the Scottish Kings at defiance. His countryman, and probably his relative, on the breaking up of the Moray province by King Malcolm Canmore, secured possessions in Sutherland. This was Hugh Freskyn, the progenitor of the Earls of Sutherland. He was liberal in bestowing land upon the Cathedral; and from the fact that Bishop Gilbert, whose will was extant in 1630, left some territory to his lay brother, Richard de Moravia, it would appear that Hugh Freskyn's gifts of land were made to Bishop Gilbert personally, and not to the Church. At any rate, certain transactions in the assignment of Church lands took place about this period, which formed a bone of contention for many years between the Church and the successors of Freskyn, the Sutherland Earls. Hugh Freskyn died in 1214 and was succeeded by William—the first Earl of Sutherland. It was during his time that Gilbert flourished as a successful ecclesiastic, builder, and agriculturist. The Bishop's Castle at Scrabster was built by him, and he is said to have discovered a mine of gold in Durness in the lands belonging to his bishoprick. He died in 1245 and was subsequently canonized. As late as 1545 John Mackay of Strathnaver makes oath to the Earl of Sutherland in the Cathedral Church at Dornoch "over the Gospels and relics of St. Gilbert."

St. Gilbert was a man of mark, and left his impress on the rude generation in which he lived. Before his time only one priest ministered in the church at Dornoch, owing, he says, to the poverty of the place, and the hostilities of the times. But before his death peace and order prevailed in his diocese, and the Romish Church had good reason to canonize him, for it was to him mainly that Roman Catholicism owed any measure of popularity which the system ever secured in Sutherland.

He was succeeded by William, the fifth bishop of the See, whose signature is adhibited to the document of Alexander III. in the defence of the liberties of the Scottish Church.

Walter de Baltrodin succeeded him. He was a canon of Caithness, and his election was not regular, but Pope Urban in 1263 offered no objections.

He was succeeded by Archibald, Archdeacon of Moray, in whose time the old dispute about the church lands came to a crisis between himself and Earl William, but it was amicably settled. About this time a general collection was made throughout the diocese in behalf of the Crusaders, and it is interesting to discover in Theiner's Monumenta in the Vatican the Sutherland churches which contributed, and the amount. Under date 1274 A.D. we find Ascend (Assynt) contributing 5s. 4d.; Haludal, 9s. 4d.; Dyrness (Durness), 14s. 8d. Again in 1275 Helwedale contributes 9s. 4d.; Ra (Reay), 9s. 4d.; Kildoninave, 2 marcs. The Caithness churches which contributed are Olrig, Thurso, Dunnet, Canisbay, Hakirk, Latheron.

Alan, an Englishman, was the next bishop. He was a tool of Edward I. He signed the letter to the King proposing a marriage between the maid of Norway and young Prince Edward.

Adam, the ninth bishop, was precentor of the church of Ross, but he died in a short time, and was succeeded by *Andrew*, Abbot of Cupar, 1273—1300. "Because of wars imminent in those parts, and dangers of the way, which are long and perilous, it is impossible for him to approach the Apostolic Seat for consecration; therefore a mandate was given to the bishops of Aberdeen, Glasgow and Ross to consecrate him."

Ferquhard, the next bishop, acknowledges in 1310 Bruce's title to the crown (1301—1328). In 1312 he witnesses the payment of 100 marks sterling by Robert the Bruce to the King of Norway for the Hebrides.

Of *Nicolas* and *David*, who succeeded him, nothing is known.

Alan was confirmed in 1341. He was Archdeacon of Aberdeen.

Thomas Murray de Fingask, confirmed in 1342, d. 1360.

Malcolm succeeded him in 1369.

Alexander Man, 1389, appears by proxy in Perth Synod, 1420.

Robert Strathbrock, 1444.

John Innes, dean, 1447.

Robert was bishop in 1434, and

William Moodie (1445—1460) was still in office when, in 1469, the Orkney Islands were ceded to the crown of Scotland.

About this date a vacancy occurs for 24 years, when the See was governed by Adam Gordon, dean and parson of Pettie. John, the ninth Earl of Sutherland (1508—1514), who inherited the mental malady of his father, was his contemporary, and his affairs were likewise in the hands of Adam Gordon.

Andrew Stewart was the next bishop of Caithness, and he acted as Treasurer for the Earl of Sutherland. An idea of the income of the Sutherland Earls may be gained from the fact that at this time the total income from the Property Lands amounted to £103 4 8 yearly, and from Tenantry Lands £147 13 4.

Andrew Stewart, son of John, Earl of Atholl, next ruled the See. He instigated the Clan Gunn to slay the Laird of Duffus. The dean of Caithness, who was the Laird's brother, in retaliation, seized the vicar of Far, and imprisoned him at Duffus (1518—1542).

Robert Stewart was the last administrator of the See. He was born in 1516, and was brother of Mathew, Earl of

Lennox. He was created Earl of March 1579. He died at St. Andrews in 1586. The Reformation had taken place before this, when he became a Protestant, and gifted away much of the rents of the See of Caithness, and the priory of St. Andrews.

The rental of the Sutherland Estates had, by the time of John, the tenth Earl (1535—1567), amounted to £666 13 4. But great difficulty was experienced in securing the teinds, and the church lands proved a bone of contention still. In 1548 Sir Robert Stewart, the last bishop, got the Earls of Sutherland and Caithness, and Mackay of Far, to promise to help him by force to secure the teinds. But the end of Roman Catholicism was drawing near. Iu 1558 such progress did the principles of the Reformation make in the North—or the *Lutheran heresy*, as the Church dignitaries called it—that a congregation of nobles was formed, with the Earl of Sutherland as one of them. Earl John was present at the Edinburgh Convention of 1558 demanding reforms of the Queen Regent, and took a prominent part in the work of Reformation. It is a pity that the nobles who were so eager to adopt the Reformation did not provide for the religious instruction of the people on the downfall of the old church. They were quite prepared to seize the patrimony of the church, but they were reluctant to provide ordinances out of the funds which fell into their hands. The rapacity of the nobles in thus secularizing the property of the Church is a slur upon the Scottish Reformation. When the Papal Jurisdiction was overthrown in 1560, the Church was very wealthy ; two-thirds of its revenues went to provide for the Romish dignitaries while they lived, and the remaining third to provide ordinances until more livings became vacant.

Knox had hoped to apply the revenues of the Church for the purposes of education, religion, and the poor; but in this he was frustrated. The territorial magnates—some of whom were eager to throw off the Roman yoke—kept a firm hold on the revenues; and when we add to this the difficulty of securing educated men for every vacant parish, there is no wonder that for fifty years after the Reformation only the most meagre provison was made for the religious instruction of the people.

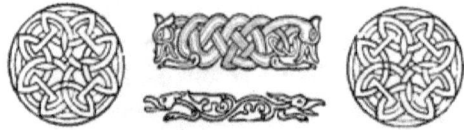

Rev. JOHN S. MACKAY.

RELIGIOUS HISTORY OF THE REAY COUNTRY AFTER THE REFORMATION.

By Rev. J. S. MACKAY, Fort-Augustus.

Chapter II.

THE first minister, so far as can be ascertained, who was settled on this coast, was Mr. Alexander Munro, who was ordained and inducted to the charge of Durness. He was a native of the burgh of Inverness, and the son of a dyer. When a young man, he had the privilege of hearing the celebrated Mr. Robert Bruce of Edinburgh, who was confined for a time, by King James VI., to Inverness. The crowds that attended on Mr. Bruce's ministry while there were immense. People came in great numbers from Nairnshire and Ross-shire, and even from Sutherlandshire. It was by no means uncommon for people from Golspie and the districts around to walk all the way to Inverness, and to consider their labour and fatigue abundantly repaid if only they got within hearing of Mr. Bruce on the Sabbath. The Earl and Countess of Sutherland went there, and remained for a month under his ministry, and reaped therefrom the salvation of their souls. Mr. Alexander Munro was also converted under Mr. Bruce's ministry. He gave early evidence of the reality of the great change he underwent, by living a life of earnest and close communion with God. On one occasion, while thus intensely exercised, he thought he heard, as it were, a voice urging him to devote himself to the Lord's service in the work of the ministry. On reflection, he attributed this impression to some vain imagination of his own heart, as he knew himself to be altogether unqualified, and thought himself unsuited for such an office. For a time he managed to drive the idea from his mind. But again, on two different occasions, the impression returned that he heard a voice in imploring tones urging him to devote himself to the ministry of the gospel. On the last of these occasions he was led to understand that the sphere of his labours was to be Durness in the Reay country. Regarding all this as a call from the Lord, he could no longer decline. He entered the University of Aberdeen; made very rapid progress in all his studies, and was ultimately licensed to preach the gospel. Soon therefore the way was opened up for his coming to Durness, and he was ordained and inducted into the charge of that parish. Whether he was preceded there by any other settled minister it is difficult to say; but there is a probability that the congregation was gathered and formed into a Presbyterian charge before his induction. The date of his ordination is not recorded. He died in 1643. But as Mr. Bruce was in Inverness about 1605, and as Mr. Munro's family were grown up and some of them married before his decease, his induction must have taken place in the early years of the century, or some fifty years after the establishment of the Reformation under Knox.

On his induction to the charge of Durness, he soon discovered that the ignorance of the people was the chief barrier to his usefulness and success in the work intrusted to him. To remedy this, he set about the cultivation of the poetic talent, of which he had a considerable share. He versified large portions of Scripture in Gaelic ; and composed hymns descriptive of creation, the fall, and the work of redemption, etc. He gave these to the people, who sang them together at their winter evening gatherings and at their work during other seasons. He thus inaugurated a mode of instruction which was afterwards effectually followed up by others,—notably by Mr. John Mackay, tacksman of Taobh-beg, Mudale, at the head of Strathnaver. It was hearing the Mackay Fencibles recite Mackay of Mudale's hymns that first suggested to Dugald Buchanan the composition of his own very beautiful Gaelic poems.

The Lord very graciously countenanced Mr. Munro's labours in the ministry, and made him the honoured means whereby a large harvest of souls was gathered in to Christ. Notices of this appear in the then Presbytery Records of Dingwall, or of Ross. The blessing bestowed upon Durness under his ministry extended in some measure to neighbouring districts. His hymns were sung in all of them, and long after his decease were known as "Laoidhean Mhaighstir Alasdair,"—Mr. Alexander's Hymns. It would thus appear that God was pleased to make use of human hymns in this instance, as He did of those of Luther, for the diffusion of gospel truths among a people who were uneducated and who had not the written Word : and through them gave instruction, guidance, comfort, and encouragement to multitudes of His people. Highlanders of those days did not esteem human hymns to be the objectionable and awfully corrupting things they are now supposed to be.

Mr. Munro was evidently held in high esteem among his people, and must have enjoyed the same among county families, inasmuch as his daughter Christina married Mr. John Mackay of Achness in Strathnaver. This Mr. Mackay became afterwards Captain of the Clan Mackay, and went by the complimentary title of "Lord John," and she by that of "Baintighearna Cursty," *i.e.* Lady Christian. He too who was Bishop of Caithness during the ascendency of Prelacy in the period immediately following Mr. Munro's death, esteemed the influence of his piety to be so great among the people, that he thought it would be a great gain to Prelacy if he could succeed in getting his son, the Rev. Hugh Munro, over to Episcopacy, and made rector of Durness. In this he succeeded, but found afterwards that Mr. Hugh, who was really a good man, made but an indifferent prelatist, as is seen from notices in the records of the Bishopric of Caithness.

Towards the close of Mr. Alexander Munro's ministry at Durness, Mr. George Squair became minister of Edderachilis and Kinlochbervie. It cannot now be ascertained what provision was made for him in the way of temporalities. After the Reformation, the lairds and great men of the period laid hold of all the Church lands they could get within their power. These and other possessions of the Church were taken by some at an earlier, and by others at a later period. The extensive possessions of the Church in Assynt were not taken possession of by the family there until after the death of the last Episcopal minister, a Mr. Gray. He died shortly before the ordination of Mr. Scobie, the first Presbyterian minister of Assynt after the Revolution Settlement. But whatever the means may have been whereby Mr. Squair was supported, he was appointed as colleague to Mr. Munro at the time mentioned. He was a man of God, faithful in all that related to his office, and the Lord set His seal very manifestly upon his ministry.

Mr. Munro, as noticed before, died in 1643 A.D., and so escaped the times of persecution. Not so Mr. Squair. He experienced great hardships and had narrow escapes during that bloody period, that has so stamped prelacy with indelible disgrace. After labouring successfully and in peace for many years in his charge, he was at last pounced upon, and hunted over mountain and glen, because of his faithfulness to Presbyterianism, and to the cause of the covenanted Reformation in Scotland. He was at this time the only Presbyterian minister in the Reay country. Though thus alone, and in the midst of many dangers, he nevertheless resolved on administering the Lord's Supper to as many of the faithful among his people as would venture on meeting with him. To do so was considered a greater crime than holding conventicles or maintaining field-preachings. He therefore went about it very quietly and cautiously, and took council with a few godly followers as to where and when it should be observed. There are two places in the parish where the people were wont to assemble for this purpose,— one in Edderachilis proper, named "Larach nam Bord," at ".Airidh nan Cruithneach," above Scourie; the other on the march between Oldshoremore and Drumnaguy, in Oldshorebeg, at a spot between Captain Mackay's house and the rising ground to the north. These places, however, were not considered in the circumstances safe from interruption. They chose, therefore, a more secluded spot in the neighbourhood of Rhicoinich, at the head of Loch Inchard, and between the little hamlet and Loch Garbad. When the spot was fixed upon, the few with whom he took counsel were enjoined to exercise the greatest prudence in diffusing the information, but to give to such as they might confide in an opportunity of being present. On the Sabbath appointed they assembled to the number of five score. These were the more devout and faithful in all the hamlets of Edderachilis and Kinlochbervie. They approached the place as if by stealth, with feelings greatly agitated, but with hearts rising in earnest supplications that the Lord might grant them His protection and gracious presence. When they came to the place, they found themselves in the centre of a glade overgrown with birchwood, and sheltered by wild and beetling rocks. The pulpit desk was a birch tree, sawn off at a considerable height, and the tables were formed of turf covered with green smooth sod. The service was opened with singing and prayer, and after reading and a short exposition, and again singing, Mr. Squair took for his text the words of Thomas when delivered from his unbelief, "My Lord, and my God." The whole service was a memorable one. The Lord was the "shield and the exceeding great reward" of His people that day. Not only was there no interruption of the service, but all there felt so much of the Lord's presence, and their bonds were so loosened, and their fears so dispelled, that all, without a single exception, felt constrained to say with Thomas, "My Lord, and my God," and without exception commemorated the dying love of their Redeemer. Many years thereafter, at a communion season in Badcall, Scourie, during the ministry of Mr. Brodie, Mr. Squair's successor, there was also a time of similar blessing. Addressing one of the oldest and most godly of his elders, Mr. Brodie asked him whether he ever before experienced a more impressive season. "Only once," said the aged patriarch, "at the memorable communion of Rhic-oinich, when Mr. Squair preached with his Bible placed before him on the stump of a tree ; and when the five score present—of whom I am the last remaining one—sat down at the Lord's table, exclaiming ' My Lord, and my God.'" It was long believed that Obsdale, in the parish of Rosskeen, was the only place in the north in which the sacrament of the Lord's Supper was administered during the twenty-eight years' persecution. It will be seen, however, that the parish of Kinlochbervie divides with Rosskeen that honourable distinction; and it is possible there may be other places which have a right to a similar claim, although the fact may now be buried in oblivion.

Mr. Squair found himself oftentimes hard pressed. His persecutors, whenever they got trace of him, were immediately in pursuit. His followers were thus obliged to seek out all manner of hidden paths to wait upon him, and all manner of secret places wherein he might minister to them the word of life. When pursued on one occasion, and as he was passing the hut of one of his people, with his pursuers close behind, he saw a girl weeding potatoes, then beginning to be raised in lazy beds (or *feannagan*) as a garden vegetable. He knew not whether he might trust her to shield him in any way, but he spoke to her, and asked what she was doing. "Weeding potatoes," she said. "And have you," he asked, "while so working, any thoughts about the interests of your soul?" "Yes," she said, "while weeding the potatoes I am praying the Lord that He may weed the love of sin out of my heart." "If that be so," said Mr. Squair, "you will try to conceal me from my pursuers, who are close behind, and try to abstain from falsehood while shielding me."

"Come quickly, then," she said, "and lie down in the deep furrow between the beds, and let me cover you with the weeds." This was scarce accomplished, and she set to work again, when the pursuers appeared. They asked her gruffly if she saw Mr. Squair pass that way lately. She said she did see him not long ago come in the direction they themselves came in, and stand where they stood; and if they were active that they were very likely to apprehend him before long. They set off immediately, exulting over their prey as if already within their grasp. No sooner were they well out of sight than Mr. Squair was liberated from under his hiding of weeds, and, after being refreshed with food, he set off in the opposite direction, and thus escaped in safety.

He was at last joined by three godly witnesses from the south, who hoped, but in vain, that coming so far north they might for a time escape the fury of the enemy. They first landed in the parish of Lochbroom, and preached here and there as they found opportunity, or a people that could understand them, and passed on through Coigeach and Assynt till they joined Mr. Squair at Edderachilis. On their arrival both he and the faithful among his people became bolder in the service of their Master, and those who were on the alert to arrest him did not feel themselves sufficiently strong to do so. A military party was therefore sent, by orders of the Bishop of Caithness, under command of an officer determined to execute his commission. His instructions were to take Mr. Squair and his companions, alive or dead! He and his friends had no help for it but to flee for protection where they might. The four set off by the passes between Foinne bheinne, Kinlochbervie, and Ben Spionnaidh in Durness. Eluding their pursuers, they passed over the slopes of Ben Hope, and reached the House of Tongue, expecting Lord Reay to afford them shelter and concealment for a season. The Mackay, however, influenced by his uncles, the Mackenzies of Seaforth and Pluscardine, was pledged to the Government, and so could only express his sympathy by not apprehending them. He made a show, indeed, openly of having apprehended them, but, after refreshing them, he secretly ordered them to proceed beyond his bounds. They met with similar treatment from the Mackays of Strathy and Bighouse. Depressed, wearied, and worn out, they now made their way for Ulbster House, the residence of the Sinclairs of Ulbster, a family known to be favourable to the cause of the Covenanters. Here they were kindly received, and concealed for some time in a vault or unused place. The fact, however, of the presence of suspicious parties in the castle began to be whispered about, and Sinclair found that soon he would be unable to shield them from the power of the Bishop. Every possible means for their safety was anxiously discussed. At last Sinclair determined on sending a private and faithful messenger to the Earl of Sutherland, requesting him to receive and shield these wanderers and sufferers for conscience' sake. The Earl and Countess were in great difficulty about the matter, as they failed in trying to protect their own minister, the Rev. John MacCulloch of Golspie. If, however, Mr. Squair and his companions could be conveyed to Dunrobin in secrecy, their protection as strangers and unknown, and for whom there might be no inquiry in that quarter, was possible. On receiving this reply, Sinclair embraced the opportunity of calm weather and dark nights, and got them conveyed by sea to Dunrobin. He got a boat, manned by the best rowers and most faithful men he could pick out. They rowed all night, and lay hidden during the day in some of the numerous creeks along the coast. They arrived at last at Dunrobin, and delivered up their charge to the Earl of Sutherland. They were kindly received, but somehow the Earl was suspicious that after all they might be spies sent by some of the prelates, or those in authority, to ensnare him and other families suspicious of being favourable to the cause of Presbyterianism. He communicated his fears to the Countess. She said she would soon discover whether or not they were true men. She therefore after dinner requested the strangers to conduct a private prayer-meeting, and an exercise of thankfulness for their preservation so far. During the meeting and throughout all the exercises the Lord's gracious presence was so manifest, that the suspicions of the Earl, who was present, were completely removed, and he immediately set about providing for the concealment and safety of his guests. There was a cave in Golspie burn, partly, it is said, the work of human hands, which was so completely shaded by trees and close underwood, so out of the ordinary route of people passing, and moreover so dry and roomy, that it was determined to make use of it as their hiding-place. Here they lay concealed for a long time, amply supplied with all things necessary to their possible comfort in such a situation. Nor was there any one engaged in conveying their provisions, or aware of their presence there, found mean enough to make it known. The day of deliverance, so long prayed for, came at last. The deceptive indulgence granted by James II. would have set them free; but whether they embraced that, or whether it was known to them, is not said. But so soon as they were free, they proceeded to Dunrobin to pour forth their hearts in thankfulness for the protection and all the other kindnesses they received during the time of their trial. They further declared to the Earl and Countess their full persuasion—as they believed from God—that there was not an inch of the land in the county, and in the hands of the Assynt family, and that of the Mackays of Reay, over which they were pursued, and from which they were driven, but would yet be in the possession of the family of Sutherland. This saying of theirs was known all over the country, and handed down through the several generations; and as said, so it happened.

Mr. Squair never returned to Kinlochbervie or Edderachilis. Like many others, the great mental strain and bodily sufferings endured told upon his constitution, which was so utterly broken down that he was unable to undertake the duties of his charge. He went and stayed with one of his family. His son is said to have lived and died at Dornoch. A daughter was married to a Mr. Munro from Ross-shire, who rented a farm that is now embraced in the Dunrobin home farm. She was the mother of the godly Mr. George Munro, who was the third minister of Farr after the Presbytery of Tongue was erected, and one highly honoured of God in the work of ingathering of souls to Christ. Mr. Munro's name, and the date of his induction and death, are to be seen on the back of his pulpit, which still remains in the Farr Church. Mr. Munro was married to a daughter of the Rev. John Mackay of Lairg, who was a near if not the immediate successor of Mr. Squair in the wide district of Durness, Edderachilis, and Tongue. He was translated thence to Lairg in 1714, A.D., and was succeeded in Durness by Mr. Brodie, already mentioned.

We already noticed that Mr. Squair's health did not permit him, after the Revolution Settlement, to return to the scene of his former labours on the north coast.. The only minister in the Reay country at that time was Mr. Hugh Munro, Durness. He was the son of Mr. Alexander Munro, the first Presbyterian minister of the country, of whom we have already given a short sketch. Mr. Hugh Munro was a man of culture, of mild temperament, of decided Christian character, and evangelical. He was a graduate of King's College, Aberdeen, and was ordained as incumbent of Durness by the bishop and clergy of Caithness, at Watten, on the 20th January, 1663.

It is not known under what influences, or motives, he was led to conform to Episcopacy; but it was manifest throughout his career that he had done so reluctantly, and was ever an indifferent Episcopalian. He was censured again and again for his non-attendance on the diocesan meetings of the clergy, and did not take the test until 1682. He retained his benefice at the Revolution Settlement, and continued thereafter sole Presbyterian minister of the Reay country until his death in 1698. Tradition, with persistent but strange inaccuracy, connects with his name an incident that occurred really in connection with his father's ministry; and as it gives us a vivid glimpse into the social condition of the times, and shows to us the lawlessness with which the ministers of the gospel were then confronted, it may be of interest to relate it briefly here. The district over which the minister of those days had oversight being so very extensive, he often took up his abode, for months at a time, at its either extremity. Mr. Alexander Munro being on one of

these occasions entertained at Tongue by Sir Donald Mackay,
—afterwards the first Lord Reay—was called upon in the
course of duty to visit some district to the west. Such were
the times, that Lord Reay did not consider even the messenger of peace safe without an armed attendant. Mr. Munro,
however, did his work unmolested, until on his return
journey he came to the river Hope, beside which there lived
a noted character of that period—a Donald MacLeod, who is
better known as Donald 'Ic Mhorchaidh 'Ic Ian mhòr. This
man, now in extreme old age, had been a powerful and lawless ruffian, whose hands were stained with the blood of no
fewer, it is said, than eighteen murders. To us now it seems
unaccountable, almost inconceivable, that any country or
condition of society could bear for any time the tyranny of
such a fiend in their midst. But he was a convenient tool
in the hands of others, who were equally bloody-minded,
though they took care not to appear so outwardly. Mr.
Munro felt it his duty to speak to this lost and lawless
sinner, if so be he might lead him in his old age to some
sense of his sin, to repentance, and to the knowledge of the
Saviour. Instead, however, of this, Donald took deadly
offence at being so spoken to, and were it not that the
infirmities of age and the fear of an armed attendant prevented, he would as readily have shed the blood of the
evangelist as he did that of his many former victims.
Donald's two sons—men of physique and spirit akin to his
own—were absent. On their return, the father charged
them instantly to follow the minister, and not show face in
his presence without the heart of him who so insulted him.
They went in pursuit, but on nearing Mr. Munro they were
challenged by his attendant, who was armed with a match-

lock, whereas they had none, so they thought discretion the better part of valour. Fearing their father even more than the matchlock, they killed a sheep, and took with them its heart, which they presented to him instead of the minister's. He viewed it attentively, and said, "Ah well! I always thought the *Munroes* cowards, but never knew until now that they had the heart of a sheep." The tomb of this ruffian is to this day an object of interest to all who visit the old church of Durness. It is built in a recess of the south wall of the church; and the tradition is that Donald, on doing some deed of violence, was taunted that soon his own carcase would be thrown into a pit, be covered with sod, and trampled upon by the meanest of God's creatures. The proud spirit, to avoid this dishonour and indignity, as he reckoned it, offered to build that side of the church at his own expense, if allowed to make a vault or recess in the wall for his coffin, and thus prevent any one from trampling on his grave. His offer was accepted, and there he was interred. The inscription on his rough tombstone is as follows:—

" Donald Mhic Mhorchaidh Heir lys lò
Vas il to his friend, var to his fò
True to his maister in veird and vò.

| D. | M | M | C | | | | | 1623." |

As Mr. Hugh Munro died in 1698, in the 59th year of his age, and so was not born for some years after Donald was dead and buried, the above incident must have occurred, as we have said, in connection with his father's ministry, for whom the old church of Durness was built in A.D. 1619.

From A.D. 1698 until 1707 there is no trace of any minister being in the Reay country. This gap of nine long years is certified by the notice of a reference to the Commission by the General Assembly, March 28, 1704, "to send a probationer having Irish (or Gaelic) to Caithness Presbytery, with special eye to Durness." Acts of Assembly, 1704.

At this point, however, the Lord was pleased to raise up and send forth as His servant in the ministry, a scion of one of the leading families of the country, and one of the ablest ministers of the gospel the Reay country has seen. In A.D. 1707, the Rev. John Mackay, son of Captain William Mackay of Borley, and cousin of General Hugh Mackay who fought the battle of Killiecrankie, was ordained and inducted as minister of Durness. He was an M.A. of Edinburgh, and thereafter studied in Utrecht, Holland. His name has been handed down from generation to generation as being eminent for his piety, and was as noted for his physical prowess as for his learning. He was also a strict and stern disciplinarian, such as the times so loudly called for; and was aided in this by the influence he wielded as a member of one of the leading families—a chief family of the Clan Mackay— the Scourie family. Tradition has handed down several stories illustrative of the man, and of his times. The ministers of those days oftentimes wielded civil and magisterial authority as well as ecclesiastical and spiritual. But their chief work, and most arduous, lay in catechizing the people. The questions and answers of the Shorter Catechism were enjoined to be repeated in every family on the Sabbath evenings, and every member of each family was expected to learn them. The minister went to every hamlet, collected the people, usually to the largest, most respectable, and most convenient house in the district, called each family in rotation, and the members of each family by name, to repeat these answers : and to be examined on their understanding of the truths they conveyed. These catechizings were the principal means of the people being educated in the great and leading truths of their salvation ; the means also that afforded the best opportunity of educating their minds and consciences in the principles of morality, and of enforcing the application of these principles to their every day life and conduct. There was a varied interest attached to the proceedings of these meetings that led the people to an attentive appreciation of what they were taught, such as could not be secured by the mere preaching of the gospel among them ; and mighty, indeed, under the blessing of God, was the change effected in the minds and manners of the generations that followed from the times of the labours of the early pioneers of the gospel in the Reay country. In every generation, however, perhaps in every district, there would be found rude and lawless characters who submitted neither to this nor any other mode of instruction ; and, indeed, the bringing of the people as a whole under the benign influences of the truth, and of the principles of morality, was then, as in every age, a very gradual process.

The thoroughness of Mr. Mackay's work and character is illustrated by many anecdotes told of him and handed down by tradition. Catechizing on one occasion, a poor imbecile or idiot member of a family examined was not presented with the others. Mr. Mackay asked if there was no other member of the family. He was told there was, but it was no use noticing him, as he was a poor creature without his natural faculties. "Call him," said the minister ; "he is one of God's creatures, and He is able to convey His own truth to his mind, however defective he may be." One of the

questions asked was, " Have you a soul?" " No," answered
the idiot. " Had you ever one?" " Yes." " And what
has become of it?" asked the minister. " God knew that I
was not able to keep it, that I would only destroy it, so He
has taken it into His own keeping," was the answer. The
examination and answers of the poor idiot turned out to be
the subject of deepest interest in that day's proceedings. At
another time Mr. Mackay was answered by a rough character
in such a way as was evidently intended to turn the subject
into ridicule. A second answer had been given in the same
way; quick as lightning the powerful hand of the minister
was laid upon the collar of the offender, and a castigation
administered as would have been done to a child. The
ridicule was now turned altogether the other way. The
minister became a hero, and never again did rudeness show
face in his presence at catechizings. The sternness and impartial character of the dicipline he enforced is illustrated by
an incident that happened in his own family. On account
of some negligence or other, one day water for Sabbath use
was not secured on the Saturday. The servant girl, with the
connivance of her mistress, took the *kits* to the spring and
brought in the needed water. The action was observed and
spoken of by the neighbours. On the minister hearing of it,
it was laid before the session; and he retired that they
might come to an independent finding with respect to the
dicipline to be exercised and administered. The finding was
that the servant girl must stand in presence of the congregation on the Sabbath, with the water *kits* one on either side,
and thus acknowledge the offence and be admonished; and
the minister was requested to admonish his wife privately.
Mr. Mackay was indignant at the partiality shown to the

mistress, so the finding had to be the same for both, and Mrs. Mackay had to stand beside her servant with the *kits*, to be admonished. Let us hope that the minister was charitable and in a tender mood when the admonition was given, and that he apportioned the guilt impartially! Mr. Mackay was translated to Lairg in A.D. 1714. He was grandfather to the late Mr. John Mackay, Rockfield, and great-grandfather to the late Mr. Sage, Resolis.

Mr. Mackay, as was noticed, was minister of Durness for only seven years—from A.D. 1707 to 1714; but this short experience led him to see how utterly impossible it was for one man to overtake the work of the ministry throughout so wide a district, or exercise any appreciable influence for the general good of a people whom he could see only occasionally, and at long intervals. The parish was from fifty to sixty miles in length, and from ten to twelve miles in breadth, and within its bounds were from 3000 to 4000 souls needing instruction in Divine things, and indeed in all things that pertained to civilized life. Their condition weighed heavily upon his mind, and he made strenuous efforts to meet their needs by raising "an action for disjunction, modification, and locality" of the parish before the Lords of Council and Session. But interested parties raised objections to this, and, after considerable loss in the way of expenses, he was doomed to disappointment and failure. This doubtless made his translation to Lairg a welcome relief. In the following year, A.D. 1715, Mr. George Brodie, a licentiate of the Inverness Presbytery, and connected with the Brodies of Brodie, was ordained as minister of Durness, by the Presbytery of Caithness. Every tradition of him, and written notices still extant, show him to have been pre-eminently a man of prayer, able and cultured as well, and greatly interested in the spiritual instruction and well-being of his people. A few years' experience led him also to see that it was altogether beyond the power of any individual minister to satisfactorily overtake the work required. He therefore moved in the same direction as Mr. Mackay, but first brought the matter before the Presbytery and Assembly of the Church. The Assembly acquiesced, and ordained a collection over the whole Church, to help to make provision for two additional ministers. Authority was also given to Mr. Brodie and the Presbytery, and an action raised before the Lords of Council and Session at their instance, and that of the Advocate-Procurator of the Church, for the disjunction of the parish into the three parishes of Tongue, Durness, and Edderachilis, with the limits of each respectively defined. The disjunction was effected in A.D. 1724; and the general collection made amounted to £1800. Lord Reay, who was member of the Assembly at which this was announced, undertook, on condition of receiving this money, to erect suitable ecclesiastical buildings, assign glebes, and contribute so much yearly as stipend to the ministers of the new charges. This arrangement being satisfactorily completed, Mr. Brodie elected to move from Durness and become minister of the newly erected parish of Edderachilis. Two years thereafter, in 1726, Mr. Murdoch MacDonald, a native of Fearn, Ross-shire, and graduate of St. Andrews, was ordained minister of Durness. Immediately after his ordination a Presbytery of Tongue was erected by order of Assembly; and consisted of four parishes, disjoined from the Caithness Presbytery, viz. Farr, Tongue, Durness, and Edderachilis; and two disjoined from Dornoch Presbytery -

Kildonan and Assynt. In the same year the Caithness Presbytery was disjoined from the Synod of Orkney, and the Dornoch Presbytery from the Synod of Ross; and the three Presbyteries were erected into the Synod of Sutherland and Caithness. The parishes of Kildonan and Assynt were again restored to the Presbytery of Dornoch in the year 1727 and 1736 respectively.

In Mr. Brodie's action for disjunction, the great difficulties met with in travelling through the country are referred to, and, down to about a century later, there was not a single yard of good road to be found in it. In this matter there is now a great change; still its natural features make travelling now, as then, very tedious and arduous at any time; and during stormy weather it is made an impossibility. As an illustration of what it was in the middle of last century, we read in Mr. MacDonald's diary that, having on one occasion during rough weather to go to a meeting of Presbytery for the purpose of translating the minister of Edderachilis to Tongue, he became ill, through over fatigue, ere he reached the west side of Loch Eriboll, and could proceed no further. An express, however, was sent to him from Tongue, saying that the corresponding member from Dornoch Presbytery, without whom they could not have a quorum, would not cross the ferry to the farther side of Loch Eriboll. The Lady Reay, who was deeply interested in the settlement, was therefore to send a boat for him, and by "her positive orders he must come over all impediments to the Presbytery seat." Alarmed at the thought of rounding Whiten Head in an open and small boat, he sent the messenger back immediately to stay their coming. But during the night the boat arrived with *feather-bed and blankets*, and the boatmen had orders to take no refusal, but to wrap the minister in these and convey him to the Presbytery! "However surprising," he says, "and disconcerting this command, finding the sea so very mild in the morning, I came off early, and before twelve o'clock we arrived at Tongue."

The social condition of the country at the period of its history which we have now reached—A.D. 1736, was considerably modified and improved from what it was at the beginning of the century. The knowledge of Divine truth was spreading among the people, and influencing their thoughts and habits socially,—their intelligence was being raised, and their moral habits bettered. As yet, however, the common people had no opportunity of learning to read; and while this continued, great ignorance must have prevailed among them. The gentry, and tacksmen generally, were educated men, and some of them well read; and because of the many bonds that bound the people to them, we find that the intelligence and character of the several communities were very much a reflex of that of their tacksmen, or of the families of their chiefs resident among them. About A.D. 1740, the ministers interested themselves—especially Mr. MacDonald of Durness—in establishing schools throughout the country, and many years had not passed when the good results of these were manifested in improved moral and social habits.

Religiously, the condition of the people was somewhat peculiar, and illustrates how slow the growth and gradual the development is of the kingdom of heaven among a people. A goodly number of men were gathered into the bosom of the Church,—men who, throughout the several communities, were living witnesses for Christ. Some of these were from among the tacksmen—men who had served in the army, and were men of breeding and education. But the greater number of them, whatever their natural intelligence, were men of no education. The difficulty, however, of overtaking the religious wants of such wide districts necessitated the making use of these men as elders and catechists among the people; but, naturally, in many instances—perhaps with the greater number—their zeal outran their knowledge, and they became filled with too high an idea of their own importance. The Fridays of communion seasons, set apart as it seems from an early period as the "Men's" day, became oftentimes the occasion of scenes that were anything but edifying. The sacrament of the Lord's Supper was at this time observed within the bounds of the Presbytery only in one congregation in the one year, and going thus the rounds of the congregations consecutively. This afforded an opportunity to all the leading professors in the country to meet once a year; and on the Friday there was oftentimes an exhibition of all manner of rivalries and jealousies, and expression given to all kinds of dissatisfaction, whether well-grounded or otherwise. Mr. MacDonald's testimony is that "it was ordinary at such conventions to start questions, either frivolous or ill-stated, and to allow ignorant people to harangue on them at random, perhaps without touching at all, or very superficially, on the subject in debate, while the ministers present allowed them, without control, correction, or direction, to ramble on in their undigested stuff." In some instances, unfortunately, the ministers afforded them an occasion of inveighing against themselves. This was especially the case with respect to him who was minister of Farr from A.D. 1733 to 1753. He was a Mr. Skeldock, who was presented to the living

by Mackay of Strathy, and translated from Kilmonivaig in
Lochaber. He was a thorough worldling, and esteemed by
the people as more of a cattle *drover* than a minister. He
was again and again admonished by his Presbytery and Synod,
but to no effect. His elders and leading men absented
themselves from his ministrations, and with them the body
of the people, and held meetings of their own throughout
the several hamlets in Strathnaver. This secession of the
people awakened a great interest among themselves, and
culminated in a religious excitement that became very
intense.

There are conflicting accounts with respect to the character of Mr. Skeldock in the latter years of his life. Mr.
MacDonald in his diary makes mention of him as hopeless;
but other accounts speak of his having undergone a great
and saving change, and that the last years of his ministry
were blessed to not a few. He died in A.D. 1753.

In 1754, the Synod of Sutherland and Caithness enjoined
that the sacrament of the Lord's Supper should be observed
yearly in all the congregations of the Tongue Presbytery;
and to prevent the unseemly occurrences formerly frequent
on the "Men's' day, they recommended the observance of
the solemnities to be on the same day in all the congregations. This, however, was considered impracticable, so it
was ordained that Scourie and Tongue should observe it on
the same day; and then Durness and Farr. This arrangement is practically that which is still followed.

After Mr. Skeldock's decease, Mr. George Munro, grandson of Mr. Squair of Edderachilis, was presented to the living
of Farr. As formerly noticed, the patronage of the parish
was alternately in the hands of the Earl of Sutherland and

the Mackays of Strathy. Mr. Munro being the presentee of the Sutherland family, he received scant courtesy at the hands of the Strathy family. He was, however, an evangelical preacher, and in the latter years of his ministry a man of great piety, of marked power in prayer, and greatly blessed of God in his work. He had three preaching stations—Achness, in the heights of Strathnaver, Farr, and Strathy. A tradition handed down of an incident in his ministry, illustrates both the rudeness of the times, and the way in which God ever honours the faithful ministers of His gospel. When, after his induction, Mr. Munro went to preach at Strathy, he was the guest of the Mackay family. The younger members of the household, seeing, no doubt, the feelings entertained towards him as the presentee of the Earl of Sutherland, thought themselves at liberty to play upon him one of their practical jokes,—especially so as they saw him to be a simple and gentle-mannered man. Mr. Munro, though considerably fatigued with his Saturday journey, was detained from rest until late in the evening. When all was quiet, the young men went and built up the outside of the window with sod, in such a manner as to exclude the faintest streak of light. Being weary, he slept on until late, and then lay long awake, waiting, as he thought, for daylight. The people assembled and waited for some time, but there was no appearance of the minister. One or two of the leading men went to the house of Strathy to ascertain whether really he had come. The situation was now made plain. Mr. Munro hastily prepared himself, and, without breaking his fast, went to meet the congregation. Never during his ministry, it is said, did he realize so great power in preaching, and so much of the Lord's presence. It was a day of great things—of marked revival in the Church, and of a numerous ingathering of souls to Christ.

A few years before Mr. Munro's death, Mr. William Mackenzie was settled at Tongue. His ministry continued for the long period of 65 years. He was a man of fine personal appearance, evangelical and pious; and was the father and grandfather respectively of Messrs. Hugh and William Mackenzie of Disruption fame. His parents had a small farm near Tain, and both father and mother were excellent, judicious persons, and greatly esteemed for their piety. Their home was a favourite resort of the godly during communion seasons. On one such occasion, the leading stranger present, as was then usual, and as in some places still is, was asked to conduct family worship. It was equally usual for him who did so to ask the most elderly person present, and most esteemed for piety, to say what portion of Scripture was to be sung and read. On the Monday of this communion Mrs. Mackenzie requested that the portion sung should be in the sixty-eighth Psalm, where it says,

> "God's chariots twenty thousand are,
> Thousands of angels strong," etc.

After worship was over, and an hour or so spent in private prayer and meditation by the many worthies present, the hour for public worship came, and, as the guests were departing, one aged saint asked her why she requested the aforesaid psalm to be sung. "Because," she said, "they are the chariots that very soon are to conduct you to the eternal Presence, where there is fulness of joy, and to His right hand, where there are pleasures evermore." He was at the moment in good health, but took ill while crossing the Meikle

Ferry on his way home after service, and died that same evening.

Mr. Mackenzie was greatly esteemed by the godly people of Strathnaver while he was yet a young man; and an incident in his history, while connected with Achness, is related of him, which shows at once his studious habits, and the intelligence and liberality of the worthies of that period. He was appointed to preach at Tongue on a certain Sabbath, with a view to his being presented with the living. His discourse was fully written, and he sought to engrave its contents on his mind, as he journeyed on the Sabbath morning from Achness to Tongue. When he came to the Ee—or ford—between Lochs Loyal and Craggie, the stream proved somewhat deep, and the wind boisterous. In crossing, he stumbled, and somehow his manuscript slipped out of his hand and was carried away. He was in great distress, as he had anything but mastered his subject, and his anxiety did not help his remembrance of it. As he came near to the church, he was met by one of the most eminent of the men, who received him kindly. After friendly greetings, he stated his trouble to this aged worthy, and told him he felt altogether unfit for the services of the day. "Well, let us carry the trouble to a Throne of Grace," said the saint of God. After a short retirement, the old man returned, and encouraged him by saying "he felt assured that, as he had diligently prepared himself, the Lord would stand by him, and that He would not allow him to be put to shame although by accident he lost his paper!" And so it was. The Lord so enabled him to preach that day, that he became endeared to all the excellent in the congregation, and the presentation was hailed with delight. But while there were a few excellent and eminent for piety among the congregation, the great body of the people were ignorant and rude, wild and godless in their habits. Especially did their drinking customs and their Sabbath conduct deeply affect him. In those days, and until a comparatively recent period, the short English service was inserted in the middle of the Gaelic. Mr. Mackenzie noticed that many of the Gaelic people who retired at the commencement of the English service returned at its close in a half-drunken state. On one occasion, having a stranger friend with him, he requested him to go and observe the doings of those who retired at the close of the first Gaelic service. The report was sad in the extreme. He was witness to all manner of bargainings about cattle, etc., and to the buying and selling and partaking of strong drink. On the following Sabbath, when the people as usual rose to retire after the Gaelic service, he asked them to resume their seats for a little, as he had something to say to them. He then made known to them what he had for long observed, and that he was aware of their doings while the English service proceeded. He exposed the godlessness of their conduct, the danger to which they exposed themselves; and urged upon them the duty and nature of a true repentance and of turning to God for forgiveness, with such deep earnestness and tenderness, that many were broken that day, and many cast themselves upon the pardoning mercy of God. So deep was the impression made, so great the power of God in their midst, that it was said that no fewer than thirty souls dated their conversion from that exhortation; and for long thereafter there were added to the Church now and again such as were the fruits of that revival.

It was immediately after this period, when so many were

added to the Church through the labours of Mr. Munro and Mr. Mackenzie, that the "men's" meetings, both on Fridays of communions and at other times, became so popular, and so honoured in the building-up of those who, by the ministry of the gospel, were gathered in to Christ. The parishes of the Reay country—especially Strathnaver—became noted at that time for the number and excellency of its outstanding men. Innumerable are the tales and anecdotes and sayings concerning them, that discover their genius and piety, and the beauty of the spirit they cherished and manifested toward one another. At first, indeed, Mr. Mackenzie and some others were jealous of the tendency of their meetings, but for a period of at least two generations—*i.e.* for sixty years, from 1780 until Disruption times—the ministrations of these godly men assisted largely both to maintain and extend the influence of the gospel throughout the whole country.

Beyond their ordinary and stated meetings and "readings" in outlying hamlets, they for long cherished the beautiful and salutary practice of question meetings on the way to and from church. As there were only four churches in so wide a country, with a few outlying preaching stations that were but rarely visited, the distances to and from regular services were necessarily long for the greater number of the people. Certain halting places on the way, in the different localities, became thus gradually recognised as spots where the people might rest and refresh their bodies with food, and their souls by starting some Scriptural and edifying question, on which the "men" discussed, touching on points doctrinal, experimental, and practical. On the home journey all had to contribute some "note" from the sermon. This tended to sustain their attention and deepen their interest in all the services of the day, and was oftentimes made instrumental in applying the truth with saving power to individual hearts.

These brief sketches of the religious history of the Reay country would be very incomplete without special notice of a class of ministers who were signally successful in establishing and building up the cause of Christ, in the more isolated corners of the district. They were known as ordained missionaries. About the year 1760 A.D., or immediately thereafter, it was felt that, notwithstanding there being now four fully-equipped charges in the country, and these constituting a Presbytery of the Church, still they were inadequate to overtake the religious wants of so wide and so populous an area. There was need of further help The same need was felt in many parts of the Highlands, and recognised by the whole Church. It was to supply this want that the Society for Propagating Christian Knowledge was instituted; and a special grant assigned from the Royal Bounty. The missions created in the Reay county were—Achness in the heights of Strathnaver; Melness; Eriboll; and Kinlochbervie in Edderachilis. In the good providence of God, a succession of men, eminent for their piety, and some of them for their natural gifts and attainments as well, supplied these missions up, we may say, to the time of the Disruption. What constituted one mission had two or more preaching stations that were supplied Sabbath about. Achness, and Achow in the heights of Kildonan were one; Melness, Eriboll, and Kinlochbervie, another. The Achness mission was supplied by such men as Mr. Wm. Mackenzie, afterwards minister of Tongue, and to whom special reference has already been made. Mr. Macgillivray of Lairg; Mr. David Mackenzie of Farr, and Mr. Donald Sage of Resolis, whose interesting "Memorabilia" was lately issued from the press. The mission of Melness, Eriboll, and Kinlochbervie was not less favoured. It had a succession of men acknowledged of God, and greatly blessed in their labours,—men such as Mr. Robertson, afterwards of Kingussie, and known as the great Mr. Robertson; Mr. Neil M'Bryde, afterwards of Kilmory, Arran; and Mr. Kennedy, afterwards of Killearnan, and father of the late Dr. John Kennedy.

Shortly after Mr. Robertson was ordained and inducted as missionary at Eriboll, it was resolved that the Sacrament of the Lord's Supper should, for the first time, be administered there. It was appointed for midsummer. The season was oppressively hot, and the drought excessive. The Eriboll district is naturally of a dry and arid soil, and with such a season all the streams, and ponds, and even springs were dried up. There was not a drop of drinkable water to be got within a great distance of Camus-an-dùin—"*the bay of the fort*"—where the people assembled for worship. When the Friday came, which with the Sabbath constitute the chief days of a communion season in the north, the day was one of scorching and exhaustive heat, but it brought with it a great multitude of people, who came from Durness, Kinlochbervie, and Edderachilis on the west; from both sides of Hope, from Melness and Tongue on the east, and from the heights of Strathnaver to the south-east. The place of meeting was one of great beauty, and the surrounding scenery of great grandeur. In front was a beautiful bay; behind, and on each hand, the hills rose to a great height, and formed a kind of amphitheatre, their sides being clothed with natural birchwood. To the right of the ministers' tent there stood the ruins of an old fort.

It being a first communion in that spot, and a great number of eminent men being gathered together, the scene was altogether a memorable one ; but especially so because of the Lord's presence being so manifestly with them. There was no moving away of any of the people from the long continued services, though many of them were faint and parched with thirst. After all the speakers were done, the venerable patriarch, eminent for piety, who gave out "the question," was called upon to pray. In doing so he evidently enjoyed great nearness to the Lord, and the multitude, so deeply impressed during the day, were now overpowered and their hearts united as one, when they heard him plead that as "the Lord gave them so richly that day of the water of life to quicken, refresh, and sustain their souls, He might now be pleased to send them supplies of earthly water, from the heavens above or earth below, to refresh and sustain their bodies, as it was the intention of the multitude, though fainting for lack of water, to continue with Him still for three days, until the solemnities of the communion season were brought to a close." After the singing of a psalm and pronouncing of the benediction, the people were dismissed, and retired to enjoy the homely but unstinted hospitality of the district, and in companies to unite again in evening and morning prayer-meetings in the several hamlets.

On Saturday, when the people began to assemble for public worship, they observed, to their great amazement and deeper joy, a stream of water issuing out from behind the tent and among the stones of the gravelly or sandy beach. Whether the spring was opened and the water made to gush forth as from Horeb of old, or whether there before and only now discovered, it matters not ; it was looked upon, and for long thereafter named, among the pious as *Tobar freagradh urnuigh*—"the spring answer to prayer;" and it continues to this day to refresh and supply the wants of storm-beaten sailors, who often, by stress of weather, are driven to take shelter in the land-locked bay.

Mr. Robertson was followed in the mission by Mr. Neil M'Bryde,—a man in every way a contrast to Mr. Robertson, still one who was greatly honoured in the work of his Master. Mr. M'Bryde, unlike Mr. Robertson, was not a man of much mental culture or ability; but like, in that he was of earnest spirit and fervent piety. Many of the leading Christian men of the Reay country about that time were gentlemen of position. They were educated; and many of them, having been in the army, had travelled and seen a good deal of the world. One such in Mr. M'Bryde's mission was Major Mackay of Eriboll. Major Mackay's daughter was wont to play the piano. Such exercise in the home of a leading Christian professor was considered by Mr. M'Bryde as sinful and scandalous, and, until the practice was put an end to, he would not so much as engage in prayer in the family when visiting it. Major Mackay told him not to burden his conscience with the matter, as he was thankful that the Lord enabled him to conduct religious exercises at all requisite times, not only in his own household, but in public among the people as well. The difference of views and feelings with respect to such matters came to a crisis on a New Year's eve, when the Major gave an entertainment and dance to all his dependents. It was his habit to do this, that he might have them all at such a time under his own supervision, and save them from congregating in questionable places, where some of them were in danger of disgracing themselves with drunkenness and riotous conduct. Entertainment he knew they must have, and he thought they ought to have it in a harmless and healthful way, that would save them from it in a way demoralizing to them. Mr. M'Bryde looked upon it differently, and thought the Major was setting others an evil example. He denounced the practice in public, and so the breach widened. Excellent as Mr. M'Bryde was, and much esteemed, still the sympathies of the good people were more with the Major than with him. This state of matters, however, led regardless characters to play a practical joke on the minister that was of a disgraceful kind. Mr. M'Bryde, like as Mr. Robertson did, observed the administration of the Lord's Supper at Kinlochbervie as was done at Eriboll. Everything necessary was not so easily obtained then as now. He had, therefore, first to take a journey across the *Mòin* to Tongue to get the bread and wine needed. On returning to Eriboll, these, together with the communion plate, were securely packed in creels, to be slung from a *cruban* and carried on horseback. All was so placed as to be ready for an early start next morning. After much fatigue endured, Kinlochbervie was reached in due time, and, when the minister's wants were attended to, they set about all necessary preparation for the communion. On unpacking the creels, both minister and elders were shocked to find that everything had been abstracted,—plate, as well as wine, etc.,—and their weight made up with stones and sod. This must have been done during the night before starting from Eriboll, and naturally enough—whoever the miscreants that did it—the doing of it was attributed to the state of feeling that existed between Mr. M'Bryde and Major Mackay. Mr. M'Bryde and those congregated for the solemnity, determined, however, that the communion should not be deferred. Before the Saturday, wine and flour were secured. Mr. M'Bryde himself is said to have baked scones for bread, and stoneware was used instead of plate. Though the outward provision was thus of the humblest and most primitive kind, still that communion Sabbath was a day to be remembered,—a day whereon the Lord vouchsafed His gracious presence in a way that filled the hearts of His people with a feast of good things. The people of Kinlochbervie were indignant at what was done, as being a slight upon them, as well as upon Mr. M'Bryde, so they determined to subscribe and present him with a new set of communion plate. They entrusted the securing of it to a Mr. Robert Mackay, who was called to Inverness or Edinburgh, for examination in connection with his being appointed as teacher in the district by the Society for Propagating Christian Knowledge. He bought the plate, and got Mr. M'Bryde's name engraved upon it. But, on his return, he found Mr. M'Bryde had left the Reay country to enter upon his charge in Arran, and, being gone, the ardour of the people cooled, and the collection to defray the expenses of the plate was never made. Mr. Mackay thereafter made a present of the plate to his friend, the Rev. Mr. Falconer, Edderachilis, and he in turn to his successor. At the Disruption it was the personal property of the Rev. George Tulloch, who joined the Free Church, and he in his turn left it to the congregation of the Free Church at Scourie, and we presume it is still used there at communion seasons. Mr. M'Bryde was succeeded by Mr. Kennedy, afterwards of Killearnan.

BIOGRAPHICAL NOTICES.

JOHN MACKAY, C.E., J.P., HEREFORD.

THERE could be no better plea for the preservation of a Highland peasantry than the existence of such families as the one to which the subject of this sketch belongs.

Mr. John Mackay, of Hereford, is a native of Rogart, Sutherland, and is the third member of a family of seven sons and two daughters, five of whom still survive, and are in good positions, four having died in distant lands. His father and grandfather were both Johns, and locally known as "M'Neills," pointing to their honourable Abrach descent. His mother, Margaret Sutherland, was an ideal housewife. His father was a quiet, shrewd man, who at the age of seventeen enlisted into the 42nd Highlanders in 1810, and retired from that noble regiment upon its return from France in 1818; at the Disruption he became an elder of the Free Church.

Mr. John Mackay was educated entirely in his native parish—first under Mr. Gunn, who dared to encourage the *banned* Gaelic even in school hours, and afterwards under Mr. Fraser. Being naturally clever, he received more than a fair share of his teacher's attention, and in addition to English and Mathematics, was taught Latin and Greek, in which he is still proficient.

At the age of twenty he resolved to try his fortunes in the south. That period, now over fifty years ago, was the time of the great railway "boom," and the young Highlander sought work in their construction. Tall, strong, and athletic, with quite a military bearing, had he not found at once congenial employment in the industrial army, he would probably have become a soldier, so fond was he of the heroic and martial achievements of his countrymen, as his forefathers were. Familiar with manual labour, and accustomed to handle horses, he was offered and accepted employment as the driver of a team, but was soon advanced to timekeeper, and then, coming more immediately under the notice of his employer, his abilities were recognised, and promotion was rapid. At twenty-four years of age he was made superintendent of a section of the Dieppe line, and remained in France during part of the trying time of the Revolution of '48. Returning to England in 1848, he found work on the Great Northern Railway, and the famous railway king—Mr. Brassey—gave him, young as he was, a portion of the line to construct as a sub-contractor. Then followed the Shrewsbury and Hereford Railway, the Sambre and Meuse Railway, and other extensive engineering works at home and abroad, in all of which he earned a well-merited reputation for skill in carrying out arduous undertakings and in dealing with men. He was, in fact, one of Mr. Brassey's right-hand men.

Arrived at middle life, his warm heart yearned to be more helpful to his fellows in the Highlands and elsewhere, and amidst the toil and cares incident to a large business he still found time to consider carefully any patriotic scheme submitted to him. None know this better than the people of his native county, where his munificence has been princely.

In 1883 he gave valuable evidence before the Napier Crofters' Commission on the land question; in 1890 to the Highlands and Islands Harbour Commission, which secured to Sutherland several harbours and piers ; in subsequent years he communicated interesting papers to the Gaelic Society of Inverness on the " Place-names of Sutherland " (*vide* " Transactions "). He is a J. P. for Herefordshire, an ex-President of the Clan Mackay Society and the Highland Association *(Comunn Gaidhealach),* and Chieftain of the Gaelic Society of London.

Mr. Mackay has been appropriately styled a true Highlander, and one of nature's noblemen. Long may we have him in our midst as a bright incentive for others to follow his lofty example.

Rev. JOHN S. MACKAY, FORT-AUGUSTUS.

The subject of our notice was born in the Reay country, and was ordained minister of the Free Church at Altnaharra in 1871. He took part in several controversies which agitated the county, especially the Crofter question ; and to his initiative the abolition of Sabbath labour and hiring is mainly due. Mr. Mackay wields a facile pen, as is evidenced from his interesting contribution to the present work, and his knowledge of the past history of the county is not excelled by many. He was translated to Fort-Augustus in 1889.

Rev. Robert Munro, B.D., F.R.S.E., F.S.A., Scot., Old Kilpatrick.

The Rev. Robert Munro, son of Hugh Munro and Christina Mackay, was born at Mudale House, Strathnaver, on 26th April, 1853. Educated at Strathy School, and at the University of St. Andrew's, where he graduated M.A. and B.D., and at the New College, Edinburgh. As a student he had a very distinguished career. In 1878 he was appointed minister of the Free Church at Old Kilpatrick. Since that time, besides devoting himself to the various interests of the parish, he has been a diligent student of the great systems of modern theological thought since the time of Schleiermacher, of philosophy as influenced by Hume and Kant, and of archæology in its different departments. In connection with his researches in anthropology and folk-lore he has for several years been honoured by the recognition of the principal archæologists in Europe and America, such as Virchow, Montelius, Mortillet, Stephens, Rygh, Sir Daniel Wilson and Dr. Joseph Anderson. He has contributed papers on theology, philosophy, anthropology and literature to the *Encyclopædia Britannica, The Quiver, British and Foreign Evangelical Review, The Journal of Speculative Philosophy, The National Observer, The Graphic, The Illustrated London News, The Celtic Monthly*, etc. In virtue of his many literary and scientific attainments he has been elected a Fellow of the Royal Society, Edinburgh, a Fellow of the Society of Antiquaries of Scotland, and a Member of the Royal Literary Fund, London.

He claims descent from the Munros of Fowlis, and the Abrach branch of the Mackays.

GEORGE J. CAMPBELL,
Sheriff of the Lews.

GEORGE J. CAMPBELL, Sheriff of the Lews.

SHERIFF CAMPBELL is a native of Farr, Sutherland, where his father, Mr. George Campbell, was a merchant. When but a very young lad Mr. Campbell went to Inverness, where he served his apprenticeship, afterwards completing his legal curriculum in Edinburgh. Returning to Inverness he began practice on his own account, and his sterling business and personal qualities quickly gained for him universal respect and confidence, his business soon becoming one of the most important in the town. He identified himself with many of the leading agencies for promoting the public good in the Highland Capital, having served for a period as a member of the Town Council, and in the crisis of 1878-79 he took the lead in preventing the liquidation of the Caledonian Bank. He was president and director of the Choral Union, and held successively the offices of hon. treasurer, secretary, and chieftain of the Gaelic Society of Inverness.

In volunteer circles the learned Sheriff is well known, having risen to be full Colonel of the Highland Volunteer Artillery, and receiving the coveted Victoria Decoration for long service. As a politician he was a strong supporter of the Liberal party, and was agent for Mr. Gilbert Beith when returned at last general election. It may be also mentioned that Mr. Campbell is a Free Churchman, and in 1888, when the General Assembly was held in the Highland Capital, he acted with marked efficiency and success as purse-bearer and secretary to the venerable Moderator, Rev. Dr. Aird of Creich. He has not lost touch with Sutherland, being a life member of the county associations of Edinburgh and Glasgow.

JAMES MACDONALD, W.S., EDINBURGH.

It is not necessary to be born in the Highlands to be a Highlander, for quite a number of those whose names are most intimately associated with Sutherland affairs were not born in the county. They are Sutherland men by descent. There are few names more closely connected with Sutherland than that of Mr. James Macdonald, W.S. He was born in Edinburgh in 1850. His father, Mr. John Macdonald, was first general treasurer of the Free Church of Scotland. His mother was Grace MacKenzie, daughter of the Rev. David MacKenzie of Farr, and through her Mr. Macdonald is the eldest representative of the family of the Gordons of Langdale, Strathnaver. In his youth the subject of our sketch spent a good deal of time in his grandfather's manse, at Farr, and became greatly attached to the place and the people. In 1870 he joined the Sutherland Association (Edinburgh), and organized the examination for school prizes which was carried on so successfully for a quarter of a century, and is now superceded in favour of a bursary scheme. During the course of these years Mr. Macdonald has been president, vice-president, secretary, and is now treasurer of this most useful association. He is also a Governor of the Highland Trust, representing Sutherland and Caithness.

In his own profession Mr. Macdonald occupies a high position. He took a good place as a law student, and became a writer to the Signet in 1874. He is a partner of the well known firm of Auld & Macdonald, W.S.; a member of the Juridical Society, Custodier of the titles of the Free Church of Scotland, Depute Keeper of the Great Seal of Scotland, and Director of various public companies.

JAMES MACDONALD, W.S.

Rev. ADAM GUNN, M.A., Durness.

Rev. ADAM GUNN, M.A., Durness.

Strathy lays claim to the distinction of providing more young men for the church than all the rest of the Reay country. The above, a son of the late Alexander Gunn and Christina Mackay, is one of a dozen from that district at the present time in the ministry. He received his early training under Mr. Anderson of Strathy Public School, a most successful teacher. After two years in the Grammar School, Aberdeen, he proceeded to St. Andrew's University, where in 1881, he gained the first bursary open to general competition of the value of £100. He had a distinguished university career, carrying off several prizes and honours : among others, the first prizes in the classes of English Literature, Logic and Metaphysics, and the second prize in Moral Philosophy. While prosecuting his theological studies at New College, Edinburgh, he took advantage of the Gaelic class taught by Professor Mackinnon, Edinburgh University, where he gained the second prize in the junior, and the first prize and medal in the senior division. On receiving license to preach from the Presbytery of Tongue in 1888, he was a few months thereafter appointed colleague and successor to the late Rev. James Ross, Durness, where he has laboured since. Mr. Gunn takes a deep interest in the temporal as well as spiritual welfare of his people, and has been member of the County Council, School Board, and Parochial Board, and latterly of the Parish Council, of which body he is now chairman. Besides his contributions to the present work he has written many articles to Celtic magazines, including *The Celtic Monthly* and *The Transactions of the Inverness Gaelic Society*.

DONALD MATHESON OF ACHANY.

So early as the fifteenth century the ancestors of Mr. Matheson were chiefs of no small repute in Sutherland. The clan took part in several of the numerous conflicts which disturbed the peace of Sutherland during the sixteenth century. The present representative of the family, Mr. Donald Matheson, was educated at the High School of Edinburgh, and spent some time in China as assistant in the great mercantile firm of Messrs. Jardine, Matheson & Co. On his return to Scotland he married, in 1849, Jane Ellen, daughter of Lieut. Horace Petley, R.N. Mr. Matheson has devoted himself mainly to mission work in Edinburgh and London. On the death of his aunt, Lady Matheson of Achany and the Lews, he succeeded to these extensive properties. Mr. Matheson has two sons, Duncan, Major of the Inniskilling Dragoons, and Donald, minister of the Presbyterian Church, Putney, London.

BAILIE ALEXANDER MURRAY, C.A., GLASGOW.

Among the numerous Sutherlandmen who have settled in Glasgow and prospered, mention should be especially made of Bailie ALEXANDER MURRAY, C.A., president of the County of Sutherland Association, Glasgow. He was born at Rogart, and is a partner in the well known firm of Carswell & Murray, C.A.. He has occupied a seat at the Municipal Board for a number of years, and is acknowledged to be one of the ablest and most respected members of the City Council. He is deeply interested in County affairs.

DONALD MATHESON,
Of Achany.

Provost WILLIAM MACKAY, Thurso.

Provost Mackay was born at Skelpick, Strathnaver, on 21st June, 1844. His father Mr. Donald Mackay, was descended from a branch of the Mackays of Kinloch, and was one of the largest and most successful farmers in the north of Scotland. Father and son were joint tenants of the farm of Melness, then the largest in Sutherland, part of which was held before the clearances by George Mackay of Hope, a relative of the family. The Provost has now given up farming.

Mr. Mackay's business connections are among the largest in the County. He is agent for the Town and County Bank, Thurso, Factor for the Freswick Estates, and the Crown Lands of Caithness, and Treasurer for the Caithness County Council. In 1878 he was elected Chief Magistrate of Thurso, which office he held for fifteen years, and is now Provost of the Burgh. In politics he is a Liberal Unionist. He is an elder in the Free Church of Scotland, and has frequently taken part in the proceedings of the General Assembly. For the last thirty years he has been Hon. President of the Thurso Y. M. C. A. He has been chairman of the Thurso Harbour Trust since its formation, and is a J.P. for Caithness.

Provost Mackay has always evinced a special interest in the Clan Mackay Society, of which he is an ex-President. He has acted as treasurer for the large fund raised on behalf of the sufferers by the Portskerra and Talmine Fishing Boat Disaster some years ago, and his management of this fund has given the greatest satisfaction to all concerned.

He married, in 1871, the youngest daughter of the late Rev. Walter Ross Taylor, D.D., Thurso, and of this marraige three sons and three daughters survive.

ANGUS SUTHERLAND,
Chairman of the Scottish Fishery Board.

Mr. Angus Sutherland was born at Helmsdale in 1848. His family had been settled for many generations on the strath of Kildonan. He was educated at the Free Church school of the parish, where he became a pupil teacher. In 1868 he entered the Edinburgh Training College, and in 1872 went to Glasgow University, and four years later became one of the mathematical masters at the Glasgow Academy. Mr. Sutherland took a prominent part in the Crofter Agitation which some twelve years ago was conducted with such energy in all parts of the country. In 1885 he was an unsuccessful candidate for the representation of his native county, but in the following year was triumphantly returned, and, till his recent appointment as Chairman of the Scottish Fishery Board, was a prominent and eloquent advocate of the cause of the crofter population. He was a member of the Deer Forests Commission, and has served on various other parliamentary committees. He is a life member of the Sutherlandshire associations of Glasgow and Edinburgh. Mr. Sutherland is still a young man, but he has already earned for himself a prominent place among the most distinguished Sutherlanders of the present day.

JOHN MACLEOD, M.P. FOR SUTHERLANDSHIRE.

Mr Macleod is the son of Mr. John Macleod, Helmsdale, where he was born in 1863. He was educated at Glasgow, and having studied gold-assaying, helped in working a gold mine in N. Wales. Returning to Sutherland he practised as surveyor, then went to Inverness in 1888, and established the *Highland News*, of which he is proprietor As secretary to the Highland Land League, Mr. Macleod has taken an active part in the land agitation in the Highlands. He was returned as member for Sutherlandshire at the last election, prior to which he was a member of the Royal Commission on Deer Forests. Mr. Macleod is a Liberal in politics.

REV. JOHN MURRAY,
CONVENER OF THE COUNTY OF SUTHERLAND.

THERE are many points of resemblance between Sutherland and the Island of Lewis. There is the same mixture of Celtic and Norse blood in the population; the same intense love of country, and the same high morality. Among other common features is the large proportion of young men who enter the church as a profession. From the district of Strathy alone, on the north coast, there are at the present moment no less than eleven ministers in various charges throughout the country—a circumstance which cannot be approached in any other district except Lewis, which may be said to supply to the largest extent the ministry of the Highlands.

Among other Lewismen labouring on the mainland is the subject of our sketch. Born near Stornoway in 1841, Mr. Murray received the rudiments of his education in his native parish, and thence proceeded to the Edinburgh University, where he finished his Arts Curriculum. He received his theological training in the New College, Edinburgh, which he entered in 1865, and where for four years he held the Highland Bursary. Hardly was he licensed to preach when the Free Church congregation of Clyne (Brora) called him to Sutherlandshire, where he was ordained in 1869.

From the outset of his ministry, Mr. Murray took a lively interest in the temporal as well as spiritual welfare of his people. It was, however, in 1880 that the young minister of Brora began to acquire that prominence in the county which ultimately led to his appointment as Convener. A keen controversy about a water supply for the village of Brora, in which a prominent estate official adopted a hostile attitude, gave occasion for the display of Mr. Murray's aptitude for the work of public bodies; and in a short time he was himself Chairman of the Parochial Board.

As might be supposed, Mr. Murray was deeply interested in the crofter agitation, and was ever a consistent advocate of the people's rights. It was therefore no surprise to the people of Sutherland when the first County Council appointed him to the high and responsible position of Convener. That the people's representatives made a wise choice has been amply proved by his re-election to the same post year by year since 1890. Notwithstanding the difficulties of the office, Mr. Murray has proved himself a capable Convener and an impartial Chairman. He never betrayed the trust reposed in him by the people of the county, and, it is hoped, that many years of useful service are yet before him. Although so much of his time and talents is taken up with county business, Mr. Murray has not allowed his public work to interfere with the discharge of his ministerial duties. In Presbytery and Synod he takes a leading place; and among Highland ministers at the General Assembly he is well known as an able and consistent supporter of the progressive party in the Free Church.

Rev. JOHN MURRAY, Brora.

DONALD MUNRO.

DONALD MUNRO, M.E., MANCHESTER.

Mr. Munro was born at Backies, Golspie, on 6th November, 1846, and was educated at the local school. In 1865, he received an appointment in connection with the Staffordshire Collieries of the late Mr. Thomas Bantock, J.P. (a distinguished Sutherlander), and he ultimately became General Manager of the great Wyrley Collieries. He also held a number of public offices in the district. After about eighteen years' service he retired in 1884 from the management, and in the following year took charge of the collieries and works of the Chesterfield Coal and Iron Co., N. Staffordshire. Afterwards Mr. Munro started business in Manchester as a Civil and Mining Engineer, and has been very successful. He is the pioneer of an important mining enterprise in the North of Ireland. In 1872 he married Mary, daughter of the late Mr. Thomas Greensill, by whom he has two daughters.

HEW MORRISON, F.S.A., Scot., EDINBURGH.

There are few better known men in Edinburgh to-day than Mr. Hew Morrison, the popular chief of the Public Library. He is a native of Torrisdale, Parish of Farr, and has had a most distinguished career. When the Carnegie Public Library was instituted, Mr. Morrison was appointed chief librarian. He is well versed in Sutherland traditions and lore, and has written a great deal on county matters, including a most interesting Tourists' Guide to Sutherland and Caithness, which has been long out of print.

JOHN MACKAY, Editor, *Celtic Monthly*.

Mr. John Mackay was born in Glasgow in 1865, his father, Donald Mackay, being a native of Strathy, in the Reay country, and his mother a native of Kintyre. He was educated at Glasgow, and when fifteen years of age entered the employment of Messrs. John Hunter & Son, Flour Merchants, where he now occupies a responsible position. Mr. Mackay's sympathies have always been strongly Celtic, and when quite a youth he was a constant contributor to the Highland press. He is well known as a naturalist, and for several years acted as secretary to the Clydesdale Naturalists Society. Some ten years ago he became a member of the Glasgow Sutherlandshire Association, of which he was vice-president.

To Mr. Mackay is due the credit of conceiving the idea of organizing the Clan Mackay Society, and to his able guidance and untiring efforts as hon. secretary, that influential society owes its present phenomenal success. In 1890, Lord Reay, in the name of the clan, presented Mr. Mackay with a handsome testimonial "in testimony of their high appreciation of his excellent services as hon. secretary."

It may be perhaps interesting to add that he is treasurer of the Gaelic Society of Glasgow; a member of the executive of the Mòd since its institution; president of the Glasgow Gaelic Musical Association and of the Cowal Shinty Club; chieftain of the Govan Highland Association; director of the County of Sutherland Association, etc. To Highlanders at home and abroad he is best known as Editor and proprietor of the *Celtic Monthly*, which has earned a popularity and circulation that no other Highland magazine has ever enjoyed.

JOHN MACKAY, Editor, *Celtic Monthly.*

GEORGE MURRAY CAMPBELL.

GEORGE MURRAY CAMPBELL, C.E., SIAM.

Mr. George Murray Campbell is a son of the late Kenneth Campbell of Eden, Rogart, and received his early education in his native parish. When twenty-three years of age he commenced his successful career in India, in connection with railway construction. Two years later he went to Ceylon to take charge of works on the Government Railway, which he carried to a successful completion. In 1880 he was made manager, and given a junior partnership in the contract for the construction of two railways in Jamaica, and on the lines being opened to traffic in 1885-6 the Governor of the Island, Sir Henry Norman, bore flattering testimony to Jamaica's indebtedness to Mr. Campbell. For the next few years he was employed in surveying and reporting on railway schemes in the Ural Mountains, Western Australia, Formosa, and the Malay Peninsula. In 1891 his tender for the equipment of 150 miles of line in Siam, was accepted for £1,200,000, and on this work he is now engaged. In November of last year he took the King of Siam over 80 miles of the new line, the trip proving most enjoyable to His Majesty. One of the principal reasons of Mr. Campbell's success has been the facility with which he has acquired the native languages, Hindustani, Tamil, Singalese, Malay, and Siamese, thus being able to give his instructions direct. This he ascribes to his knowledge of Gaelic.

In 1887 Mr. Campbell was married to Lily, third daughter of the late Mr. Wm. Haynes, of Hampstead, a most accomplished lady, who has accompanied her husband in all his Eastern travels.

Rev. JAMES ABERIGH-MACKAY, M.A., D.D.,

THE subject of this brief sketch is chieftain of that gallant and powerful branch of the Clan Mackay, which for so many centuries inhabited Strathnaver, and were the "wardens" of the Mackay country against invasion, a trust which they never once betrayed. To them also was entrusted in battle the famous White Banner *(Bratach Bhàn Chlann Aoidh)* of the clan, so renowned in song and story. The Rev. J. Aberigh-Mackay was born at Inverness in 1820, and after taking his degree at Aberdeen, he spent seven years in the United States, where he married. On his return home he officiated at St. John's Chapel, Inverness, for some time. In March, 1857, accompanied by his wife, he went out to India on the Bengal Establishment, and found himself immediately in the midst of the turmoil and bloodshed of the Indian Mutiny. He was shut up in Cawnpore during the terrible siege, and after its relief by Sir Colin Campbell, saw a good deal of active service with his regiment, the 9th Lancers, his experiences being related in his "London to Lucknow," published in two vols. in 1860. Thereafter he officiated at Penang, Meerut, Simla, and Calcutta, returning to Britain on pension, having served eighteen years. In 1881 his *alma mater* conferred on him the degree of D.D. Since then Dr. Mackay has officiated in Paris, America, and Scotland.

His elder son, James L. Aberigh-Mackay, is Lieut.-Colonel of the 8th Bengal Cavalry, and is acknowledged to be one of the most brilliant cavalry officers in the British service. His younger son, George Robert, was principal of Rajkumar College, and died in 1881. His only daughter is married to Mr. W. E. Maxwell, C.M.G., Colonial Secretary at Singapore.

The late JOHN MACKAY, (Ben Reay.)

Mr. John Mackay, whose recent death was lamented by Highlanders at home and abroad, was one of the most enthusiastic of Gaels. He was born at Restalrig, near Edinburgh, nearly seventy years ago. When a young man he went to Canada, where he spent twenty years, engaged chiefly in fruit growing and experimental farming. Here he found scope for his military instincts, and was captain of a company of Home Guards which he organised during the Fenian troubles of 1865-6. He returned to Scotland in 1875, but since he sold Herriesdale a small estate in Dumfries-shire, he resided in Germany, and latterly at Bridge of Allan. He died in Edinburgh on 14th November, 1896.

Besides his contributions to the *Celtic Monthly* and various other magazines and *Transactions* Mr. Mackay was the author of "An Old Scots Brigade," being a history of the famous regiment raised by Donald, first Lord Reay, a full account of which is included in the interesting chapter on "Sutherland Regiments" which he contributed to the present work (see p. 183). For many years past he was engaged on the preparation of a new History and Genealogy of the Clan Mackay, which we hope may yet be published. He was the senior representative, in the male line, of the Mackays of Melness, and took a lively interest in all matters pertaining to his clan, and especially to the Clan Mackay Society, of which he was an Honorary Member, a distinction which, so far, has only been conferred on three members.

Mr. Mackay married, in 1877, the younger daughter of the Hon. A. Ware, a Judge of the District Court of the United States, and has an only child, Ethel Reay, born in 1879.

Lieut.-Colonel DUNCAN MENZIES.

The subject of this sketch was born at Glengoulandie, Perthshire. In early life he evinced a liking for farming, and engaged in this avocation for several years with his father, who held several large farms. He afterwards went to New Zealand, where he remained for a time, and acquired an enlarged experience of his profession. He is now tenant of the large farm of Blarich in Sutherland, which he conducts with marked ability and success. Colonel Menzies has always evinced a deep practical interest in all matters relating to the Parish of Rogart, and his valuable services in the Parochial and School Boards for many years have been deservedly and gratefully acknowledged.

Colonel Menzies is inspired with an intense love for the Highlands, its people, and indeed everything that is considered of good repute in connection with his native land. He is deeply interested in Celtic literature, and passionately fond of Gaelic music, especially the inspiring notes of the *piob-mhor*, and every movement intended to preserve the best traditions of our race has his sympathy and generous support.

The 1st Sutherland Highland Rifle Volunteers, which the Colonel has the honour to command, is admitted to be one of the finest bodies of men in Her Majesty's service. It need hardly be said that the subject of our sketch is extremely popular among the men of his regiment, and this warm feeling of respect took practical form when the officers and men of the Rogart Company in July, 1890, presented him with an address, congratulating him on his promotion to the rank of Major in the Battalion.

SOME NOTABLE SUTHERLANDERS.

It would be quite impossible, in the limited space at our disposal, to treat of notable Sutherlanders at any length; indeed, it would require the entire volume to do this interesting subject the justice it deserves. We are not prepared to state that Sutherland, in proportion to its population, has produced more men of note than any other Highland county, but it was only when we commenced to note down the names of such as we considered deserving of notice that we realised how considerable the list was. We have already given short sketches of a few of these, but there are scores of others equally deserving of mention, and to a number of them we should like now to briefly refer.

That excellent institution, "The Sutherland Association, Edinburgh, instituted 1866," includes among its members many of the most prominent men of our county. Several have been already referred to, but we should like to mention one who is known to our countrymen in all parts of the world, namely, Mr. D. W. KEMP, J.P. He is not a native of the county, but he has written more books relating to it than perhaps any man living. Of these we might mention *Pococke's Tour in 1760*; *Notes on Early Iron-Smelting in Sutherland*; *The Sutherland Democracy*, etc. We believe he has one or two new works on hand of a particularly interesting nature. He is a J.P. of the county, and has a residence at Altass, Rosehall. Then there is Mr. ALEXANDER MACKAY, a native of Swordly, who for twenty years acted as treasurer to the association, and wrote a delightful book, *Sketches of Sutherland Characters*, which is now out of print. Another most eminent member of this association is Mr. NEIL J. D. KENNEDY, advocate, a native of the parish of Creich. He was a candidate for the representation of Inverness-shire at last election, but being too ill at the time to contest the county in person, was defeated by a small majority. Mr. HUGH MACKAY MATHESON, Banker, London, belongs to the Achany family, and occupies a high position in mercantile circles in London. The Hon. JAMES MUNRO, late premier of Victoria, was born at Armadale, in the Reay country, and has had a most distinguished career. A few years ago Mr. Munro gifted £100 for prizes to the children in Armadale school. Mr. DONALD MACKAY, of Ceylon, was born at Rogart, and has spent the greater part of his life in distant lands, engaged principally in planting. Like his brother, Mr. John Mackay of Hereford, he has been very successful. Among other notable Sutherlanders, connected with this association, may be mentioned Messrs. ALEXANDER MACKAY, LL.D., Editor of the *Educational News* and late president of the association: J. L. ANDERSON, of the Commercial Bank (an ex-president); DONALD MACLEOD, M.A., Principal of Forfar Academy, and a native of Assynt; ALEXANDER SUTHERLAND, Prestonkirk (of Portskerra); DONALD MACKAY, "Strathnaver" House, a native of Kirtomy, Farr; HUGH MACKAY, M.A., born on Melness-side, who has acted for a number of years as educational secretary; Captain WILLIAM MORRISON, a Durness-man, who rose from the ranks by his own native ability; A. MACKAY ROBSON, president, HUGH M. MATHESON, ALEXANDER ROSS MACKAY, who is also assistant secretary to the Clan Mackay Society, and others.

There are two county associations in Glasgow, where there should only be one, but we hope that before long they will amalgamate and form one powerful organization. Mr. ALEXANDER BRUCE, of Pollokshields, president of the "Sutherlandshire Association," is a native of the parish of Clyne. As a business man he has been most successful, and is principal partner in the firm of Alexander Bruce & Co. The energy and zeal which he exerts in matters relating to the association and his native county, do him credit. He is favoured with literary and musical gifts of no common order, and frequently contributes at the meetings. Messrs. ALEXANDER MACDONALD, M.A., F.E.I.S., a native of Dornoch, and DONALD MACLEOD, born in Assynt, are both H. M Inspectors of Schools, and have distinguished themselves in various ways. In addition to these, mention should be made of Messrs. MURDO MACLEOD, ex-president, who also belongs to Assynt : JOHN SIMPSON (parish of Clyne) : DONALD MACKENZIE (Creich), a successful business man, and one who is expected before long to occupy a seat at the City Council Board ; J. G. MACKAY, C.C., Portree, and Dr. HUGH MURRAY, L.R.C.S., of the Cancer Institution.

"The County of Sutherland Association (Glasgow)," includes among its members a number of gentlemen of distinction. Among the officials reference should be made to Messrs. HUGH BANNERMAN, Southport (a native of Helmsdale) : JOHN MUNRO, Hanley (parish of Creich), the proprietor of a large number of flourishing concerns in Staffordshire, and one who takes a deep interest in all matters affecting his native county : Dr. JOHN GUNN (Helmsdale), and Dr. GEORGE GORDON (Helmsdale), both enjoying large practices in Glasgow, and George Mackay (Bonar Bridge).

There is a "Sutherlandshire Association" in Edinburgh which devotes itself specially to political and social questions, and which has done good service. A social gathering is held each year, which is largely attended. Its moving spirit is Mr. John Macdonald, a gifted native of Helmsdale.

A Sutherland association was started several years ago in London, of which Mr. ANGUS H. R. MACKAY was secretary, but during the past year or two it seems to have altogether disappeared. It does not seem to have been a success.

Just as we go to press we notice public announcements of the formation of a Sutherlandshire Association in Inverness; and a Clan Sutherland Society in Edinburgh. We wish them both every success.

"The Clan Mackay Society" may be looked upon practically as a Sutherland society, for the great bulk of its members are either natives or descendants of natives. The Clan Mackay had the honour of first banding themselves in the south as a society, in 1808, and the present society has the largest membership, and is the most energetic and influential of all the clan societies. Although only eight years old, it has published volumes, instituted a clan bursary, and otherwise shown evidence of its desire to do good work. Among its members will be found the most eminent persons of the name Mackay in all parts of the world, among whom may be mentioned Baron ÆNEAS MACKAY, late Prime Minister of the Netherlands (of the Scourie branch); Sheriff ÆNEAS J. G. MACKAY, M.A., LL.D. (of Sandwood); Surgeon-General GEORGE MACKAY, M.D., J.P. (of Bighouse); Mr. GEORGE J. MACKAY, Ex-Mayor of Kendal (son of a native of Farr); Sir JAMES LYLE MACKAY, and many other distinguished clansmen.

Apart from the county associations there are many Sutherland men at home and abroad who have done credit to themselves and the county of their nativity. Among them are politicians and statesmen, merchants, governors, and professional men, explorers, missionaries, officers in the army and navy,—indeed, they seem to have distinguished themselves in every sphere of life, and in every part of the globe. To attempt even to refer to them would occupy a great deal more space than we can afford, but there is ample material for a delightful volume, should anyone care to take up the subject.

INDEX.

Abrachs, The, a sept of the Mackays, ...	29, 48, 50, 52, 63, 67
Aldgowne, Conflict of, Gunns defeat the Sinclairs,	... 51
Antiquities of Sutherland, ...	87-115
Artillery Companies, Sutherland, ...	281, 282
Assynt, Macleods of, ...	32, 43, 47, 50, 53, 70, 146
,, Place-names of, ...	159, 161
,, Dialectic peculiarities of,	177
Bannockburn, Battle of,	12, 13
Bards, The minor,	284, 285
Bharruich, Castle, ...	27, 112
Biographical Sketches of Notable Sutherlanders,	367
Births, Superstitions concerning, ...	... 117
Borve Castle, ...	... 40, 41, 112
Brochs, Large number of, ...	106, 107
Brodie, Rev. George, ...	 350
Bronze Age, ...	97, 105
Cairns, Chambered, ...	90, 95
Campbell, Sir Colin, ...	247
Catechising, Diets of, ...	348
Catholicism, Roman, ...	325-332
Charters, The Sutherland, ...	143
,, The Mackay, ..., ...	20, 32, 38, 44
Clyne, The place-names of, ...	168, 169
Columban Missionaries, ...	2, 322, 324
Conventicles, Suppression of,	 72
Covenanters, The, ...	... 64, 65, 69, 70, 72
Crimean War, The, ...	 241

INDEX. 391

Creich, Place-names of,	161, 162
Cromarty, Earl of,	75
Cromwell, Oliver,	70
Culloden, Battle of,	195
Dalriadic Scots,	2, 3
David, King of Scotland,	16
Death, Superstitions concerning,	121
Dialect of Sutherland, The,	172-181
Divinations,	128
Dornadilla, Castle of,	107
Dornoch, Battle of,	7
,, Place-names of,	163, 165
Druidic Circles,	321, 322
Druim-na-cupa, Battle of,	25
Drummond, Lady Jane,	63
Dunrobin, Castle of,	36, 70, 110
Durness,	3, 8, 64
,, Macleods of,	43, 48, 52
,, Place-names of,	154, 156
Earth-houses, Underground dwellings,	109
Eddrachilis, Place-names of,	150
Edward I., King of England,	10, 11
Episcopacy,	63, 64
Fairies,	136, 140
Farr, Sculptured Stone at,	111
,, Place-names of,	146, 153
Felting Cloth,	84
Fencibles, The Reay,	230
,, Sutherland,	227, 230
Fishermen, Their Superstitions,	130
Folk-lore,	116, 140
Freskyn, Hugh, Ancestor of Sutherland Earls,	7

INDEX.

Gaelic, Peculiarities of Sutherland,	172-182
Galloway, Origin of Mackays,	7
Gilbert, Bishop of Caithness,	7
Golspie, Place-names of,	165
,, The Stone of,	110
Gordons, Advent of the,	33, 36
Gordon, Adam, Earl of,	34
,, George, of Garty,	53
,, Lady Jane,	59
,, Sir Robert, The Historian,	58, 61, 67
Gower, George Granville Leveson,	77
Gunn, The Clan,	30, 46, 50, 51
,, Sir William, Colonel,	65
,, George,	52
,, William,	58
,, John-Mac-Ian-Mac-Rob,	52
Haco,	8, 9, 113
Halidon Hill, Battle of,	13
Hamilton, Marquis of,	62, 63
Harald Maddadson, Earl,	6
Harpsdale, Battle of,	21
Hazard, Sloop of war, Story of the.	75, 194
Helmsdale Castle.	45, 113
Homespun, Treatise on,	78-86
Huntly, Earl of,	38, 39, 40
Iberian,	142
Iron Age,	105
Isles, Lord of the,	19
Keiths' Conflict with the Gunns,	30
Kildonan, Place-names of,	170, 171
Killiecrankie,	72, 190

INDEX.

La-na-creich-mor, The day of the great spoil, ...	... 54
Lairg, Place-names of, ...	... 162, 163
Lewis, Macleods of, ...	16, 18, 32, 33
Loth, Place-names of, ...	1. 40, 169
Loudon, Earl of, ..	75, 193
Lovat, ...-	... 75
Lucknow, Sutherland Highlanders at, ...	... 250
M'Bryde, Rev. Neil, of Eriboll, ...	364
MacCulloch, Rev. John, of Golspie,	... 341
Macdonald, Rev. Murdo, of Durness,	351, 353
Macdonalds of Glengarry, Raids of the, ...	... 31
Macdonald, Samuel, " Big Sam,"	... 229
Mackay, Alexander, 1st Chief, ...	6
,, Iye of Farr, Chief, ...	16
,, Angus, Chief, ...	16
,, Hugh, his brother, ...	18
,, Angus Du, Chief, Leader of 4,000 men, ...	19
,, Thomas, Morgan, and Neil, nephews,, ...	20, 21, 27
,, Neil of the Bass, Chief, ...	22, 30
,, John Abrach, ...	25, 28
,, Angus, son of Neil, Chief, ...	30, 31
,, John, Chief, ...	31
,, Iye II., or Hugh, Chief, favourite of James IV.,	32
,, John, son of Iye, chief, ...	36
,, Donald, brother of John, Chief, aids James V., ...	37
,, Iye III., or Hugh, Chief, ...	39, 40, 42, 44, 47
,, John Mor, Cousin of Iye, ...	40, 42, 48
,, Niel, Chief of Abrach Mackays, ...	48
,, Hugh, Chief, ...	50, 51, 52, 53, 55, 59
,, William, of Bighouse, ...	51, 53, 57
,, Donald, of Scourie,	53, 55

Mackay, Sir Donald, 1st Lord Reay,	57, 60
,, John, 2nd Lord Reay, ...	64, 65, 67, 69, 70
,, Hugh, of Scourie, Colonel, ...	69, 70
,, John, of Dilred and Strathy, ...	70
,, Hugh, of Scourie, General of King William's forces,	72
,, George, 3rd Lord Reay,	73
,, William, of Melness, ...	75
,, Donald, 4th Lord Reay, ...	76, 77, 293
,, Hugh, of Bighouse, Lieutenant-Colonel,	77, 296, 299
,, George, 5th Lord Reay,	77, 298
. Hugh, 6th Lord Reay,	... 77
.. Eric, 7th Lord Reay, ...	77
.. Donald James, present Lord Reay,	77
.. Rev. John, of Durness and Lairg,	... 347
Robert Donn, the bard of Reay,	286-313
.. John Donn, son of Rob Donn, ...	303
., Mackay, John of Achness, ...	336
., John MacEachainn, patron of Rob Donn,	289
,, Major, of Eriboll, ...	364
Mackenzie, Rev. William, of Tongue,	355
Malcolm, King of Scotland,... ...	4
Marriage, Superstitions concerning.	119
" Men," The, ...	234-354
Monar, Loch, modern Bethesda, ...	... 126
Munro, Rev. Alexander, ...	333
,, Rev. George, of Farr, —	... 355
,, Rev. Hugh, ...	... 333
., of Fowlis, ...	53, 54
,, Regiment of,	... 225
Murkle, Laird of, ...	55
Murray, Earl of, ...	 44
Murrays of Sutherland, The,	20, 22, 46, 57

National Covenant, The,	64
Naver, Etymology of,	1, 142
Neville's Cross, Battle of,	14
Nordlingen, Battle of,	225
Norse Rule,	2, 9
„ Influence on Language,	178
Ordained Missionaries,	361
Picts, Northern,	2
Pictish element in Place-names,	164
Poetry and Music,	283-320
Privy Council, Proceedings before the,	56, 60, 64
Queen's Prizeman, Robert Mackay,	277, 278
Reay Country, Etymology of,	145
„ „ Sale of,	146
Reformation, Attitude of Chiefs to the,	44, 71
Regiments, The,	183-282
Revolution, The,	72
Robbers, Ord of Caithness,	69
Robertson, Rev. Mr., of Eriboll,	362
Rogart, Place-names of,	166
Rosses of Balnagown,	31, 191
Seaforth, Earl of,	69, 75
Sigurd, Earl of Orkney,	2, 3
Sinclair, John, Earl of Caithness,	34, 36
Sinclair, George, Earl of Caithness,	45, 46, 48, 53, 55, 56
„ John, Master of Caithness,	47
„ Henry, „ „	51
Smith, Arthur, The Coiner,	58
Stone Age, The,	88
„ „ Circles,	104

INDEX.

Strathnaver, Place-names of,	151
Superstitions, ...	117
Sutherland, William, 1st Earl of, ...	7, 8
,, William, 3rd Earl of, ...	10
,, Kenneth, 4th Earl of,	13
,, William, 5th Earl of, ...	13, 14
,, Robert, 6th Earl of, ...	20
,, John, 7th Earl of, ...	3
,, Alexander, 8th Earl of, ...	34, 36, 37
,, John, 9th Earl of, last of Freskyn race,	34
,, John, 10th Earl of, ...	44
,, Alexander, 11th Earl of,	46
,, John, 12th Earl of, ...	55, 56, 63
,, John, 13th Earl of, ...	69
,, George, 14th	71
,, John, 15th Earl of, ...	73
,, William, 16th Earl of, ...	76
,, William, 17th Earl of,	76
,, Elizabeth, Countess of, ...	77
Sutherland Fencibles of 1759, '79, and '93, ...	227, 230
,, Highlanders (the 93rd), ...	235
,, John, of Forse, ...	193
,, John, of Berriedale, ...	57
Tacksmen, ...	354
Thorfinn, Earl of Sutherland and Caithness, ...	4
Thorstein, the Red, ...	2
Victoria Crosses won by Sutherland Highlanders, ...	254
Visit of Northern Chiefs to Orkney, ...	56
Volunteers, The, ...	260-282
Wallace, Sir William, ...	11
Witchcraft, ...	133, 136

APPENDIX I.

Ministers of the Reay Country since the Reformation.

DURNESS.

1567.	John Reid, *Exhorter*.
16—.	Alexander Munro.
1663.	Hugh Munro.
1707.	John Mackay.
1726.	Murdoch Macdonald
1764.	John Thomson.
1812.	William Findlater.

FARR.

1567.	Donald Reid, *Reader*.
1574.	Ferquhard Reid.
1664.	John Munro
16—.	Daniel Mackintosh.
1727.	Andrew Robertson.
1734.	John Skeldoch.
1754.	George Munro.
1780.	James Dingwall.
1815.	David MacKenzie.

TONGUE.

1727.	William Mackay.
1730.	Walter Ross.
1762.	John Mackay.
1769.	William Mackenzie.
1806.	H. M. Mackenzie.

EDDRACHILIS.

1726.	George Brodie.
1741.	George Mackay.
1743.	William Henderson.
1744.	John Munro.

EDDRACHILIS.—*cont*.

1756.	John Mackay.
1762.	Alexander Falconer.
1803.	John Mackenzie.
1831.	George Tulloch.

KINLOCHBERVIE.

1829.	David Mackenzie.
1834.	Robert Clarke.

MELNESS AND ERIBOLL.

1794.	John Robertson.
1800.	Neil MacBryde.
1802.	John Kennedy.
1808.	William Findlater.
1816.	Hugh Mackenzie.
1819.	Robert Clarke.
1829.	George Tulloch.
1833.	Hugh Macleod.
1838.	William Macintyre.

STRATHY.

1828.	Angus MacGillivray.
1842.	David Sutherland.

ACHNESS MISSION.

1767.	William Mackenzie.
1772.	James Dingwall.
1781.	—— Urquhart.
1796.	George Gordon.
1813.	David Mackenzie.
1819.	Donald Sage.

APPENDIX II.

Ministers of the Presbytery of Dornoch since the Reformation.

DORNOCH.

- 1569. William Gray.
- 1588. William Paip, Pape, Paipe or Papp.
- 1614. John Gray.
- 1639. Alexander Munro.
- 1680. John Ross.
- 1690. William Mackay.
- 1702. Archibald Bouie.
- 1713. Robert Kirk.
- 1759. John Sutherland.
- 1778. John Bethune.
- 1817. Angus Kennedy.
- 1837. George Rainy Kennedy.

ASSYNT.

- 1576. William Gray.
- 1590. Alexander Ross.
- 16--. John Gray.
- 1713. Robert Thomson.
- 1719. Francis Robertson.
- 1764. George Gordon.
- 1771. Harry Robertson.
- 1777. Walter Ross.
- 1825. Hugh Mackenzie.
- 1828. George Mackay.

CREICH.

- 1585. Donald Logane.
- 1607. James Gray.
- 16 . Robert Monro *alias* Ferguson.
- 16- . John Hosack.
- 16--. John Dempster.
- 1668. John Alexander.
- 1682. Hugh Rose.
- 1707. Andrew Munro.
- 1714. Walter Ross.

CREICH.—*cont.*

- 1731. James Smith.
- 1759 Hugh Rose.
- 1771. George Rainy.
- 1811. Murdo Cameron.

GOLSPIE (formerly) KILMALLIE.

- 1632. Alexander Monro.
- 1656. John Macculloch.
- 1682. Hugh Rose.
- 1690. Walter Denoone.
- 1731. John Sutherland.
- 1754 Martin Macpherson.
- 1774. John Campbell.
- 1776. William Gunn.
- 1787. William Keith.
- 1817. Alexander Macpherson.

KILDONAN.

- 1577. George Ruthven.
- 1584. William Levingston.
- 1656. Andrew Anderson.
- 1673. James Hay.
- 1712. Alexander Brodie.
- 1725. William Rose.
- 1740. Hugh Sutherland.
- 1755. Hugh Ross.
- 1761. John Ross.
- 1776. William Keith.
- 1787. Alexander Sage.
- 1824. James Campbell.

LAIRG.

- 1580. William Gray.
- 1607. James Gray.
- 1658. Robert Ross.

LAIRG.—cont.

1663.	David Monroe.
1668.	William Mackay.
1682.	John Dempster.
1706.	John Robertson.
1714.	John Mackay.
1749.	Thomas Mackay.
1804.	Angus Kennedy
1817.	Duncan MacGillivray.

LOTH.

1590.	Andrew Anderson.
16—.	Hector Munro.
1656.	John Rose.
1682.	Hector Paip.
1721.	Robert Robertson.
1732.	James Gilchrist.
1739.	William Rose.
1756.	George MacCulloch.

LOTH.—cont.

1802.	George Gordon.
1823.	Donald Ross.

ROGART.

1574.	George Sinclair.
1574.	William Gray.
1590.	Thomas Pape.
1614.	John Sutherland.
1639.	George Sutherland.
1656.	Thomas Ross.
1662.	William Mackay.
1683.	Walter Ross.
1725.	John Monro.
1755.	Hugh Sutherland.
1774.	Æneas MacLeod.
1795.	Alexander Urquhart.
1813.	George Urquhart.
1822.	Donald Ross.
1823.	John Mackenzie.

ARCHIBALD SINCLAIR, PRINTER, GLASGOW.

www.ingramcontent.com/pod-product-compliance
Lightning Source LLC
Chambersburg PA
CBHW032002300426
44117CB00008B/867